HOMELANDS

HOMELANDS

*Four Friends, Two Countries,
and the Fate of the Great
Mexican-American Migration*

ALFREDO CORCHADO

BLOOMSBURY PUBLISHING
NEW YORK · LONDON · OXFORD · NEW DELHI · SYDNEY

BLOOMSBURY PUBLISHING
Bloomsbury Publishing Inc.
1385 Broadway, New York, NY 10018, USA

BLOOMSBURY, BLOOMSBURY PUBLISHING, and the Diana logo are trademarks of
Bloomsbury Publishing Plc

First published in the United States 2018

ISBN: HB: 978-1-63286-554-0; eBook: 978-1-63286-556-4

Library of Congress Cataloging-in-Publication Data is available

2 4 6 8 10 9 7 5 3 1

Typeset by Westchester Publishing Services
Printed and bound in the U.S.A. by Berryville Graphics Inc., Berryville, Virginia

To find out more about our authors and books visit www.bloomsbury.com
and sign up for our newsletters.

Bloomsbury books may be purchased for business or promotional use. For information
on bulk purchases please contact Macmillan Corporate and Premium Sales Department at
specialmarkets@macmillan.com.

To the faceless shadows at dawn for
still dreaming and believing

I

In-between
all that comes of *outside* where homelands break,
throw up their barriers
and the cloudless sky threatens endless rain.

To remain here
might be to plant a flag
in nowhere
entredeaux
words like talismans go—be free—dream,
go figure

II

Somewhere between sound and sense a relentless driving forward

in and down—
you leave the roots on
let them dangle, and show
for all those who might question

where *from* is from
where home is hidden
where children become their mothers where saints are just as sinister

Sigurd Selby Stoneyroad the avenues broad below me

divided in allegiance to marks
my own breath makes on the rainwet panes
again and again and again these worlds come back to me
in the full force of their movement

a quality of sky and earth and heaven behind histories of two countries

beyond *patois*, a singular difference: that here we speak simply
and say what we mean to say
that we meet somewhere in the middle by night, or by day

ever wandering—
till love slips, laughter holds,
and life calls us back again

IRISH POET JONATHAN C. CREASY, PARIS, 2017

CONTENTS

PROLOGUE

One Wintry Night at Tequilas

It took days of calling on the spin-dial phone before Primo picked up with a heavily accented *¿Hola?*

I introduced myself in Spanish.

I had been told by a friend in El Paso that Primitivo "Primo" Rodríguez Oceguera could be the only other Mexican in Philadelphia. Just me and a Jesuit-educated human rights activist with Marxist tendencies. Not the type of guy I'd usually hang out with, but it was my first winter away from home—the U.S.-Mexico border—and I was lonely and desperate.

We spoke briefly and agreed to meet. At my suggestion and because the place was near my apartment, we met at an Indian restaurant and made a tradition out of it, every Saturday. I didn't know much about Primo but, by virtue of being Mexican, I counted him as my only friend in *Filadelfia*.

One night, feeling like curry wasn't going to cut it anymore and yearning for Mexican food, we took a gamble on a place Primo had heard about.

Tequilas, read the sign outside the restaurant.

We swung the door open against the icy wind to a blast of warmth radiating from inside. We entered with a bad attitude, skeptical that this Mexican restaurant could be the real thing. I was greeted by an altar to the Virgin of Guadalupe with photos of Cuban revolutionaries Ernesto "Che" Guevara and Fidel Castro, Mexican revolutionaries Pancho Villa and Emiliano Zapata and the leftist Uruguayan writer Eduardo Galeano.

I rolled my eyes.

Another phony capitalist capitalizing on Latin America's romantic leftist leaders and the revered brown saint. Really, the Virgin of

Guadalupe? I imagined my mother and her daily prayers back home, hoping they would be enough to guide me through this new life.

What did this *cabrón* know about our faith? All this, just to make a few bucks from tacos.

Insulting.

We grabbed two chairs at the bar. It smelled surprisingly authentic. Not quite like my mother's cooking—but close.

"Cruz de Navajas," a popular song about love and betrayal by the Spanish pop group Mecano, was playing, not some generic instrumental mariachi music. Ana Torroja's angelic voice hooked me. I mouthed the lyrics as we sat studying a menu that seemed straight out of Mexico. In classic Mexican satire, the menu lampooned Tex-Mex food, mockingly listing *nachos obligatorios* as an obligatory item to appease those who believe that any Mexican restaurant had to include nachos. But the sarcasm wasn't all. The menu seemed to educate ignorant patrons about the history of the U.S.-Mexico border.

Genius marketing, I thought. The dishes included mole, complete with *trenza de carne*, beef in a braided pastry.

Somebody here knows Mexico intimately, I thought. The Spanish pop music and menu began to seduce me. I lowered my guard.

Primo was older than me but I couldn't place his age—and didn't dare ask. He had a receding hairline and tiny mustache that gave him the look of a Don Juan with matador instincts. His eyes popped behind his Hemingway eyeglasses when he talked about something that he was passionate about. His top four? Politics, immigration, salsa music and women. But not always in that order.

I had learned from our Saturdays together that he was working to help undocumented immigrants legalize under the generous new amnesty program. President Ronald Reagan had just signed the Immigration Reform and Control Act (IRCA) into law. He called it "amnesty" during a presidential debate with Democratic presidential candidate Walter Mondale in 1984: "I believe in the idea of amnesty for those who have put down roots and lived here, even though some time back they may have entered illegally." The concept stuck.

Primo and I rarely spoke about anything personal except nostalgia and policy.

I told him about my family's background, how we emigrated from Mexico, thanks to the 1965 Immigration Act that President Kennedy had advocated for before his assassination. I told him how my family once worked as migrants in the fields of California and how I managed—by luck, I confessed—to nail down this *Wall Street Journal* gig. From working at a scrappy afternoon newspaper, the *El Paso Herald-Post*, now here I was, working on the ninth floor of the twenty-one-story redbrick North American Building on South Broad Street commissioned by Thomas Wanamaker. It felt surreal.

On those few first days to work, I'd take the train with my bureau chief, Frank Edward Allen, who had generously been hosting me at his home while I found a place to live. I sat shoulder to shoulder with commuters rustling the pages of the *Philadelphia Inquirer*, the *Wall Street Journal* or the *New York Times*, occasionally sharing a section but hardly ever saying a word.

If all of these people were Mexican, I thought, this train would be so loud every morning. Everyone would know each other, all smiles and laughter. Kisses on the cheek and long, familiar hugs. But, no, Philadelphia felt sterile and soulless.

The very first day of my new job, Frank and I walked out of Suburban Station, an art deco building with commuter trains underneath. Onward to Fifteenth Street across a park with a statue with the word LOVE in red. On my left was the impressive City Hall, a Gothic-looking brick structure façade adorned with marble. The North American Building was once the tallest in Philadelphia, back when it was completed in 1900, a title it held for a year before being eclipsed by City Hall and its statue of William Penn. Wanamaker housed his own newspaper, the *North American*, in the building until it went out of print in 1925. Now the building had new, highly esteemed journalism credentials.

The statue of Penn that sits atop City Hall honors the founder of the city and state, Frank said. Ever the teacher, Frank patiently took me by the shoulder and pointed to Penn and said the city was laid out as a holy experiment based on Penn's Quaker neighborly beliefs.

I nodded, confused as to how I was on my way to work at a place obsessed with stocks, earnings reports, mergers and acquisitions, hostile takeovers, insider trading—all concepts I barely grasped. From my vantage point, I could swear it looked like Billy was pissing on me.

I was now part of the "diversity" experiment.

When we were inside at the *Journal* office, Frank took me around the room and briefly introduced me to everyone, all nice and pleasant, all buried in work, most of them from big universities: Harvard, Princeton, Northwestern and so on. In contrast, I had managed to get my education by overstaying my welcome at El Paso Community College before transferring to the University of Texas at El Paso, or UTEP.

Although I didn't even have a diploma from UTEP, I told others it was the Harvard of the border—a joke that I often heard back home.

No one laughed.

Thankfully, one colleague stood out: Julie Amparano, a native of Phoenix, who had attended the University of Arizona in Tucson. She covered the new casinos going up in Atlantic City. It was 1987, and the stock market was climbing. Rock-bottom bargains could be had in real estate, especially downtown, so businessmen began flocking to the area, some cutting deals with Italian mobsters like Salvatore Testa, who controlled construction sites. She was new to the *Journal* and was keeping a close eye on a young playboy billionaire from New York City simply known as The Donald. Donald J. Trump, a young, brash businessman, a graduate of the Wharton School of Business at the University of Pennsylvania, was the flashiest of deal makers.

Julie looked Italian, maybe Greek, but she said her mother was from El Paso. Other than the janitors, she seemed to be the only other Hispanic at the *Journal*'s Philadelphia bureau. She promised we'd grab lunch and share experiences. But I had a feeling lunch wouldn't happen anytime soon. In her twenties, with short, curly black hair, Julie gave off an air of professional ambition and personal style. She seemed to be afraid that I was going to embarrass her. Embracing a clumsy Mexican American reporter like myself wasn't in her best interests.

In a country and city obsessed with its black-white racial conflicts, Hispanics like us were flying under the radar, quietly trying to hide, attempting to join the white mainstream. I represented what Julie was running away from. I had no style, and I saw her glance disapprovingly at my sports coat, the only one I had, a once-in-a-lifetime deal bought off the rack at JCPenney at an after-Christmas sale in El Paso. I cut the price tag off but left a cloth tag on the cuff, which came down to the middle of my hands. Frank noticed it, too, and pulled me back into his office with "art work" of animals drawn with crayons by his three young sons, Zack, Josh, and Nick. They'd often visit to watch their dad work.

That's a sharp look, he said, pulling out scissors and snipping off the tag.

Frank rattled off the names of the companies on my beat, urging me to do research, to read up on every public corporation, because quarterly reports would be out soon and I needed to be prepared. I would cover corporate news from companies like Hershey's, Campbell's, and Black & Decker—names I knew from my school days when I would jump off the bus and run to the corner store in Oro Loma, across the Delta–Mendota Canal, to buy a Hershey's bar.

I'd sit down at my bare desk and listen to the white noise of tapping on IBM keyboards; journalists conducting interviews in hushed tones, heavy phone receivers cradled on their shoulders; gatherings in conference rooms to talk to editors back in New York City. The furniture was made by Steelcase, all metal and done in shades of gray, fitting for a newspaper with no photos or color at the time. The desks had laminate tops with fake colored patterns made to look like wood.

Each reporter had a lockable file cabinet next to the desk. In the back of the office we had a small room with one window, one desk and one chair. We called it the Writing Room, where reporters could go, one at a time, to work on their Page One features. It was quiet. No phones ringing. No "spot news" hassles to bother the reporter.

Yes, this was the epicenter of economic and political power, I was told, but something didn't feel authentic. It was as if the rest of the country didn't exist—this was the only thing that mattered, not the fringe. I looked around and saw a cookie-cutter existence.

I missed the heat from the *Herald-Post*. The *Wall Street Journal* had a different vibe. Every day felt the same. I would stare out the window from the bus or train at Broad Street, at the new buildings going up and up in a city that, like me, was in the midst of an identity crisis. My soul whined. Nothing about Philadelphia seemed familiar. Hoagies, Philly cheesesteaks and Rolling Rocks replaced enchiladas, *huevos rancheros* and a Coors. Homesick, I kept my watch on El Paso time. Frank once missed a deadline because I was on the wrong time zone and he was glancing at my watch, sitting next to me, covering a corporate forecast.

At my desk, I would wait for the janitors to walk into the restrooms to follow them, just to say *buenos días, buenas noches*, to hear the sound of Spanish again. They were mostly Puerto Ricans, and they were as stunned as I was that a Mexican had found his way east of the Mississippi.

At night, back at my apartment, I found bitter solace in the music that took me home. When nostalgia ached even more I turned to Juan Gabriel and pushed play on "Se Me Olvidó Otra Vez," reminiscing about the "same place and the same people," the lyrics of a song I believed was dedicated to Ciudad Juárez.

I had never lived alone. I kept the volume low, concerned that my neighbors might hear my Mexican music. Yet I began to tap my foot to the music they listened to—the soulful sounds of Miles Davis, John

Coltrane, Louis Armstrong and Duke Ellington, whose song "Haupe" would set me off on an endless search for sleep. My "furniture" was limited to a rocking chair and a rectangular sleeping bag that Frank's father used in his days of elk and moose hunting back in Wyoming. I couldn't wait to snuggle inside the bag filled with goose down and a zipper that ran all the way down the side and across the bottom. Both were gifts from Frank and his wife, Maggie. I was plain broke. I'd turn the lights off and hear the wind roar, the snow gathering in a hush. I would imagine the white powder swallowing up the brick stone façade and I'd lie in bed, listening to the traffic clatter outside, wondering whether I would ever be a part of Philadelphia.

Stop complaining, I'd tell myself. You could be picking cantaloupes.

THE CHIPS AND SALSA soon arrived, interrupting my daydreaming and debate with Primo about whether immigration reform would really lift millions out of the shadows and signal the end of Mexican migration, or whether the stream would go on forever. Mexico was in the midst of rapid demographic change; women were having far fewer children. There had to be a limit to the northward flow, right?

Ever the reporter, I took notes that, unbeknownst to me, my mother would meticulously preserve in plastic containers for decades to come.

A waiter swooped in with our plates of *enchiladas rojas*. They looked and smelled amazing. I took a bite and swallowed. For a second I wasn't sure I knew where I was anymore. Whoever was doing the cooking must have taken a class from my mother. Miguel Bosé was now singing "La Gran Ciudad" ("The Big City"), a song about leaving—*no mamá, no llores asi, papá mío dame bendición*—that my brothers and I had listened to in sadness before I left for Philadelphia. Mother, don't cry for me; Father, give me your blessing. Whoever had put on this music shared my pain, my longing for home, and was as miserable as I was in Philadelphia.

As we dug into our food, I watched the waiter, who had turned on his heel with an empty tray and headed to the kitchen, calling out to the bartender, a young man who looked about my age but was far more handsome, fiddling with glasses and wiping the bar counter. He eyed us intently, apparently trying to listen to our conversation. I figured he was Italian, cleverly disguised as a Mexican to give his restaurant authenticity—complete with a bushy black mustache across his upper lip and a long mane of black hair that hung over his ears. He was tall, with broad shoulders, and built like a linebacker. Puffy chest.

Clever marketers, I thought. They think of everything.

That mustache is right out of that picture of Zapata, I told Primo.

Supongo que sí, I suppose so, he responded.

The bartender walked toward us like an oversized teddy bear with a big smile on his face.

Caballeros, ¿en qué les puedo servir? the man asked in polite, flawless Spanish. How can I help you?

Estamos buscando al dueño, I said, in shock, asking for the owner.

He speaks Spanish. *Putísima madre.* I'm so, so fucked, I thought.

I was momentarily horrified that he might have been listening to my doubts and earlier jabs about his mustache. My theory that he was a fake Mexican. I told him we wanted to know where the owner had gotten the idea for this place, because it felt like the real thing.

David Suro-Piñera *a sus órdenes*, he said, indicating he owned the place and adding courteously that he was at our service.

Primo and I looked at each other, unsure how to respond.

No se asusten, he said. Don't be frightened. I was just eavesdropping. Didn't mean to, but this is a new place, just a few months old. It's my place, and I want to make sure the service is up to your standards, *jóvenes*. I'm trying to build a business from the ground up. You seem to know your food, and your . . . music.

We looked at him suspiciously. He said all the graceful things a Mexican would say, in the standard passive-aggressive manner to which we were accustomed. We looked away quietly, not saying a thing, overcome by the joy of eating real Mexican food again in a restaurant owned by what appeared to be a real Mexican in this cold city where, until very recently, we had felt completely alone.

We finished our enchiladas and were about to leave, when David blocked our exit with a skip in his step. He looked persistent, like a goalie who wasn't about to let anything get through.

Stay for another drink, he said, and then rattled off the most complete list of tequilas I had ever heard in my life—not that I knew anything about tequila at the time. I liked beer, preferably Budweiser or Coors. He began mentioning tequilas he didn't even have in stock, the ones he really liked but couldn't find in the United States. In fact, he confessed, his supply was so bad, he refused to even drink what he had stocked on his shelves, yet he knew detailed information about their different origins and distilling processes.

He didn't belong in a restaurant, I thought. He should be roaming the wild blue agave fields back in Mexico's northwestern state of Jalisco.

I later discovered he was from Jalisco's capital, Guadalajara.

It's cold outside, he insisted. The tequila is on the house.

Primo and I hesitated for a split second. What were we going to do, say no? David walked us to a table near the door. He sat us at Table 21, the first of many nights in the very same spot. David poured a generous serving for each of us, smiled mischievously, then headed back to the bar with its thatched-palm-frond awning. He looked happy with himself.

I tossed back the tequila, much the way I did back at Juárez's Electric Q discotheque, and much to David's dismay. He stared at me in shock from behind the bar and quickly came back with the same bottle and poured another. He shook his head as if saying, *Don't you dare toss it back again or I will slam this bottle across your head. Pendejo.* Moron.

Despacito, he said. Kiss it slowly. Savor it. Don't slam it. I drank it slowly, not sure what had just happened. He seemed pleased. We both nodded, as if I had just been baptized.

I remembered looking at Primo sheepishly. But Primo's eyes were already locked elsewhere. Raul Yzaguirre, perhaps the most influential Latino in America, the man making news nationwide over amnesty for immigrants, was headed our way. A Texan born to Mexican American parents, Raul was head of the National Council of La Raza, the leading powerful lobbying group that advocated for the rights of Hispanics and immigrants in the United States. Under Raul's leadership, NCLR was a key player in the immigration debate. La Raza was now under fire: How could an organization that advocated for immigrant rights be aligned with giant corporations, having lobbied for amnesty alongside the men and women who preyed on the cheap labor of these workers? Raul had been dining with what looked like a banker or lawyer or politician.

On his way out, Raul recognized Primo—a well-known immigrant organizer in his own right—and stopped at our table. He was a consummate D.C. insider, a mover and shaker, and greeted us in Spanish.

I gave Raul my business card and solicited an interview about the challenges of representing a group radically changing the face of America. He readily accepted the request and told me that on my next visit to Washington we could sit down and talk politics alongside his deputy, Cecilia Muñoz.

He presented his dinner companion, Kenneth I. Trujillo, or Ken. He wore a sharp three-piece suit and stylish round glasses. Of course he was an attorney. He had wavy hair, a square chin and smooth skin; he also talked fast and flashed perfect teeth, the kind that made me insecure about my own. I was glad the lights were dimmed for that reason, and also to better hide my acne-scarred face.

I forced a half smile.

The guy looked like a Hispanic Tom Cruise, I thought. His face was still caked with powder. Earlier that evening both had appeared on a TV show debating local and nationwide efforts to make English the official language of Pennsylvania. We offered Ken a seat and he quickly took it, as Raul had to run to hail down a cab back to Thirtieth Street Station to catch the last train for Washington.

Ken spoke Spanish far from perfectly, but we admired his effort. Mine wasn't so great, either, so I felt comfortable with him. At times he sounded Puerto Rican, but I later discovered he wasn't from Puerto Rico or Mexico but had been born and raised in New Mexico. There, people need to remind outsiders that the border crossed their Mexican family, not the other way around. His family had been cut off from the homeland for generations. Like many New Mexicans he felt more wedded to his Spanish heritage than any roots to Mexico. He didn't know anyone back in Mexico. He never missed his cousins or felt the familiar heartbreak many Mexican immigrants endure during birthdays or holidays, because he was already surrounded by family. Ken's family had never actually left. Like me, Ken missed the sunsets in the Southwest that color the skies purple and orange.

David strolled over again and introduced himself to Ken. He poured him a drink, happy that he had met three other homesick souls all in the same evening. At our insistence, he poured one for himself, too. With our glasses full, we looked at each other and tried to size one another up. We quickly adopted an Old World tradition that became our own, looking into each other's eyes when saying cheers—*salud*.

In that brief moment we must have sensed a common heartbreak. We forged a bond conversing in Spanish that evening over music, cuisine and our shared roots, thousands of miles from the southern border. The four of us, the unlikeliest of friends, had nowhere else to go that night. It was late, almost midnight, and the tables were mostly cleared of guests. With every round poured, the tequila bottle became lighter and we became louder as we began to pick apart every aspect of the historic migration sweeping the country. We dug deeper into the currents reshaping America.

Except for Ken, we were the sons of a failed and incomplete revolution in Mexico now living in Philadelphia, which was supposed to embody the best of a revolution and where the nation's Founders drew up a constitution that would be the envy of the world for centuries over. We were testing the tolerance of a city built in 1691 by William Penn, an aristocrat turned rabble-rouser who saw in his new landholdings a haven for refugees fleeing religious persecution and immigrants looking to reinvent themselves.

David spoke of his passion for food and how he sought to seduce Americans with Mexican culinary culture and spirits—"soft power," a term I would later learn. Ken talked of judicial justice, a vision for a more equal and inclusive country. Primo only hinted at what he was up to: secretly connecting workers on both sides of the border and devising efforts to empower Mexicans in the U.S. I told them I just wanted to go home, to find a way back to the border or the Mexico of my childhood, hopefully as a "foreign" correspondent for a big U.S. newspaper, an illusion that felt like a pipe dream at that moment.

Years later, looking back on that evening in Philadelphia, it felt as if we were destined to come together that night, in that moment, at Tequilas' Table 21. Four strangers bound for the unknown, unhinged from our old comfort zones, embarking on a chaotic journey. Three immigrants from prominent migrant-exporting states in Mexico: Jalisco, Michoacán and Durango. Ken, the New Mexican, an unwitting ambassador of mainstream America, still searching for his Mexican roots along the way. Our friendships would withstand the passage of time, some better than others.

That night we began a conversation that has lasted more than thirty years, turning on a fundamental and deeply personal question: How do we fit in? What does it mean to be American and become part of its diverse mainstream, integrate into its colorful tapestry, its noble ideals and timeless democratic principles? Whenever we thought we had figured it out, somehow the entire concept would again escape us. We seek the original idea, then destroy it—a cruel irony.

Outside Tequilas, dawn began to envelop Philadelphia. Workers headed home, while others were about to begin as the city slept. Trucks plowed piles of snow, clearing Locust Street between Broad and Rittenhouse Square, exposing all that was left of a wintry darkness: four strangers searching for their own shadows at dawn.

SECTION I

Leaving Home

1.

El Pajarito & Superwoman in El Norte

The realization that I would have to leave Mexico for the United States literally startled me from a dream.

I was just a young boy in San Luis de Cordero, napping in the middle of my maternal grandmother Nina's courtyard, filled with parrots and plants, dahlias and geraniums. The sweet scents and sounds of birds chirping were drowned out by the mournful whimpering coming from my mother as she and my grandmother plotted our new future. My mother told Nina she needed her to join us: she couldn't make it alone raising the family; plus, my father insisted that she join us.

News of the impending departure was met with fierce resistance by inconsolable tantrums, my mother recalled many years later, those of my five-year-old self and my brother Juan, a year younger than me.

But what choice did we have?

We didn't really know our father. As a child, I never called him *papá*—just *señor*. I didn't even know his real name. Pajarito was his nickname, an homage to his band. He loved music. As a *bracero*, part of the U.S. guest-worker program, he lived in Texas and later California like his other siblings. They had been inspired to go north thanks to their eldest sister, Felicidad, known to us as Tía Chala. She was the first immigrant in the family if not the town. She had been forced to close down her small grocery store because the latest drought meant her clients were forced to ask for store credit. They had no money. She originally left for the northern city of Monterrey, but once there she made a beeline for the border because she was told opportunities were greater. Stories of her grew to legendary proportions: a woman who found her freedom sewing clothes, earning *dólares*. Tía Chala arrived on the border in Ciudad Juárez in the 1940s with her daughters: Odelva, Alicia, Irma and Olga. And now, thanks to a provision in the Bracero Program, we qualified for green cards. My mother wanted my father to be part of our lives, to guide us and lead us in the right direction.

At night Tía Chala would head to bed and eye the city of El Paso from her battered home in Juárez. She pledged to her daughters they would all cross someday. A fiercely independent woman, she fulfilled her promise and made it to El Paso in 1948. The stories inspired many back in Durango but none more than her brothers. Juan Pablo, the youngest, was particularly fascinated by Tía Chala. Sure, some of his brothers had already left, but if a woman could make it in the United States, he thought, his chances were even greater.

In a rare moment, my father, who wasn't very affectionate, sent me a postcard of California's state capitol. Are we there yet? my brothers would ask each time the bus rumbled into a new town. I'd take out my crumpled postcard, look at it and compare every house in front of us. No, I'd respond. Go back to sleep. I grew worried, as no home looked like the postcard. But faith reigned in that Bible my mother carried.

When we arrived in California in 1966, the population was about 196.5 million and whites made up about 85 percent of the population. The remaining 15 percent was overwhelming African-Americans, with Mexicans quietly in the mix, small and nearly invisible, unless you were out in the fields under the earth's elements. The Sosa, Perez, Jiménez, Ramirez and Corchado families—some of whom I knew back home— had already settled in. Imagine my disappointment when we finally arrived and in front of us wasn't even a home but a dilapidated trailer house where two of my uncles, Mundo and Eutemio, and a cousin, Chalio—lived and worked alongside my father picking cantaloupes. My parents lived inside and my brothers, my uncles and I would sleep outside with weeds and rats around us. We'd cry in unison and beg my parents to take us back home to San Luis de Cordero, to walk those friendly cobblestone streets that felt like they belonged to us. I'd angrily confront my father after work and point to the fields around us, the trailer house on its last legs, and shout, *¡Esto está gacho!* This is garbage! We want to go home again. We're so lonely here. Lost.

My father would look to my mother, embarrassed that a little twit like me would raise his voice and question him. Rather than address my concerns, he asked her to calm me down. Tell me something. Make me stop screaming. Tell him life will get better. My mother was seven months pregnant, so she pleaded for peace. She was just as depressed.

It was the summer of 1966 and we had no babysitter—didn't even know what that was—so my brother Juan and I joined our father and our aunts in the fields, helping them pick tomatoes and filling our father's buckets, child labor laws be damned. When my brother David was born, we'd carry him with joy and pick rocks that looked like cars and pretend we were driving back to Mexico. Some rocks were bigger, and we piled smaller ones on top to make it look like large trucks pulling cargo all the way to Mexico. We told him that somewhere south was a place that was beautiful. A place where people were friendly and didn't work all the time. They worked to live.

The more my parents talked about the American dream, the more we rebelled against the notion. I wanted nothing to do with this American dream, not if we had to go to sleep fearful that rats would jump on us. Not if that meant I would lose my parents to "work."

Months after David was born, we hardly saw my mother anymore.

We lost her to the fields.

Gone were the days when she'd serenade us at home or spend the day planning what we would eat for lunch and dinner—those simple days when she would stock our tiny grocery store with the dollars my father sent from up north.

Following in my father's footsteps, she, too, became invaluable to and inseparable from work. Mama became the queen of the tomato fields, filling up bins in record time. She was so good that contractors, including her two sisters, fought for her, quibbling over five cents or ten cents more per bin: one penny more meant everything to her. She filled her sacks with lettuce and oranges, jumping off ladders, defying gravity. We tried to imitate her on weekends or during summer, only to make her work double, triple and more as she bailed out my three brothers and me, forcing her to take over four rows, leaving us out.

My mom was Superwoman and Batwoman rolled into one. She was also a wizard with the long hoe and short hoe, working through the fields in a blink of an eye until the California Supreme Court banned the short hoe in 1975, calling it an "unsafe tool," as it required workers to stoop over as they used it to cultivate crops. In fact, the short hoe led to long-term health consequences for her: a bad back and bad bones.

Politically speaking, my mother came of age in the fields. Shortly after she arrived, she took part in the fight for equal pay and justice for farm-workers led by union leader Cesar Chavez, who saw Mexicans as a hindrance, an obstacle to making the union stronger, as illegal Mexican workers were bringing down wages for union members. Not my mother.

She supported the union's goal of fair wages, justice and respect. Quiet and even meek at home, in the fields my mother would lead sit-ins and urge workers to rise up. My aunts were mortified by the mutiny orchestrated by their sister, Herlinda, the meek one who was afraid of cats, who made a living selling *gorditas* on weekends and afternoons.

The *patrones* needed workers more than the workers needed them, she'd tell them. Their precious crops would rot because the fields would spoil without us. Have courage, she would whisper as workers gathered around her seeking direction.

At home she dedicated her time to us but she would go to sleep by eight. Her day started at 3:30 a.m., when she'd wake to prepare lunch, a couple of egg-and-bean burritos, and she was off to the next field, greeting sugar beets at dawn. My mother would not let us get used to California. She prohibited us from the beach in Carmel, Monterey or Santa Cruz for fear we'd drown like my sister did back in Durango, or Disneyland because we were too busy, particularly my parents, working sunrise to sunset, making sure Americans had vegetables on their tables or fine wines for their fancy parties. California was temporary, she reminded us. Bigger dreams awaited us closer to Mexico.

Back in Durango, a terrible drought showed no mercy. The exodus from Mexico grew, on both sides of the family. Two, three or six would arrive at a time. We were increasingly surrounded by cousins, uncles and aunts. One night Javier, Abel, Joel, Edmundo, Roberto, Armando, Richie and Rosa arrived and shared a room in Eagle Field, sleeping on mattresses on the floor.

Later came cousins Hector, Abel, Geno, Leticia and Carmen. They moved in our cramped government housing, fresh from Ciudad Juárez, and stayed with us for nearly a year as they waited for their own housing, thanks to my uncle Guero's work as a *bracero*.

They were followed by a whole new set of cousins, which included Martha, who was so pretty the much older labor contractor, Pilar, fell hard for her.

By now my brothers and I spoke a little English, so we stayed up late at night teaching the newcomers basic words with the help of songs like "I Think I Love You": "This morning I woke up with this feeling . . ." I pretended to be Keith of the Partridge Family, played by David Cassidy.

The Bracero Program, which grew out of a series of bilateral agreements between Mexico and the United States, allowed millions of mostly Mexican men from rural villages to work in the United States via temporary contracts to help with labor shortages generated by wars. The program ended in 1964, but employers continued craving the tireless laborers. More cousins, uncles, aunts and Mexicans in general kept popping up gradually in Oro Loma, Eagle Field, Firebaugh, Mendota, Dos Palos and South Dos Palos. They came from Zacatecas, Michoacán, Jalisco, Guanajuato.

Farmers would stop by our trailer after work, visit our parents, sometimes subtly urging them to spread the word back in Durango. They needed more workers, *como sea*, and everyone knew that meant illegal. The farmers wanted workers like my mother and father, people unafraid of manual labor, people who never refused a job. Some were illegal immigrants, but to us they were just family and friends. Some came with the help of *coyotes*, smugglers. Others on their own. One time Cousin Lupe crossed the El Paso–Juárez border after a Christmas visit without having to declare or say a thing. She sat between my brother Juan and me and simply smiled at the officer. Maybe because she is light-skinned with hazel eyes, or this was her lucky moment, the customs officer at the bridge just waved us in.

Cousins Cayo, Lucy and Mary came with the help of a *coyote*. To us, the smugglers weren't criminals but neighbors we knew from back in San Luis de Cordero. They were small-timers, not the hired guns of violent criminal organizations as many *coyotes* are today. They stayed for coffee and *pan dulce*, which we offered with gratitude for having brought the family over safely. The new immigrants made financial arrangements upon arrival, paying half the debt that night and the remainder after their first paychecks.

My mother's older brothers, uncles Rosalio—or, as we know him, Chey—and Alejo, were among the last to arrive. Like those before them, they also promised to return to Mexico. They missed their families, but going back wasn't so simple when jobs stared at them year-round. They added to the growing population of undocumented immigrants, who soon included their own children, cousins Ruben, Armando, Chavela, Catalina and Irma, among them.

The endless drought back in Mexico dragged on through the late 1960s.

But who needed rain when we had California? I was part of a human chain. San Luis de Cordero had been transplanted in the San Joaquin Valley. One evening my mother walked over to me, kneeled down, ruffled my hair and whispered, Don't feel lonely anymore. They're all here now.

But family did little to comfort my heartbreak. I dropped out of high school—simply walked out of my music class and brought my guitar along with me. I sneaked out for a shake and burger at Don's Frosty and just kept walking out of Dos Palos until I found a place with weeds along the Surgo canal, its waters running high. The long weeds helped conceal me from my uncle Chey, who irrigated fields from the canal during harvest season.

Dropping out of school would be my secret. No one would know.

I strummed my guitar and attempted to write a song in Spanish—I would be the next Juan Gabriel, the beloved crooner from Juárez—but realized I was well on my way toward assimilation because all I could do was sing the Eagles' "Best of My Love." If the fields are my destiny, I convinced myself as I walked the canal, then by the time they graduate I will be the foreman of my graduating class.

My parents eventually found out and didn't take the news well. My father stopped talking to me. One day he was so disgusted, he took a large piece of ice and smashed it on my face, causing blood to gush down my face and neck. I vowed never to talk to him again. He wouldn't even look me in the eye. He was too hurt. What about the sacrifices we made? he screamed at my mother. Why did we even come here, buy a home? We were now living in our first home in South Dos Palos, just across from our favorite store, Jerry's Dry Goods.

Neighbors like Larry Willis and Melvin Littlejohn would peek through the curtains to see what all the commotion was about. They'd knock on the door: Alfredo, wanna come out and play? They carried with them our favorite weapon, a basketball to get my frustrations out on the court. I was hooked on the bank shot, pretending I played for UCLA.

My mother wouldn't give up on me. She convinced me to get an education by promising to make the down payment on my favorite car, a white 1978 Camaro, after I pledged I would leave California for El Paso, where Hispanics didn't stoop in the fields. I would enroll in college and I would not marry until I had a college degree.

When we moved to El Paso, my parents took over a home they'd made payments on for more than a decade, a house a few doors down from my *tía* Chala. They knew nothing other than the fields. But they would try to add something else to their résumés: they would be entrepreneurs. They realized how well loved my mother's cooking was in California, as folks from far and wide asked for it. So they decided they would open their own restaurant, Freddy's Café.

Inspired by the encouragement of my community college counselor and teacher Penny Byrne, I studied journalism and eventually finished up at the University of Texas at El Paso. I became a reporter for the *El Paso Herald-Post*, a scrappy afternoon newspaper haunted by the fiery legacy of E. M. Pooley, a cranky, opinionated Scripps Howard newsman who used investigative journalism to stir things up in El Paso. We reported on the mistreatment of Mexican immigrants and questioned why, in a city with so many Mexican Americans, so few were in power.

Eventually, I realized I was in love. With reporting. With the border. With life.

The *Post* rumbled like a loud stampede, out to uncover the surface for the real story. The border was chaotic and exciting. With political upheaval, public protests, heartbreak and hope. In 1986 the protests in Ciudad Juárez embodied a people's revolution. The longtime opposition, the National Action Party (the Partido Acción Nacional, or PAN), was blasting open political battlegrounds against the Revolutionary Institutional Party (the Partido Revolucionario Institucional, or PRI), which had held an iron first over Mexican politics and society for more than fifty years. Juárez was increasingly opening up to progressive change. My blood boiled.

We fought for every scoop and wanted to tell stories no one else dared to. We had journalists who became their own institutions, with names like Joe Olvera, a hard-hitting Chicano columnist, Joe Old, from the gritty streets of Chicago, and Betty Ligon, an airplane pilot and a pioneering journalist who made sure she got names right by calling everyone "luv." And then there was the cuddly Ken Flynn, a Catholic deacon on weekends and the most foulmouthed reporter I've ever been around. Fuck them, he said, if ever—and rarely this was the case—the *El Paso Times* got a scoop over us. Let's beat the shit out of them tomorrow, he'd add, making me proud to be Catholic.

I also had my inseparable wingman, Billy Calzada. Our editor called us the Juárez Vice after the hit series *Miami Vice*. Billy and I could hop across the border with journalist colleagues Sonny Lopez and Maria Barron inside her white convertible and cover the demonstrations for democracy that were growing larger and louder by the week. And within that same breath I could cross back and be home in time for dinner with my family. From the protests at the U.S.-Mexico port of entry, *el puente* Santa Fe, I sometimes recognized faces, like my mother's. She fought against her petite frame, making her way from the U.S. side, balancing a heavy basket of steaming-hot burritos on her hip to hand out in solidarity to protesters on the bridge from El Paso to Ciudad Juárez.

We have to help from both sides of the border to make sure Mexico becomes a great nation, she said. A country that provides opportunities rather than exports us as cheap labor to the United States.

I felt like I already had it all on the border. That's why the eventual advances at the *Wall Street Journal* were difficult to appreciate.

Frank Allen had a vision way ahead of his time to make the *Journal*'s largely white male newsroom more diverse. Having once lived in Tucson, he believed that editors didn't understand the demographic changes America was going through, or the fact that Spanish was quickly overtaking English in some communities.

Marketers took to calling the 1980s the "Decade of Hispanics." The Hispanic population was surging, with Mexican immigration leading the way. Over the course of the decade, nearly two million Mexican immigrants would enter the U.S. legally, with an average of one million undocumented Mexicans apprehended each year by the U.S. Border Patrol. In 1980 about 2.2 million Mexicans were living in the U.S. By the end of the decade that number would more than double to 4.3 million. Hispanics were quickly becoming the largest minority group, having grown by more than seven million during the 1980s, and thereafter were projected to lead a plurality of other ethnic groups.

Newsrooms have to reflect those numbers, Frank said. Otherwise, journalism—the storytelling—would suffer. How could the *Journal* tell the full story without reporters who truly got it? Newsrooms had to become browner. By the end of the decade, one survey of newspapers in California showed that fewer than 5 percent of journalists were Hispanic.

Sure, not every Hispanic reporter wanted to do stories about immigration or be pigeonholed, Frank recognized that. But if that was your passion and you could speak the language, even better. You could learn Spanish, but culture was something inherent in us. Maybe I could write a story like the one about Mexican immigrants keeping their communities economically afloat back home through remittances, he said, referring to an article I had clipped and kept by my desk for inspiration even before I knew the author actually worked at the *Wall Street Journal*.

Maybe this is the kind of newspaper I'm looking for, I thought.

But while that was my passion, I still had doubts, mostly because I felt uncomfortable being a token. Plus I didn't even apply for the job in the first place.

I had attended the second National Association of Hispanic Journalists (NAHJ) convention in Tucson. Given its novelty, the *New York Times* came to cover it—and to scout for up-and-coming Hispanic journalists. The *Times* also needed to achieve "diversity," a concept that made me cringe, as though it wasn't Hispanic journalists with knowledge of their own community that they needed but a means to reach some magical number that implied well-roundedness. A *Times* reporter zeroed in on me, a clueless young man with boat shoes, no socks, torn Levi's 501 jeans and a photo album stuffed with newspaper clips from the *Prospector*, the college newspaper at UTEP.

I must have fit the profile.

I ended up in his story, which ignited a firestorm of attention from America's most prestigious newspapers, including the *New York Times*, the *Los Angeles Times*, the *Wall Street Journal* and other, smaller publications, including one from Utah. They began to court me at the convention.

It seemed a bit ridiculous.

My mentor, Ray Chavez, a UTEP journalism professor, sat with me at a dining table at the convention, where we met Frank. The two became quick friends.

Alfredo was fired by a TV anchorwoman, Ray told Frank. The anchorwoman told him he had no future in journalism. That only made him hungrier. More passionate. Alfredo is trying to prove her and everyone else wrong. He's got a chip on his shoulder and that's good. He's known defeat all his life.

I was grateful to Ray for seeing something in me. Still, I felt skeptical of all the attention, uncomfortable in my role as a "Hispanic journalist," a term I reluctantly accepted.

I got internship offers at the *Times* and *Journal*, but Ray advised me to turn both down: You don't want to go to the Northeast and be a tourist, he said. You want to wander into white America and test yourself first.

Frank, meanwhile, delivered on the promise he had made over lunch and kept in touch with me and even read my clips, offering much-needed criticism as he marked my clippings from the *Prospector* and from my internships at the *El Paso Herald-Post* and *Ogden Standard-Examiner* in Utah—the whitest place I had ever lived in. A year later, in April 1986, Frank called with an offer of nearly $30,000 a year and benefits—nearly twice my salary at the *Post*—to work at the *Journal* office in Philadelphia.

You should take the job, Ray said, or risk having no career at all.

I ignored Ray, just that once. But Frank would not take no for an answer. The NAHJ had just awarded me first place for a series of stories about migrant workers in the state of Utah. Frank wouldn't give up. He said he wanted me to start in May. But May came and went. So did the summer and fall, and now winter was looming.

Get your experience and get out, Ray scolded me. I caved in and agreed, although, like a real Mexican, I was obsessed with *mañana*. The not-today-but-maybe-tomorrow mentality. I couldn't tear myself away. I couldn't find the last story, the one good enough to say goodbye.

By November, Frank had had enough of my broken promises and flew to El Paso. He thought I was reluctant to leave because of my parents. He was partly right. I did feel like I had to be there for my mother, after all we had been through together in Mexico and the fields. We now lived together as a family, although my father was often absent. He didn't really understand what it meant to be a father. He left parenting up to my mother. We ran Freddy's Café as a family and I felt the responsibility to help and take care of my younger siblings, five brothers in their teens and twenties and two girls, ten-year-old Monica and toddler Linda—half of us born in Mexico, half in the United States.

We lived in a gang-infested neighborhood not far from the border, in a long, narrow three-bedroom house just behind a newly renovated mall that drew Mexican shoppers in droves. They loved spending their dollars there.

When Frank arrived, my parents, Juan Pablo and Herlinda, and my brothers and sisters were there to meet him. Their warm welcome felt like a betrayal. He brought a bottle of red wine. We all looked at one another, confused. We didn't drink wine but doused every meal in spicy salsa, and some of us drank ice-cold beer.

Little did I know that I would be facing the most consequential negotiation of my life: Frank and my mother. At stake was my future and a quest deep into another America. A place far from the border, unforgiving, less tolerant and not ready for me.

I was the interpreter.

My mother served up red enchiladas.

Frank, with a warm smile, dark mustache and silvered hair, rose to the occasion and served up dreams.

Frank told my mother about the *Wall Street Journal*, the bible of business leaders. He conjured Philadelphia in terms she could understand: the birth of a nation; a city made for and by immigrants. He explained my potential. He said I was someone who, thanks to my parents, understood and appreciated hard work.

My mother nodded. Her deep-green eyes began to fill with sadness, maybe pride or a deeper understanding of life and how these things must go.

As I looked at Frank across the table, I began wishing my parents would just put me out of my misery and say, *No, he can't go.* Su familia lo necesita. *He stays with his family, where he belongs. His family needs him.*

But instead my mother asked Frank if I could stay through Christmas; it was almost Thanksgiving, after all.

Frank agreed.

When Frank left, she began to wash the dishes. She said it was my time to go now. He believes in you, my mother said. Your father and I have nothing but an elementary school education, if even that. All your father knows is how to drive a tractor, which he can't do anymore because of his bad back. So he sells burritos from his catering truck and he drinks too much. I know how to pick tomatoes, make burritos, tacos and enchiladas, and clear our table. We don't speak English. I don't know journalism. This is what you love. This is what you chose.

I can stay if you want, I told my mother.

She looked at me and my brothers and sisters sitting in the living room, watching some holiday rerun. They didn't seem very cheery now. All glum.

Do it for them, she said, always speaking Spanish even after more than two decades in the United States. Set an example. Who better than you? You're more than their brother. You're like a father to them. Show them they, too, can become someone in their new country.

But isn't our country still Mexico?

It's mine, not yours.

I was too sad to argue.

Don't go west like all of us. Go there—later she would tell me she didn't know where "there" really was—and help chart new paths. Be the new immigrant and show them opportunities in new communities. Inspire them to dream. Maybe some will join you, follow in your footsteps, just like those back in Durango when they followed us to California. We'll miss you and always will; you know that.

The weight of her worlds fell heavy on my shoulders.

I looked around the living room and saw my siblings sitting sadly around the television set. How could I ever leave them and still look them in the eyes. When the Navy recruited my brother Panchito earlier that year—they picked him up at the house and took him from us—we all cried hysterically and made a promise to each other that our bond would never be broken again. But his departure was more like a hairline crack forming in the walls of our old home. When Panchito left, we did something we used to do as farmworkers when we'd circle the wagons and protect each other before moving to a new camp, or from the encroaching Border Patrol agents in their dark green uniforms circling our migrant camps. We huddled close together and I promised them I would never abandon them.

It was my turn now, I said to myself sadly as I made my bed on the living room couch. I stared at the ceiling that evening, afraid of dawn and what would come with the new morning.

On January 3, 1987, I boarded a plane to Philadelphia from El Paso. I was leaving the border—*my* border: The sprawling cities with a fast-growing industry of assembly factories on the south side and the Asarco copper and lead smelter in El Paso on the other. The spot where Mexico begins and Texas ends, an invisible line. Both cities so tolerant, generous and yet so poor and hopeful. I remember the plane leaving the tarmac and wondered whether I would ever see those Franklin Mountains again or the ravines that were more like open veins exposing my city from above the clouds. On the verge of tears, I wondered whether by searching for opportunity I was leaving behind what I cared for the most. And at what cost? Was it worth the separation? I felt my heart still beating on the border below, home of the constant wretched refuge, our jewel in the desert, our Ellis Island in the Southwest.

From above the clouds I saw the landscape slowly change from desert to the green tree-lined streets of Dallas. Another flight, and just before touchdown the sky grew dark and the ground below turned white. Snowy white.

My father had been roped in by ranchers who envisioned him picking every cotton field in West Texas. I was lured by the prospect of telling his story. *Our* story.

2.

David, un Caminero in Philly

I often thought of my father when I arrived in Philadelphia. Was his soul as tortured as mine when he was alone in El Norte, forsaken in a strange land, afraid of failure?

Philadelphia back then was no comparison to a glamorous, elegant and powerful city like New York. It was dreary. Frightful. Desolate. A shell of the glorious past I had read about in history books, limited to an Amtrak stop between New York City and Washington, D.C. Just what exactly did the Founding Fathers find in this city that I wasn't seeing?

My colleagues seemed worried about my homesickness and reminded me Mexican food in the city was slim pickings, although the food at a place called ChiChis wasn't bad.

I was horrified. "ChiChis" in Spanish translated literally to "Titties."

Instead, most of my nights in Philadelphia were spent at Tequilas, where I'd stay long after the dining room emptied out. Out of nowhere, David would turn into Dracula, the fictional vampire, as if his soul unfurled with the departure of his last customer. His obsession would take over. David had a passion, and it wasn't just serving up tacos: He wanted to tempt Americans with the finest in Mexico's cuisine, open their minds with its sophisticated gastronomy, then blow them away with the complexity of its spirits, chiefly tequila.

If anything, I'd think, this friendship will lead us to find the perfect tequila.

We had our work cut out. Pennsylvania controlled liquor sales through state-run stores, making it difficult for a variety of tequilas to enter the market. On his trips to Guadalajara, David would carry as many bottles as he could for "personal use." We would study the labels on tequila bottles, savor the taste and analyze its content. At first I worried that we might become alcoholics giving into nostalgia, something immigrants are prone to do. But David was more disciplined than that. He drank to enrich his mind and taste all that Mexico had to offer.

Esto es Mexico, he'd say with pride, as if saying, *This is who we are and who we can become.*

I simply drank to forget and imagine I was somewhere else.

David came from a long line of merchants. His family believed their ancestors were from the Middle East, possibly what is now Israel or Turkey. He had an unshakable confidence—guts I sometimes envied—and, like me, David also had a chip on his shoulder. He wanted to prove everyone wrong, beginning with his wife and her overly traditional Italian American family. Other than being a good father to his newborn baby, Dave, David was determined to be able to go home to Mexico again *on his terms.*

When he spoke of growing economic ties and amnesty, he saw consequences in the agave fields of Jalisco. He worried that amnesty and the rumblings of economic opening in Mexico would mean the exodus of too many of our countrymen. What would be lost? Would there be any *jimadores* left to hand down the ancient art of cultivating the blue agave fields, stripping the cactus down to its *piña*, roasting it in hot-fired chambers and crushing the agave hearts until the *aguamiel* ran out, ready to ferment and age into real tequila? Or would they all leave and go north? He wanted to rescue something that was left of his childhood.

He wasn't talking about a cheap bottle of Sauza or Cuervo, either. He was talking about something most Americans didn't know about: high-end, high-quality tequila with real terroir.

Another immigrant dreamer, I thought, dismissing his fiery talk.

Like me, David was a high school dropout, but in Mexico. He had had to work harder for everything. His upbringing had been harder than mine. I mean, he grew up in Mexico with all its obstacles of inequality, rampant government corruption and elitist systems. I had been given a chance—a good chance—in the U.S., replete with inspiration and opportunities. I could dream, and anytime doubt crept in, I'd remember the words of Robert F. Kennedy: "Some men see things as they are and say 'Why?' I dream of things that never were and say, 'Why not?'" My mother lived by those words, too.

David had to create his every chance from the bottom up. He knew that to be an immigrant meant taking risks, dreaming big, always being one wrong step away from losing it all. He grew up barely knowing his father, a government secret agent. I often wondered whether his father's right-wing, extremist past sparked David's love of leftist movements in Latin America, something he's always denied. He would often keep the music of Silvio Rodríguez, artistic icon of revolutionary Cuba, playing low. I was intrigued that he knew so much about history. He was a voracious reader, picking up books about everything and anything. He was intrigued by how the Cubans considered themselves equals, not inferiors, to the Spaniards in the New World, and not victims of the conquest like Mexicans and so many others throughout Latin America. They understood the difference, as author Earl Shorris once wrote, between the survivors and the ghosts.

He liked to poke fun at me, much like I did with my younger brothers back home. They saw it as bullying, and I was beginning to understand why. David's latest kick was that I had an uncanny resemblance to Che, the Argentine Marxist revolutionary, who along with Fidel Castro drove the Americans and their U.S. puppet dictator, Fulgencio Batista, out of Cuba. I had grown out a patchy, scruffy beard like Che's—a small, personal rebellion against my clean-cut, corporate-minded journal colleagues—although that wasn't working for me, either.

Maybe you should think like Che more, David said. Be bold. Cut loose. Take on the capitalist world through your pen. You do work for the *Wall Street Journal*, right? Teach them humanity. Rebel against the suits. *No te dejes.*

As annoying as he was, I found David fascinating.

We have a history, a proud history, he'd tell me. Not everything begins and ends in the United States.

But what do I know? I just want to sell tacos.

Unlike most of the guys he grew up with, who had dollar signs in their eyes, he saw the American dream as a myth. Stubborn and obsessive, he believed more in his own will than the "opportunity" of a nation and its capitalistic system that he saw as flawed. The country had no soul. Humans were really robots who could turn on you whenever things didn't go their way. He was above it; he would preach this even as he polished the glasses behind the bar of a restaurant that I told him he would never have opened in Mexico, not as a poor kid with a single mom and no connections.

An only child, he roamed the streets of Calle Apeninos, a middle-class neighborhood in Guadalajara in the western state of Jalisco, Mexico's most dynamic state responsible for exporting everything from music, tequila, cuisine—its own soul and charm.

David was charismatic and a magnet for friends, both Mexican and American, older and younger than he, picking up bohemian habits—drinking and talking through thick layers of smoke by his early teens. He was so rebellious, his overly protective and image-conscious mother kicked him out of the house. Grow up, she said. He moved in with his grandparents.

His parents had split when his mother discovered her husband lived a double life and had another family. David knew only that his father had worked for Mexican intelligence and was part of the White Brigades, which included a death squad, during the brutal administration of Adolfo López Mateos in the 1950s. The Mexican president was alleged to have been responsible for hundreds of deaths and disappearances.

David found his father through a cousin who knew him. He wrote his father letters, never quite telling him how much his absence had left a void in his life. He had too much pride for that. The two finally agreed to meet at a café in Guadalajara. David was seventeen. His father was a dapper man with an aura of elegance. The two agreed to keep in touch, and they did, although the relationship remained strained and never flourished. David reached out more out of curiosity after he and his mother were estranged over David's carousing ways.

He left Guadalajara after being dumped by his girlfriend, who caught him cheating on her. Heartbroken, he went looking for opportunity, not across the border like so many did in the state of Jalisco, but rather in Cancún, Mexico's mecca of white sands and Caribbean beaches. He worked for Carlos' n Charlie's as a waiter and later manager. There he believed he could make his fortune, get a piece of the burgeoning tourism industry that lured gringos looking for fun and sun. The tourist hub was like a slice of America on Mexican soil. All Cancún needed was a giant U.S. flag to tell the world that this land, too, belonged to them.

David learned quickly and became an expert on American tastes. His natural congeniality helped. He looked people in the eye. He made the time. No detail was too small. He studied his American customers closely, learning to pamper them, cater to their every whim and listen to their stories and their bad Spanish. He would encourage them to keep practicing their Spanish. Another tequila, *señor*? He was the ultimate ambassador.

One night one of his customers captivated him.

Annette Cipolloni, an employee of American Airlines, regularly flew in and out of Cancún to accompany a colleague and best friend who was dating David's roommate. It was 1983. Annette was on the verge of engagement, but soon after returning to Philadelphia she called David, who was working the late shift at Carlos' n Charlie's.

She told him she'd like to return to Cancún and see him. David's English was limited to the crucial information he needed to get by: "How was your dinner? Are you finished? Would you like the check? Another *cerveza* or a tequila to make you very happy, sir, ma'am?" He didn't understand English and thought she wanted to make a reservation at the restaurant.

Sure, he told her. How many?

No, a waiter who took the call, told him. Don't be an idiot. She's asking you out.

Okay . . . he said, somewhat perplexed. Isn't she getting married?

That was the beginning of a different kind of migration. Love migration. In one year Annette made nearly sixty trips to Cancún. Needless to say, her relationship with her boyfriend in Philadelphia fell apart. She and David became an item.

Their affair was punctuated by her long layovers. So when she told him she was pregnant, he begged her to stay and make a life with him in Cancún. She said no, pointing out her strict Italian upbringing. David bit his lip and succumbed to the idea of living in the United States. He couldn't bear the thought of his newborn growing up without a father, repeating his own story.

He used his connections in Guadalajara to get a special visa. He was best friends with a young American, the eldest son of the head of the DEA in Guadalajara. As teens, the two grew up together, which was one reason why his mother was so protective of her only son. Many of the kids of the U.S. senior drug enforcement officials were heavy users of pot and coke, vices he stayed away from at the stern warning of his mother, whose wrath he feared the most.

David overlooked his friend's addiction and they remained friends; they were so close that when David had to head north, he turned to his friend for help. The friend confided to his father, who ordered his agent, Enrique "Kiki" Camarena, a native of the San Joaquin Valley, to issue David a special permit, a ten-year tourist visa. Kiki worked at the consulate as cover for his undercover activities as a DEA agent. During the interview, David found the officer quite affable, polite and empathetic as he listened to David's love saga. The consular assignment ended up becoming one of the last tasks Camarena did. Weeks later, in February 1985, the undercover agent was kidnapped and later found tortured and killed, a tragic episode that became a watershed moment that transformed the

U.S.-Mexico relationship. The killing sparked one of the biggest manhunts the U.S. government has ever launched in North America and provided an ominous warning of things to come between both countries.

After Camarena's death, the U.S. government concluded it could no longer trust the Mexican government and questioned the very essence of the country's political machine, the PRI, the party the U.S. government had supported through crisis after crisis. The Americans had overlooked the injustices, student massacres, corruption, and impunity under the PRI in return for stability. A stable neighbor along a two-thousand-mile border was essential, no matter how messy the house was inside.

That had been the case for nearly fifty years, until that afternoon in February when their agent went missing and weeks later his body was discovered; it had been mutilated. The Americans suspected the PRI. The border was shut temporarily, much the way Richard Nixon had ordered it closed decades before. Security became the overriding issue for the United States.

Before any of that, Camarena was simply the agent who had closed the gap between David's past and his future in America. Weeks later David saw the international drama unfolding as he prepared to move to the United States and talked daily with his American friend, whose life grew weary because of the stress on the family and personal strain with his father following Camarena's death. Months later and with limited English, David set out with his newly issued visa to provide for his new family and find his place in a strange land.

David was twenty-three.

He walked the streets of Philadelphia, applying for jobs at restaurants. There weren't that many restaurants downtown then, maybe twenty altogether, he recalled. Center City Philadelphia offered few opportunities. One stood out: El Metate, which claimed to sell Mexican food. He applied and got a job as a waiter. Less than two years later, David's knowledge of the restaurant industry had impressed the owner so much that he offered him a chance to lease the place.

David went looking for money; he had visions of opening a restaurant with a menu of high-end Mexican cuisine. Puerto Rican clients put him in touch with a community development corporation, an organization that "helped minorities," as they put it.

David was confused: What the hell is a minority? he wondered.

By then it was 1986, the economy was collapsing and the group's government funding began drying up. He tried another development corporation. They took one look at the Mexican kid in front of them and sent him packing. Watching the drama unfold was his father-in-law, George J. Cipolloni Sr., an Italian immigrant. Mr. Cipolloni arranged to get David an $85,000 loan to take over the lease. Mr. Cipolloni put up the family home as collateral. The bankers initially envisioned a restaurant to revitalize a downtrodden Puerto Rican neighborhood, but the more they studied David's plan—a high-end restaurant—the more they realized a new, ambitious business could help bring Center City Philadelphia back to life.

Philadelphia was plagued by crack cocaine, ravaged by AIDS, and struggling to recover from the 1985 MOVE siege, in which Philadelphia police dropped a bomb on a residential neighborhood, leaving eleven dead, including five children. David looked around City Center and saw opportunity. He would inject life back into the streets where Philadelphia's aristocrats and luminaries, from Benjamin Franklin to Grace Kelly, once roamed. This would be a cross-border effort. He'd lure friends from Cancún, Guadalajara and across Mexico to help. David wanted to build the very best Mexican restaurant north of the border and leave nothing to chance. He wanted quality, authenticity, fantastic service.

Detail-oriented, he was meticulous about everything from the server uniforms—making sure everyone buttoned their shirts up to necklines—to the handpicked music. He would stay up late to produce homemade mix tapes for his restaurant's music. David turned to other friends in Guadalajara and debated what to name the new place. Tequilas, they suggested. More than a drink, they told him, the word "tequila" also meant a place of work.

He looked for a highly sought-after Mexican chef. He sniffed out leads and found several contenders between Cancún and Guadalajara. It was a rocky beginning. The first chef, José, created such exquisite dishes that a smuggler, a Mexican customs agent, took the chef as his personal hostage to cook his favorite dishes. Arrangements were made to negotiate his freedom, and days later the chef was in Philadelphia. Unfortunately, that chef turned out to be a drunkard who was too jealous with his recipes and refused to teach the cooks, some of them African Americans, in the kitchen.

Chef aside, from day one the restaurant was a smashing success. Food critics raved over the sharp service and the "new" kind of Mexican food: David was offering so much more than tacos and nachos. Lines stretched around the block, with patrons waiting more than two hours to be seated. One evening a wealthy, well-dressed man walked up to David and offered him $50 for a table. He had a date and wanted to impress her. No, David said. What about $100? Or $200? David shook his head, although he was intrigued by the customer's determination. Rejected, the man drove off in his chauffeured convertible and minutes later drove back again.

How about $300? he asked.

No. But I'll tell you what, bring your convertible around and we'll serve the food in your backseat. The man's date was overwhelmed by the attention.

Word of mouth exploded. Everyone wanted to go to and be seen at Tequilas.

One night a woman showed up with a guitar and asked David if she could sing on weekends for tips.

I'm sure you sing great, but I have no space, he said. This is not the right setup. Years later the celebrated Grammy-winning singer, Lila Downs, reminded David of his rejection.

Everything seemed to be working out except for the thing his restaurant was named for: his tequila selection. David couldn't vouch for its quality. In fact, he despised his own selection and darkly warned Ken, Primo and me to drink at our own peril. He feared that the *época de oro del cine mexicano*—the Golden Age of Mexican cinema—had deceived the public with movies that depicted the clichéd character doing the salt-shot-lime cheap-drink version of his beloved tequila. Iconic figures from movie star Pedro Infante (who in real life didn't even drink) to writer Ernest Hemingway didn't help.

You don't toss it back like Hemingway, he'd tell customers. You sip it slowly, like making love to a woman, very slowly, as though it's the last thing you'll ever taste in your mouth. Take in the flavor, the aroma . . .

After his clients left, he'd take out his own favorite tequilas, those he smuggled in his luggage on his frequent trips to Mexico, brands like Siete Leguas, Tapatio, Tres Magueyes. I quickly came to understand the difference. The stuff he sold, along with the rest of America's bars, left lingering headaches and terrible hangovers, because those tequilas were rarely 100 percent agave. Instead the cheap stuff often contained just 51 percent blue agave with sugarcane-based fillers. The stuff he gave us—100 percent agave—lifted our spirits, left no headache and made us pine for home even more. But the good stuff wasn't easy to come by.

We're getting the worst tequila possible. People don't know any better, he said.

He would someday make the *perfect* tequila.

Those long nights at the bar he would talk of his childhood, of driving to the agave fields and being mesmerized by the beauty that lay before him. He'd walk with elders through those fields, admiring the burly *jima-dores*, learning their names, their stories, and wishing he was one of them. They owned their own plot of land and worked for themselves, made their own tequila and sold it locally. He liked their independence.

Sometimes Primo and Ken would join us and we changed the subject to more contemporary topics, away from the dreams we shared. The contentious discussions revolved around Mexico's political and economic strife and looming trade deals.

The consequences of the changes under way could be horrendous for Mexico, Primo repeatedly warned, growing weary of the *Philadelphia Inquirer* headlines.

David would sip his tequila and state his anticapitalist, pseudo-communist position, swearing up and down that *his own willpower* was pivotal to whatever success he'd achieved, not the U.S. American dream.

I never backed down in my belief that he was wrong, especially when the first buzz hit me. Ken agreed with me. The opportunities available in the U.S. were greater than anywhere else, we would tell him. David would accuse Ken and me of lacking imagination, of not believing in our own instincts enough to take risks, of putting too much faith in the American economy, its way of life, the failed status quo. I'd remind him of the benefits of capitalism and how far we'd come, how we had already achieved milestones we never would have achieved in Mexico—at least not without wealth and connections, which none of us had growing up. Mexico was opening up politically, and now economically. Mexicans, with their work ethic, will build a country that's as generous as this one, I'd say.

We'd look for Primo's approval. Mexico has no chance, Primo would respond—the wise one. Not so long as U.S. interests come first.

Bullshit, I'd say, feeling the jolt of tequila refining my brash opinions. Look at us: we're in the Northeast. We're not in some California melon field filling buckets for small change or looking for any sightings of the Border Patrol to warn our friends and family to run and hide in some ditch or brush. We're in the Northeast! *En la vanguardia.* We're building our own network, part of the so-called Decade of the Hispanic, among the fine bluebloods of Philadelphia, even as the city felt like it was crum-bling around us at the time. We would pick it up, fix it, I told them, return it to its former luster. Isn't that what we do as immigrants? Transform cities? Turn them around? Rebuild them with our own sweat, blood? Me, a high school dropout; you, David, another dropout; and you, Primo, having attended the prestigious University of Chicago, and El Colegio de Mexico? And you, Ken, you flunked algebra, still got your Ivy League education—a lawyer surrounded by the bastion of Ivy League schools.

Hey, *chacho*—a common diminutive for *muchacho*—I made As in college, Ken would say in his nerdy way. But, yes, I did flunk algebra.

And me, at the amazing *Wall Street Journal*, uninspiring but incredible.

El pinche Wall Street Journal, they'd mock me right back, rolling their eyes, knowing I had found my tequila limit.

We're making it, right? We're here now, this very moment, together.

I didn't stop there. Imagine what will happen now with amnesty? Who will stay behind in Mexico? We should be lucky we left—or, in my case, that my parents brought me here for a better life. You, David, should be happy you came for love, *cabrón*—the slight implying we were now comfortable with one another.

And then I'd take special aim at him and ask, my words slurring, the tequila taking its full effect: How do you think we got here, sitting here in your own place, Tequilas? *Oportunidades. The American dream*. I uttered the words slowly, aimed as much for me as for David. By the end of the night, I was trying to convince myself of my own promise—that somehow things would get better, because I increasingly found myself drowning.

I was desperate to believe in what I was told about the American dream, which didn't seem to exist for people who looked like me. As much as I tried not to admit it, my colleagues were back at the office burning the midnight oil, climbing the ladder. That wasn't me. I was holed up at Tequilas looking for the courage and a white flag to surrender.

Really? The American dream? David would ask. No more Neruda or tequila for you. Then he'd grin at me and ask, *¿Otro?*—perhaps feeling bad about giving me so much crap. It's on me, he'd say, and reach for his secret stash.

Make that a double, I'd joke.

We were clueless in Philadelphia, a city going through its own growing pains, down on its luck, bankruptcy and an exodus of the wealthy to the suburbs. We were all restless and, by the look of things at Table 21, uneasy.

One of David's music mixes featured nearly the entire Miguel Bosé album *XXX*. Miguel Bosé, son of a Spanish bullfighter and an Italian actress and ballet dancer, smoothed over our philosophical differences.

We could take apart Bosé's lyrics without any disagreement, diving into the meaning of his words, writing them down on napkins and taking a hard look at his genius and ourselves.

Primo and Ken looked at us like we were romantic fools—maybe we were—as we closed our eyes and hummed the lyrics, floating away:

> *Falso paraíso yo . . .*
> *Contradicción, extraña invención*
> *Y al ser vulnerable me vuelvo invencible . . .*

> False paradise, me . . .
> Contradiction, strange invention
> And by being vulnerable I become invincible . . .

3.

Ken, Barbie & Brooks Brothers

Despite my cluelessness, or perhaps because of it, my *Journal* colleague Julie and I had become close. In retrospect, I realize she was just intrigued by Ken, eyeing him with curiosity, constantly asking what his secret was. How did someone from some small town in New Mexico, with an impoverished upbringing, get so polished that he felt he could fit right in? It seemed hard for us to believe, and at the same time it felt to Julie and me that Ken somehow held the key. Plus I'm pretty sure she was attracted to Ken, though she said she saw him like a long-lost cousin. He always seemed oblivious to her and so she often palled around with me.

I argued with Julie: Hey, look at us. How did we end up here?

But he has no Mexico baggage like us, she said. *Corchadito*, your closet is full of baggage.

Ken was generations removed from Mexico. We were flirting with the mainstream, while Ken was casually floating in it, cutting a path into the future of mainstream political involvement. He had worked hard to get to where he was. But meeting us, this budding club of Mexicans in Philadelphia, had inspired Ken to reexamine his roots. He was looking for his own Mexican identity and we were looking for the opposite.

Ken couldn't have been more wholesome and driven if he tried. He was the son of a Protestant preacher in a region colonized by the Spaniards in 1598 when Juan de Oñate established a small pueblo in Santa Fe, a region not new to conflicts. In 1680 the Pueblo Indians rebelled against efforts to replace their traditional religion by the Spanish Catholic Church. They killed most of the priests and drove the rest of the Spaniards south—momentarily at least. By 1696, Spain was once again in control of New Mexico, but never so comfortable and entitled as before.

A tree-studded bend in the hills near where he grew up is called Trujillo Pass, named for his ancestors. He could trace his lineage back to the seventeenth century.

The only boy among four sisters, Ken was born in Española and raised across northern New Mexico and in Durango, Colorado. He spent many summers at his grandmother's home in Cañones, a tiny four room place made of adobe with no indoor plumbing and an outhouse. In the middle was a wood-burning stove with fireplaces to stay warm. They grew vegetables.

A few feet away from his grandmother's home was a tiny church where Ken's father preached. When Ken was five, he told his father he too wanted to preach during Christmas service and his dad agreed. He put a chair behind the pulpit. Ken still laughs when he tells the story. I got up, looked around, got scared and said, *Arrepientansen pecadores y no miren tanto para aca.* In other words, Repent, you sinners—and don't look up here so much! That was Ken's first and only sermon. Everyone laughed gently, he said.

For Ken, food stamps, "government cheese" and peanut butter were childhood staples. He wore the same pair of shoes for much of high school, the soles nearly worn-out completely by senior year.

Ken's mother, Eileen, was a homemaker raised in the small New Mexico town of Cañones, near the iconic Cerro Pedernal mesa, the same foothills that inspired Georgia O'Keeffe to paint her masterpieces: a place where the landscape unfolded—blue sky, brown hills one way, snow-covered peaks the other, clay-colored adobe ranches in the distance. The farther he got away from the cities like Albuquerque and Santa Fe, Ken said, the wilder the land became.

This was the same land deeded to Ken's family at the turn of the nineteenth century, before the U.S.-Mexico war divided land possessions and families, before nations were separated, a stinging humiliation that still lingers for some. At the end of the Mexican-American War, the United States took control of the present-day states of California, Nevada, Utah, New Mexico, Arizona and Colorado, asserting the English language in these lands. The 1848 Treaty of Guadalupe Hidalgo transferred the territories to the U.S. and upheld land grants, formalizing the annexation of an estimated 500,000 square miles of territory, half of Mexico's most valued land, complete with seaports that pointed toward Asia. Up to 100,000 Mexicans remained in those territories, including Ken's family.

In Texas, which had already seceded from Mexico, the southern boundary was marked along the Rio Grande (Río Bravo to Mexicans) all the way to California. The cession of Alta California would include the port of San Diego. The land grab turned the United States into an instant world superpower and left Mexico with a stinging sense of humiliation and an unshakable suspicion of its imperialist northern neighbor. To help ease any lasting resentment, the U.S. paid $15 million for the lands—a pittance even then—and retrieved its troops from Mexico City.

The United States could have taken all of Mexico, as Americans believed it was "God's will" or manifest destiny that the U.S. should absorb their southern neighbor—perhaps Central and South America as well. Opponents, however, worried about one fundamental matter: How do you incorporate so many Mexicans, nonwhite, non–English speaking people into the United States without fundamentally changing the character of the country? Historian David Gutiérrez at the University of California, San Diego, noted that the annexation of Mexico was about territory, not people. There was no way to absorb so many Mexicans. Such a move would create a race problem and residents of the territory had the option to head south into what remained of Mexico.

Moreover, New Mexicans had always felt that swaps of territory, from the time when Spain and Mexico ruled the region, were illegal. To add fuel to the fire, the provision upholding land grants in the Treaty of Guadalupe Hidalgo was later revoked by the U.S. Congress.

The 1960s saw New Mexican land grant movements led by activists like Reies Tijerina, a fiery, charismatic Texas-born preacher. Tijerina argued that land grants were still valid and founded the Alianza Federal de Mercedes to stage a number of protests, often fueled by his religious fervor and belief that the United States had used its laws to steal and connive hundreds of poor landowners who didn't know about their rights to those deeds. In his prophetic zeal, he referred to the Mexicans of indigenous origins of New Mexico as "Indo-Hispanos."

On June 5, 1967, Tijerina led a group of armed men to storm a courthouse in the small New Mexico community of Tierra Amarilla to free prisoners arrested earlier in the dispute over land. In the bungled attack and mayhem that ensued, a jailer and sheriff deputy were wounded. Tijerina was arrested and later released, vaulting him into the national spotlight. He is considered one of the Four Horsemen of the Chicano Rights Movement, alongside Cesar Chavez, Rodolfo "Corky" Gonzales and José Ángel Gutiérrez. His determination to seek redress for landless, impoverished New Mexicans left a mark on the region, especially on Ken's family. But Ken himself seemed unscathed, unscarred.

It would take many cigarettes and shots of tequila before I would learn any of this from Ken. He always drank quietly with us, listening while David, Primo and I droned on, debated politics, gave each other shit. He later confessed that he—Mr. Ivy League—felt out of his league, sometimes even intimidated by us, by our Spanish and our connection to our culture. Yet when he was alone with me—perhaps because I wasn't as brash as David or as intellectual as Primo—Ken opened up.

His entire situation seemed odd to me. I couldn't get my mind around how a kid growing up so close to Mexico could still feel estranged from it. For me, Mexico was just a way of life; I never had to reconnect. But as an immigrant myself, my family hadn't lived through the Treaty of Guadalupe Hidalgo, the way Ken's family had. Moreover, the animosity toward Mexicans in the region had never quite receded.

In New Mexico, Ken's minister father was no activist, but he did believe in fighting for justice. Once, Ken accompanied his father down to southern New Mexico to pick up undocumented Mexican workers to help them return to the San Luis Valley fields in southern Colorado. For his father, whose annual income was $4,500 a year, it was an opportunity to do good and make a few extra dollars. Ken never forgot that lesson. He'd travel everywhere with his father, and along those paved and dirt roads he developed a deep interest in helping others. He took to his father's philosophy: that dreams sail higher with the boost of an education.

His father, Gene, spoke to everyone in Spanish with pride in their deep family roots, pointing to the lands the Spaniards had crisscrossed in their search for gold mines, the same lands now under U.S. possession. He was particularly proud of the vitality that Spanish still enjoyed, tracing the power of language to decisions made centuries ago.

This was well before Spain began colonizing the New World in 1492, back to the thirteenth century, when the Spanish king Alfonso X assembled a collection of Jews, Arabs and Christians, as Mexican writer Carlos Fuentes noted in his book *The Buried Mirror*, to promote Spanish at a time when Latin and Arabic still influenced the Iberian Peninsula. Ken's father cringed at how the language had since been butchered—Spanglish—although a semblance of its origins remained intact.

Despite pride in their roots, the family didn't expect much from life. But Ken did. No family member, teacher or guidance counselor expected him to amount to much, but Ken had an urgent drive to succeed. And he was smart—very smart—despite the low expectations. Ken once came home from winning a spelling bee with a black eye, having angered the kids who were expected to win. The Boys & Girls Club of La Plata County taught Ken chess and gave him a used pair of skis. Ken took the chess lessons and won a contest that netted him an introduction to his boyhood hero, NFL quarterback Bart Starr. Not able to afford a ski lift pass, Ken taught himself to ski in the hills behind his house to get on Durango's legendary high school ski team. His fifth-grade teacher, Mrs. Gore, saw a spark that others missed, watching Ken learn to play tennis from books and magazines. A sixth-grade teacher taught Ken the basics of golf in the high school gym. Under the radar, Ken was feeding a hungry mind while learning country club sports.

Low expectations didn't stop Ken from becoming a voracious reader: he devoured everything from Ayn Rand to history tomes to *The Spook Who Sat by the Door* by Sam Greenlee. Early in high school, Ken was generally a B-minus student while barely cracking a book. Why would he? He had no plans to go to a competitive school. He assumed he'd head for a state school, which wasn't difficult to get into. When Russell Yates, a Durango lawyer, visited his classroom and urged others like him to become lawyers, Ken took the challenge to heart. He joined his high school Model United Nations team and won a state competition as the delegate from Romania, prompting one of his teammates to grouse, *Ken's not all that smart, he's just clever.*

Unlike me, Ken figured early that his ticket out was higher education. He graduated high school at seventeen and worked the summer so he and a close friend could to travel to Europe on Laker Airways' peanut fares. While I was still working the fields in California as a high school dropout, Ken was applying to Evangel College in Springfield, Missouri, the liberal arts college of his father's church, the Assemblies of God. As he filled out his applications, his father's W2 form confirmed what he already knew: his father could barely afford to provide for his family. Ken had to do better than that but had no clue where to even start. He followed his instincts.

Later, when I pressed him about how he even thought to apply to college, Ken told me that he didn't really have a plan or role models or anyone to ask for guidance. He improvised. He told me, This was all new to me. I just acted as if I belonged.

In Philadelphia, Julie seemed almost as comfortable as Ken, acting the part of the savvy professional. That's why—even though I could pour my heart out to David at Tequilas about anything and everything—I felt closer to Ken in a way. I so desperately wanted to emulate him.

Once in college, Ken felt his world had come alive. He loved history, political science and philosophy. He wanted and needed to graduate quickly and he overloaded on courses at Evangel and took summer courses back in Durango. He did it all while working the midnight shift at a nursing home. He majored in political science and was intrigued by how power worked. He snagged a Washington, D.C., internship and then got his first job after college with Senator Pete Domenici of New Mexico. He quickly got rid of the John Travolta look, cropping his long locks short and polishing up on the formalities of East Coast life. The Capitol Hill crowd wore Brooks Brothers suits, button-down oxford shirts and penny loafers. He arrived with two suits, a few shirts, a couple of slacks and a brand-new pair of penny loafers to help fit in. Ken longed for the look but had no budget for it. He managed to buy an affordable blue button-down shirt but could hardly put together a presentable suit. The envy he had felt back at Evangel around his wealthier friends only grew.

He still planned on going to law school, but politics in Washington was intoxicating. He was more excited than intimidated, especially since he was surrounded by wide-eyed college-age kids who seemed to run Washington in the summer. He was awed by the beauty of the city, its statues, monuments and green grass. But the nasty partisan politics put him off and made him, for the moment, discard any idea of becoming just another politician obsessed with reelection. He was more interested in the actual governance. The allure of D.C. hooked Ken on another adventure, one course short of graduating from college.

He also quickly understood the importance of connections.

One of his friends was the son of the deacon at a Baptist church where President Jimmy Carter was to attend. Ken suddenly found himself in Washington in front of the leader of the free world.

Power had its appeal, too. Getting there hadn't been easy.

Just as Ken was going to apply to law schools, his father called him back to Colorado. In addition to serving as a minister to migrant laborers, Ken's father had a small contract delivering mail for the U.S. Postal Service. But his diabetes was robbing his eyesight and he couldn't do the only job that provided for the family financially. So Ken returned to Durango to drive his dad's mail truck while he applied to law schools.

As an aspiring lawyer, Ken read *The Partners: Inside America's Most Powerful Law Firms* by James B. Stewart, a bestselling nonfiction account that offered a rare view into the world of white-shoe New York law firms in the 1970s. Vacations were rare, if ever, but the payoff was in the millions. Ken was enthralled, using the book as a bible, reading it everywhere he could. He kept it on the seat in the mail truck. Or next to him in bed.

Ken had found his calling. He imagined a day when he would walk New York avenues wearing a sleek suit and tie and with a wallet thick with dollars and credit cards. He spent evenings applying to law schools from California to Wisconsin to Harvard and Penn. He liked the idea of the Northeast and he wanted to fashion himself after those pricey lawyers in Stewart's book.

Ironically, Stewart later became the page one editor at the *Wall Street Journal*, overseeing some of my work, and later won the Pulitzer for his coverage on the 1987 stock market crash and insider trading.

University of Pennsylvania School of Law came calling. He got in. The Ivy League. Ken could not believe it. He took a Greyhound bus to Philadelphia with two suitcases, a box of books and a college dorm refrigerator. Most of his classmates came from money, prep schools and the Ivy League. His first year, he could only afford a meal plan for one meal a day. No matter. Ken was going to be a lawyer.

He arrived at Penn Law in Philadelphia in 1983 with plans of graduating and returning to Colorado to practice. Although penniless, he quickly fit in, dating the daughters of WASPs and the Jewish elite. He timed his escapes to brief hours on weekends so nothing would get in the way of his ambitions. His idea of fun was hanging out with law students and doing frat-boy things he'd missed in strict college experience like drinking beer, playing squash, and watching *Monty Python* movies and reruns on TV. He never spoke Spanish and rarely talked about where he came from.

He got his first law job with Schnader, one of the top firms in the city. It changed Ken's fate. Although he dabbled in immigration and tried corporate law, immigration cases drained him and at times seemed too repetitive and predictable. He loved complex civil litigation laced with jurisdictional issues and big money: he found it more profitable and less taxing on him personally.

Ken soon started to forget about ever going back to the Southwest. By the time I met him, he had earned the highest bonus of any associate in his firm the late 1980s, resulting from a lawsuit against the Salvation Army for wrongful death. His job was loaded with perks. For example, if he stayed beyond 7:00 p.m., he earned a meal allowance of $12 and a free ride home. Almost invariably, he'd work past 7:00 p.m. and eat at Tequilas.

At a time when I struggled to afford a hoagie, Ken's assimilation into the U.S. mainstream was almost complete. Unlike me, he seemed comfortable in his skin, walking inside Tequilas with dapper wool scarves and Allen Edmonds shoes. I usually took time to study his dress, asking about the designer and dumbfounded at the prices he'd paid. Each suit would cost me the same price as maybe three round-trip tickets to El Paso.

Yet beyond the world Ken was now a part of, he was looking for ways to retain what was left of his roots. He missed his father, his family and the sound of Spanish. He was so curious about Mexico that Primo and I immediately adopted him, if just for the sake of increasing our pitiful number. Plus he was charitable. Ken generously helped pay much of the tab, which at times was sucking away at least one-third of our weekly earnings. He also offered me hand-me-downs.

Stop by my place this weekend, he'd say. I've got a couple of sports jackets, a tweed one, and some shirts and ties that may fit you.

I declined, telling him not to worry about me.

He looked me up and down and quipped: *Chacho*, you work at the *WSJ*. You need them.

I was a little taller than him, so swapping slacks was out of the question. Plus I rarely parted with my jeans, a proud reminder of my days as a farmworker. But I took the blazers, grudgingly grateful for his generosity.

Julie took me on as her pet project, maybe out of pity or to save her own skin. My failure could have ramifications for her and many more of us after. Either way, I was grateful. My situation was so desperate that I needed her help. Unsurprisingly, Julie enlisted Ken.

Julie and Ken, a.k.a. Ann Taylor and Brooks Brothers. That was what they called each other, a testament to their aspirations. Wading in American culture, swimming in its vanilla waters, undetected. In contrast, I struggled to find any other Mexican Americans of equal stature in Philadelphia. This reality made their aspirations and achievements even more remarkable—that they could break so many barriers to get where they were. Julie's presence at the *Journal* and Ken's power in court made them groundbreakers and trailblazers.

But to me, at that time, well, they were more like Barbie and Ken.

I just dreamed of being half as polished as Julie or anywhere near as eloquent as Ken. Presciently, the two bonded over Donald Trump, better known at the time as The Donald since people still referred to his father as "Trump." The Donald was the brashest developer in the region, bent on tearing New York City apart to build huge monuments to his young, privileged, egomaniacal self. He was only in his late thirties and already his net worth, according to a *New York Times* article, was estimated at $3 billion. He was coy, treating the media as his lapdog. Tasked with covering The Donald's rise in New York, Julie had her hands full. That year, 1987, The Donald floated trial balloons for a presidential run—if not the following year, sometime later. He took out three full-page $93,000 ads in key newspapers—the *New York Times*, the *Boston Globe* and the *Washington Post*—touting his foreign policy mettle and ridiculing Ronald Reagan.

"There's nothing wrong with America's Foreign Defense Policy that a little backbone can't cure," read one ad.

Trump was talking about nuclear disarmament as he trotted around the world. One article in the *New York Times* said he had visited Moscow that year and met with Soviet leader Mikhail S. Gorbachev. Trump told the *Times* the two talked about a luxury hotel development in the Soviet Union.

Was Trump running for president? Editors wanted to know. And what about those alleged ties to the Mafia? Speculation about a presidential run grew with a scheduled visit to New Hampshire that fall. The spokesman replied: "There is absolutely no plan to run for mayor, governor or United States senator. He will not comment about the presidency."

Even so, Julie was a bit underwhelmed when Trump personally called to invite her to Atlantic City to see his latest wonder. Julie putting him off, I learned, was part of the *Journal* game, or that of any major newspaper. I was quickly discovering that when you work at the *Journal* just about everyone wants to talk to you. You are supposed to play every invitation cool, to be smug about it. To play hard to get. This was against everything I had learned at the *El Paso Herald-Post*, where we were usually eager to get out of the office. The best stories were in the streets.

Julie pondered the idea of covering what Trump billed as the biggest, most beautiful casino ever built in run-down Atlantic City, just over an hour's drive from Philadelphia. Julie talked to Frank, who thought it would be of interest to *Journal* readers to see what The Donald was up to. She agreed to ride with Trump from Philadelphia to Atlantic City in his helicopter, named after his wife, Ivana. Julie later returned to Atlantic City and asked Ken to join her at the grand opening of Trump's newest jewel, the Showboat Casino. The reporting didn't go as planned.

The whole time I'm trying to get information from him for the story, she told me, and nothing! He didn't answer my questions. Not one single question. No matter what I asked—how many people will be employed, how much money you expect to make, specifics—he would go off on a tangent about himself, his "tremendous" business know-how.

God, Alfredo, it was infuriating. I couldn't crack his façade. Such a waste of time, she recalled.

But to Frank that was the story. Trump doesn't want to talk about anything else but himself. And Frank's right, Julie said. That's the story. Trump can't focus. He's narcissistic.

And yet, when it came to writing the story, Julie couldn't get beyond the lead. She couldn't see the story even though the media had a strange fixation on The Donald. So she wrote another story, a lighthearted feature about a Mexican American lawyer bowling in a tuxedo at Trump's new casino. She wrote about Ken.

Now here we were at Wanamaker's looking for suits, my last-ditch effort to fit in and save face. I had lost my self-worth, thinking I couldn't write anything beyond stories I cared little about, like earnings reports and hostile takeovers. I took a stab at features, like concert promoters creating a so-called quiet room for beleaguered parents of rock concert attendees. They waited quietly, reading, while their kids banged heads to Iron Maiden's music onstage. Or a story about cops in Penn State frisking students not for booze or guns but for marshmallows, which could lead to a sticky situation for players on the field. Get it?

I regained my self-esteem only when I walked into Tequilas. Some magic happened when I turned on Locust Street, on that block, where I would beam again with confidence like I did back home, walk with the rooster strut of the *gallo* that I thought only macho Mexican men and John Travolta could pull off. With Ken and Julie's help, I bought four somewhat stylish but affordable suits—gray, black, khaki and navy blue— to see if I could somehow find the confidence to fit into this new culture and go unnoticed around the people I reported on, the investors, corporate executives, Wall Street types. Sure, Ken wanted me to buy pricey suits identical to his, but I needed to save my money for Tequilas.

Besides, regardless of what I wore, I couldn't mask who I really was. As much as I wanted to be him, I just couldn't.

4.

Primo, the Mystery Man

One evening between midnight and dawn, after one of those debates over Mexico's grim future—the kind that left us drained and yet feeling like we still had more to say—I asked David to drop off Primo and me at our homes. It was getting late and cabs rarely passed through downtown at that time. He readily agreed. We headed for what was planned as our first stop, Primo's apartment in West Philly, at Thirty-Fifth and Baring Street. We lived blocks away from one another.

But as we got in David's deep-red VW van, I suddenly envisioned a far more sinister plan. I would snoop through Primo's apartment and search for clues as to what he was really up to in Philadelphia. David had never been inside his apartment and the thought never even crossed Ken's mind, but the desire to dig deeper into Primo's life was something I couldn't shake.

Primo would disappear on trips that he would rarely tell us about, then days later show up at Tequilas and tell us about the women he had met and how he had danced all night, and launch into his never-ending rants on politics. He'd also spend entire days walking the streets with a small camera, taking pictures of reflections taken from mirrors, windows and puddles.

Primo was the most complex and mysterious of the four of us. I couldn't help but wonder: Did he have a secret phone somewhere lying in the house with direct access to a government handler in Mexico City? What made this guy tick? What was he doing in Philadelphia? Did he belong to the Communist party? In fact, years before, in 1982, while at the University of Chicago, Primo was accused by the Chicago Boys that he fought against for their support of the Chilean dictator Augosto Pinochet, of working for Russia. He seemed so accomplished, dapper, to be a night owl, a ladies' man, defying that straitlaced Quaker type. What was behind that façade? I wondered as we neared his apartment.

As I had hoped, Primo invited us in for a *caminero*, or one for the road, his first offering from his own place.

Wow, I thought, Primo had had too much to drink. He was dropping his guard. He usually seemed private about his apartment—had never even come close to extending an invitation to us, a rarity for Mexicans who dish out such invitations amid pleasantries. Not Primo. He'd usually walk out discreetly from the restaurant, saying he needed a smoke, take in the Philadelphia evening and disappear.

David and I exchanged glances. I urged him to come inside, winking. *Vamos*, no? He said he'd have to pass as he had a long drive home and wanted to see his son Dave in the morning. Be wide awake. Sunday was his best day to be with his family. But he discreetly winked back as if to say *GO!* I eagerly accepted Primo's offer and walked into his tiny apartment.

The place looked like a hotel room, barren and sad, in spite of the white walls and blue ceiling. He lived frugally, surrounded by books. He had an empty refrigerator, except for Wonder Bread, ham, turkey, slices of cheese, ketchup, mayonnaise, mustard and enough salsa and jalapeños to feed the entire Mexican army back home. No TV set. No special phone in sight other than the spin-dial, the one he used to answer my call months before. He had a radio–cassette player with salsa songs that included a collection by Rubén Blades. He loved the song "Buscando América"—America is a continent and anyone born in the continent is an American, he'd remind me.

We're all stuck here in the same neighborhood, *joven* Alfredo. Let's make the best of our time in our diverse playground.

Of course, I'd say.

At times, inspired by the song, and in his desperation to teach me to dance and loosen up, he'd do a few steps in front of me, his cigarette hanging from his mouth. The act had the opposite effect on me. I would only become more intimidated, as I tried controlling my laugh. As it turned out, there was something in the apartment revealing Primo's innermost and iconoclastic thoughts. His choice of heroes was underscored by three posters. The first one from the entrance to the bedroom, a black-and-white portrait of a smiling Harold Washington, the first and only African American mayor of Chicago; the second, in red and white with a blue background, was a stylized version of the iconic picture of Che Guevara by photographer Alberto Korda; and the third one was the emblematic face of the most popular religious figure in Mexico and throughout the Americas, the Virgin of Guadalupe.

What's going on here, Primo? I asked as I headed for his restroom, thinking maybe the secret listening devices were there somewhere underneath his toilet. Nothing. Are you a Democrat, like Harold, an idealist revolutionary à la Che or a militant Guadalupano Catholic? I asked. *¿Qué pedo?*

I admire those who stand up for justice, he said.

That evening, he introduced me to Billie Holiday's music, he later said, to keep hope alive.

As much as I criticized the U.S. government and Wall Street, Primo added, I have lots of respect, let's say, for people who change the face of this country for good. From Native Americans, women and Chicano struggles to civil rights and anti-war movements.

But why, then, does your apartment look like mine, like you're ready to take off, get on a plane at any moment? I insisted. You have nothing here. No memories, no roots.

I'm just waiting for the revolution to begin, he'd say.

Words that only intrigued me more.

He told me he had no intention of staying in the U.S. long term. Even after stints in the Midwest and Northeast, he was always one suitcase away from Mexico City. I browsed through his books, autobiographies and history tomes and I realized he was the most educated compared to us—with a college degree, a master's and nearly a PhD from prestigious institutions in Mexico and the U.S.—and yet he held fast to poverty, never acquiring much. Living without much fanfare. A simple life. Maybe he *was* a Quaker.

Primo sensed I was in no hurry to leave and brought the tequila bottle to the living room. He said the magical words: You're welcome to stay.

Got a pillow? I quickly asked before he changed his mind. You may be right. I'm not sure I should walk home so late at night, and I'm low on cash for a cab and I hear West Philly is dangerous at night, I said, making myself comfortable on his tiny sofa.

Of course, Alfredo. I wouldn't want you to walk around on streets still filled with snow and ice. You could fall and break your restless and much-admired head.

What a compliment, but I wouldn't want to burden you.

Not at all, *hermano*, he said.

Good, I thought.

Primo brought an extra pillow and blanket.

Make yourself at home, *joven galán*.

Gracias, Primo.

What I really wanted to do was wait for him to fall asleep so I could walk around the room and start digging.

Instead, I realized Primo was a lot more open than I had originally thought. He sat across me puffing on another cigarette. He was just getting started. No sign of fatigue.

Tell me your story, Primo. Tomorrow is Sunday. We have all night.

Primo's family has their own migration tale, symbolic because Primo's family was the first of any of our families to embrace immigration. Primo was born and raised in Ixtlán de los Hervores, a small town in the western state of Michoacán, bordering Jalisco, a region with deep, historic routes to the United States. His grandfather, Don José, worked in an Ohio factory during World War I, a participant in the factory-driven northward migration led by Henry Ford in the 1910s that continued through the two world wars into the 1940s. It wasn't Mexico sending people north; it was American factories and American agriculture pulling Mexicans like a giant magnet. America was hungry for labor.

For seven years Don José harvested fields, waited on tables and sang in cantinas throughout the Midwest, states like Kansas, Indiana and Michigan. He then worked in construction in Toledo, Ohio, where he settled down. During this time he saved money to return to Mexico. Economic times in the United States seemed ominous, and Don José dreamed of building a store in Ixtlán de los Hervores. He also wrote and sang songs for those Ohio bars, Primo later discovered. He recorded some of those songs in Ohio, and when Primo learned that, he knew he wanted to someday find them, any remnants of the music, to better understand his grandfather.

On the eve of the Great Depression, with the future of the U.S. economy looking bleak, Don José feared the worst. Don José returned to Ixtlán de los Hervores on his own. He didn't arrive empty-handed, but in a new truck, with enough money to build his dream grocery store. Many others returned and each one started his or her own small business. His experience and that of tens of thousands of other migrant workers would inspire many hundreds of thousands more to head north for generations to come, beginning with World War II, when the fickle United States once again implored Mexicans to give the U.S. a hand while its sons fought overseas.

The exodus for the U.S. never ended. It only grew. Like many before him, Primo was destined to head north. He was expected to pack his sack and wave goodbye. That he did, but he took a new route. He dreamed of traveling, seeing the world, the volcanoes in Japan, the jungles of Africa; all he knew was what was pictured in the Tarzan movie that he saw in the theater where his mother worked, the theater he had frequented as a young boy. He just wanted to travel. So he became a seminarian at Misioneros de Guadalupe in Mexico City. They had missions in Japan and Kenya.

He began his adventure in Texas. In 1963, when Primo was nineteen years old, he and four young seminarians traveled by bus to Laredo, where they put their dollars together and bought a used Chevy pickup truck. Inspired by Alexis de Tocqueville and Jack Kerouac and guided by Catholic connections, they made their way to Chicago and Clearwater, Nebraska, where they lived for three months with farmers of German ancestry and learned to raise chickens, grow wheat, make marmalade and butter and become everyday handymen, plumbers and construction workers.

There were no other Mexicans around, he recalled: We were a novelty in town, like Martians, and everyone wanted to invite us to dinner, to schools to talk about Mexico, the Virgin of Guadalupe, bullfighting, soccer . . .

One afternoon Primo and one of the four young men were dancing *Jarabe Tapatío*—known in English as the Mexican hat dance—in front of a big crowd of students inside a gym, when the news broke: John F. Kennedy had been shot. The room fell silent and everyone got on their knees and prayed. Minutes later they were told the young Catholic president who was also worshipped throughout Mexico was dead.

That moment—especially the way the American community fell to prayer and unity in a moment of such terrible tragedy—struck Primo. He knew his trip was at its end but he wanted to come back. His friendship with America had just begun.

We all cried and prayed for the country and its countrymen, he said. There was something beautiful, so beautiful, about the United States that I wanted to return. I was intrigued.

Thus began long visits to the United States, trips sponsored by seminaries, journeys that went beyond wanting to understand the northern neighbor. He also wanted to lose his virginity—or, conversely, to test the will of his abstinence. Just how devoted was he to a life of a seminarian? Would he perhaps join the priesthood one day? He needed to search out temptation in a new land to know those answers.

One seminarian's family lived in Franklin Lakes, New Jersey. They owned a construction company and Primo worked there for three months, alongside African Americans building a golf course, shoveling dirt, smashing rocks with pickaxes, working ten-hour workdays at $2.30 an hour. On weekends he'd take a bus to New York City, where the layers of Catholic guilt were slowly wearing off.

I walked by bars and I was afraid that if I walked inside them I would be walking into hell's inferno, he said. One day I finally gave in to temptation and walked into a topless bar and came out a changed man. It was the summer of 1965.

Primo knew his days as a seminarian were numbered. He returned two years later to Franklin Lakes to work, this time alongside Puerto Ricans. His escapades to New York City continued. He met a Portuguese American, Elya, a sweet and beautiful woman who tried to release his repressed sensuality. But Primo still maintained some resistance and saved his virginity that night, something he later regretted.

I was an idiot, he said. So high and mighty, so preachy, a complete idiot.

The year 1968, the last year of his Jesuit training, was spent working in Mexico City as a volunteer in poor communities. Mexico was to host the Olympics, amid a student movement that demanded three fundamental democratic changes in Mexican politics: freedom of speech, the right to assemble and government accountability. Primo had many friends in the movement and joined them. A student uprising in Mexico City that fall fueled what many in Mexico consider the beginning of the end for Mexico's ruling party and first steps toward a more open system. For Primo it marked the end of his seminary studies.

The year 1968 definitely turned me into a leftist, an activist within the Catholic Church, he said. He later joined the Socialist Party and became active in causes on both sides of the border, including in Austin. In 1971, while doing research work at the Latin American Collection at the University of Texas, Primo joined a Chicano commune. Soon he was hooked on Texas burgers and blues music—and he was still obsessed with losing his virginity. The monumental moment happened at the commune when a Chicana seduced him, leaving Primo mesmerized not just with sex but with a woman who embraced both sides of the border, who spoke to him in broken Spanish and yet was connected to her roots in Mexico.

Primo returned to Mexico City, lived on a scholarship and attended El Colegio de México, a progressive university for future standout classmates, including Sergio Aguayo, Roberta Lajous and Jaime Serra Puche. He wanted to be a historian, an intellectual, and in 1977, without finishing his dissertation, he left for the University of Chicago to study with the legendary historian Frederick Katz, who later penned a book on Pancho Villa, and John H. Coatsworth, who years later became provost of Columbia University. He joined groups of women and men fighting for social justice, constantly haunted by his grandfather and what he saw in the States. What caught his attention as an activist was a growing and courageous immigrant movement.

He showed me a picture of himself dressed in jeans, a black turtleneck, a black leather jacket and a black beret. He thought that growing globalization was absolutely driven by corporations. He feared that workers' rights would be disregarded as the world became more interconnected. An admirer of farmworker organizers Cesar Chavez and Baldemar Velásquez, Primo believed Chavez had a point: in their search for a job, any job, Mexican immigrants worked for such cheap wages that they sabotaged themselves and hurt their own cause. He also came to appreciate their political insights and convictions in improving labor conditions for the immigrant worker, documented or not.

Primo joined movements as well as campaigns to elect progressive candidates, even though his student visa prohibited him from doing so. In fact, he joined the movement to elect Harold Washington mayor of Chicago, politicking in Mexican and Puerto Rican neighborhoods and making a last call outside polling places on Election Day. He was on the streets so much, he didn't finish his dissertation.

In 1982, Primo and other Mexican immigrants got behind Washington, who became a link between the African American and Hispanic communities, channeling their frustrations into a political movement. As a member of the U.S. House of Representatives, Washington had served one of Chicago's poorest, most racially segregated districts. He was progressive. He vowed to represent Chicago's immigrants—including the "illegals"—because they deserved the same rights as black and white Americans. Washington won and became the first black mayor of Chicago, capturing more than 90 percent of the black vote and about 60 percent of the Hispanic vote, and squeaking by with less than 10 percent of the white vote.

After his election, Washington held a press conference where he reiterated: he had been elected to govern for everyone in Chicago, independent of their race, nationality, gender and immigration status.

"Chicago," he said, "belongs to all of the people living in the city. Everyone has the right to have a job if she or he is qualified for it." And the media defiantly asked, *Even illegals?* Washington replied, "Anyone living in this city has a right." Journalists fired back: *You are the mayor of Chicago with a large African American population, many of whom do not have a job. You were elected mostly by blacks who needed a job. You promised jobs to them, and now you are offering jobs to illegals. What do you say about it?*

He said, "I will keep fighting for jobs for every worker, any person who qualifies. I was elected mostly by the black voters, but I am the mayor of everybody." Second, he said, "Yes, I know there is a law against giving jobs to people illegally in the States. I don't care. And if what I'm doing doesn't please the feds, they know where I work. So I'm ready."

In 1985, with Primo's help, Washington was invited to Mexico to receive an honorary Mexican citizenship from President Miguel de la Madrid. He stood with his fellow activists Carlos Arango, Lupe Lozano, and Jesús "Chuy" Garcia, and felt this was just the beginning.

The political empowerment of Mexicans in the United States had reached a new stage. Transnational politics was just around the corner. As newly legalized Mexicans began moving around the country, they brought their families up from Mexico. Much to his chagrin, Mexico was becoming a nation without borders. Tensions began to grow—subtly— in towns and cities far from the Southwest. The rest of the country was not Chicago, a city used to embracing newcomers and transforming them into something else: new Americans.

He later backed Illinois U.S. representative Paul Simon, who ran for the Senate and won. Primo saw his role as similar to that of many immigrants who served as peace brokers or defenders of human rights who felt compelled to shed light on misguided U.S. policies.

Primo would hold evening sessions with Mexican immigrants and others to teach them about their rights in the United States and immigration policies being debated by Congress. He'd tell them to stand and fight. They weren't in Mexico anymore, he said. Legal or not, they had rights here.

He never finished his degree, he said, because he was busy being an activist. Busy pushing for change in the company of women and men of all nationalities and skin colors.

He took the job as national director of the U.S.-Mexico Border Program at the American Friends Service Committee as a way to formally take on the issues of undocumented immigration in the U.S. It was a program that straddled the border, and took particular aim at assembly plants, or *maquiladoras*, filled with women making a pittance. He arrived in Philadelphia in September 1985, days before a violent 8.1 magnitude earthquake shattered Mexico City, causing serious damage and the deaths of as many as ten thousand people. Primo faced TV cameras to talk about the devastation back in his homeland. He became a media celebrity almost overnight, the go-to person on just about any issue involving Mexico.

Now in Philadelphia, he'd travel regularly to Washington, where he'd meet with now Senator Simon and later with Senator Ted Kennedy to talk about the thorny issues of immigration reform and amnesty.

Amnesty wasn't the panacea some activists were making it out to be, or even a benign plan, Primo said. He opened the bottle of tequila.

He explained that he worried what amnesty would mean for the communities and politics of his homeland. Unlike the orderly, legal migration of his grandfather, my father, my mother, my brothers and me, this wave was different, more pervasive, intense and chaotic.

He feared Mexico would empty itself out and the United States, frustrated over the rapid change and newcomers, would have little choice but to annex what was left of his cherished homeland.

Sounds like a conspiracy theory, I suggested.

History is on my side, he responded.

Every immigrant equaled a lost vote for change. Mexicans abroad still didn't have the right to an absentee vote in their homeland. Mexico had no tradition of democratic change.

Of course, immigrants represented a huge human resource drain, although the remittances sent from abroad kept the communities back home afloat, I said.

But remittances came at an extraordinary cost, Primo argued.

He'd often fantasize about returning to Mexico to visit some of these immigrant-sending communities and taking over the town square with a megaphone to shout from the top of his skinny lungs: *America is a myth! We can build the country we want here!*

He'd tell me he was in favor of building fences on the Mexican side to keep his countrymen from leaving, a mile-high wall to force Mexicans to rebuild a better country, a prosperous nation with accountability and the rule of law.

That sounds so hypocritical, I told Primo. What are we doing here, then? Drinking tequila in Philadelphia. *¡Vamonos con una chingada!* Screw this, let's all go back to Mexico!

If it was only so easy, he said. Immigration ran deep in the blood of just about every Mexican; it was part of their heritage, their DNA. Every Mexican, including Primo's own mother.

By the time Primo came of age, the latest exodus for the U.S. from his hometown was almost complete. Just about everyone had at one point left except his mother, and that was about to change. His mother, Jovita, felt she didn't belong in her community and the only way she could become someone in Ixtlán de los Hervores, a real native, was if she, too, followed the journey north. She wanted to work in the United States, even without papers, going through the same process as thousands had done before her.

At the age of fifty-seven Jovita finally crossed inside the trunk of a car from Reynosa to McAllen and from there took a Greyhound bus to Dallas. There she worked two jobs. During the day she took care of an elderly person confined to a wheelchair, and at night she would clean an office building. After a year she returned to Guadalajara, where she had moved years before with her family, wishing to visit Ixtlán de los Hervores, to tell everybody that she was now fully one of them. She now could talk about working in the United States. She was finally part of the Ixtlán immigrant fabric. She could tell stories and be part of the community. Ironically, Jovita felt that leaving, embarking on the same journey as so many of her neighbors, would be the only way to feel at home.

Can you believe that? Primo said. Immigration is what makes you. It is a rite of passage.

Not losing your virginity? I asked, yawning.

He laughed and called it a night.

Get some sleep, *hermano. Estás en tu casa.*

I couldn't wait to close my eyes. I was too tired to stroll around his one-bedroom apartment. Besides, at first glance, what was there in front of me was likely all he had. Salsa, ketchup, ham and a vast array of music. I did look under the sofa to see if maybe he had wires hanging somewhere. Nothing. I curled up in his sofa, lay my head on the pillow, threw the cover over me and fell asleep to the sound of the howling winds outside. Maybe I shouldn't be so nosy, I thought. Primo, Ken and David were the only friends I had in Philadelphia. I couldn't even begin to imagine my life without them. There were things I didn't need to know, not when my own personal survival was at stake.

The next morning I quietly strolled out of Primo's apartment as he slept in. I had learned more about Primo the night before but he remained an enigmatic man, and my curiosity was not fully satisfied. I walked to Forty-First and Spruce and later called David at home.

I failed, I said.

Let it go, he said, laughing, as I heard his son playing with toys in the background.

5.

Crawling out of the Shadows

Before the fields unionized, Campbell's paid its produce suppliers prices so little that the farmers were practically forced to exploit their workers, many of them Mexican, many of them hired and fired in between the planting and harvest seasons. Workers like my parents.

It was practices like these, originating at the top of the food chain with famous brands like Campbell's, that helped create a massive migrant and eventually undocumented workforce. Broad-based guest-worker programs that gave migrant laborers some sense of dignity had ended two decades before, and supervisors couldn't complete the season's harvest without Mexicans, who proved to be pliant hardworkers, sweat pouring down their foreheads, from 6:00 a.m. to 6:00 p.m.

At a Campbell's shareholder meeting, I stood alongside other business reporters and felt like a fraud. I had spent my childhood in the fields of California alongside my parents, and now I had the gatekeepers and the decision makers before me. I had a chance to do what I thought journalists were supposed to do: dig, find something more beneath the surface and hold the powerful accountable.

Amid the noise, I asked a Campbell's executive point-blank about the company's plans to improve working conditions for tomato pickers in California.

The silence in the room roared.

Frank was impressed that I was bold enough to ask such tough questions, but that was not the time or place, he lectured me. I was there to find out about the company's financial forecast and keep an ear open to future stories.

I felt claustrophobic.

I began practicing my speech of defeat, the one about how I failed as a wannabe journalist in the Northeast, on the Septa bus from West Philly to Center City. Nothing was working. The pull of home was always there, unless I was hanging out with new friends, but nostalgia had a price tag, and Tequilas was high-end. My reporter's notepad became a diary. One morning I literally wrote, "I wished I could be stronger and say I was finding my firm step, but I'm not."

The bus had stopped on Chestnut Street when I heard the Simply Red song "Holding Back the Years" flowing from an open window of a pizza joint by the name of Freddy's. For that one moment I was in two places at once. I closed my eyes and wished that the song would never end, that the bus would never move. I realized the drops falling on one of my new suits were my own tears. I wiped my eyes, half worried that someone would see me, half wanting someone to notice and actually make a connection. But no one did. No one ever did: they were always preoccupied with their own lives, reading newspapers or looking away.

Just days before, I had made another mad dash to the local department store with Julie, thinking clothes would save me from myself. Maybe new clothes would change my outlook. People, especially my colleagues, would see me differently, as if I belonged.

Frank noticed the mood swings, the cheap new suits, the sudden appetite for hoagies. I stopped asking for jalapeños on my cheesesteak. One afternoon, Frank had enough. We went for a ride to the Brandywine Region and he pointed at the rolling hills of Pennsylvania. We drove mostly in silence. I knew in my gut this was the end, a goodbye road trip less than six months after I had arrived. I felt ashamed, yet relieved that the adventure was over.

We returned to the *Journal* building and Frank finally exploded. He pulled me into his office and scolded me for trying to go Ivy League on him, transforming myself into a northeasterner. Lying to myself.

I'm on to you, he said.

I'm not fitting in no matter how I try, I responded.

I didn't tell him I could see how hard he was trying, too, taking me out on a ride, checking up on me on weekends and even evenings. When I walked into Tequilas, I would tell everyone that if an American man called for me, I was either not there or doing an interview. Frank, I later learned, was growing impatient with my spending habits. I didn't have credit, so I'd use the company card to charge my expenses, whether the suits or Tequilas, and then pay the amount at the end of the month. I got admonished for that, too.

This is only for company expenses, he said. Plus, how are you getting by? You're throwing all your money away. I had no idea about the culture of saving money, so I just looked at him with a dumb stare.

Frank, I'm so sorry, I said. This isn't working out like I thought it would, I finally told him. I really wanted to say, *Let's save face and go our separate ways.*

Give it time, he said. And then he went silent for a long minute.

I recruited you because your background is different, I remembered words to that effect. You bring a different perspective to the story, to stories this country needs to know about. You went to Utah and wrote about migrant workers. You found your way. Give this some time. Be yourself. This country is looking more and more like you. Aren't you aware of that? You represent the future. Show pride, not fear.

I stared back, inspired but doubtful.

One morning Frank called me into his office. He had news for me: good news, he said. In addition to my regular corporate beat, he would like for me to focus on stories about immigration, the process of legalizing millions of undocumented immigrants. The Immigration Reform and Control Act was upending industries from the fields to factories, and the *Journal* wanted to go deeper. What was happening in the workplace? Where were these millions living? Why hadn't they come forward?

The U.S. government was offering amnesty to undocumented immigrants who had lived in the U.S. continuously since 1982. The deadline to apply, May 1988, loomed, but there was no rush to sign up. People were reluctant to come out of the shadows, too suspicious of the government. Was "amnesty" a ruse for another mass deportation under way?

The offer to "legalize" millions was paired with "employer sanctions" for businesses that hired undocumented workers. The goal was to reduce the number of jobs that lured Mexicans across the border. But IRCA didn't do that. Employer sanctions were rarely enforced. With about a year away from the deadline, the massive exodus out from the shadows hadn't taken place. But for every person granted amnesty, five to ten more relatives would come to the U.S., critics worried.

If the 1965 law changed the face of America in America's cities, IRCA in 1986 made those modifications permanent and pushed immigrants, particularly Mexicans, out of California, Texas and the Southwest and into the middle of America, the Northeast and the Southeast in greater numbers. Amnesty, paired with more than two decades of steady economic growth in the U.S., would spark a new wave of Mexican migration that would rival any that had come before it.

Much to the dismay of many Republicans, the Simpson-Rodino Act, as IRCA was originally known, passed with the help of the Reagan administration. Senator Alan Simpson, a Republican from Wyoming, lacked the votes in 1986 to pass a reform bill without making a compromise on the so-called one-time-only amnesty. Democratic representative Peter Rodino of New Jersey agreed to negotiate: in order to be naturalized, an undocumented immigrant would need to show four years of continuous residency rather than two, which Rodino had originally hoped for.

The Reagan administration also had an interest in protecting recent immigrants, and not for altruistic motives but for political ones. During the 1980s, nearly a million refugees from El Salvador were sending about $3 million a day back to their relatives in the war-torn country. These remittances played a key role in propping up a U.S. ally defending itself against Marxist insurgents who would undermine Reagan's Cold War tactics.

IRCA granted an opportunity for millions of undocumented immigrants, mainly from Latin America, to legalize their status if they met certain conditions, including letters of recommendation from their employers, proof of continuous residence and no criminal record. It took five tries, including early proposals during the Ford and Carter administrations, before Reagan succeeded in securing the support for reform.

Many skeptics had their doubts. IRCA was the first legislative attempt to regulate illegal migration outside of a guest-worker program. Representative Charles "Chuck" Schumer, who helped foster a compromise that would push the bill to enactment, described the legislation as "a riverboat gamble."

This form of amnesty also sparked fears of an invasion of undesirable immigrants. In order to appease conservatives, IRCA mandated tighter border security and provided funding to ramp up enforcement. The law also imposed sanctions on employers who hired unauthorized immigrants. Those three components were referred to as the "three-legged stool."

The buy-in among immigrants may have been off to a slow start, but as it gained traction things became clear. First, workers previously bound to their employers because of their illegal status could, upon gaining a green card, move wherever they wanted and work whatever job they wanted; the workforce in the country's toughest jobs could now aim for higher wages. Second, many of the millions of newly legal immigrants would have the opportunity to sponsor family members, igniting a great exodus of wives and children and parents from Mexico, creating a backlog in visa quotas. The law transformed the previously transnational migrant into a future American citizen, creating a permanency that compelled extended family members to cross illegally in order to reunite with their families.

Lastly, employers who depended on cheap, available—albeit illegal— labor suddenly found themselves scrambling for workers or stressing about the new documentation required by IRCA. Many business owners questioned why they should be responsible for enforcing immigration law. Around the same time as IRCA's passage, the federal government developed a pilot program that would later transform into E-Verify, the online system that today allows employers to check whether Social Security numbers are valid and if an employee can work legally in the U.S. The system is voluntary with the exception of federal government contracts. IRCA essentially tried to transform millions of employers into INS agents: business owners were responsible for checking the immigration status of their employees.

For the first time, it was expressly against the law to hire an illegal immigrant. Fines ranged from $539 per unauthorized worker for a single offense to more than $21,000 per unauthorized worker for a third offense. Many employers neither welcomed the responsibility nor understood it.

Frank had recommended that I be part of a team of *Journal* reporters that included Dianne Solis, who was the best immigration reporter in the country, a smart, ambitious Mexican American woman from the San Joaquin Valley based in the Houston bureau. I had been a fan of Dianne's since I was a student and met her at a LULAC (League of United Latin American Citizens) convention in El Paso. She had been lobbying for me to help her and be a part of the national team. Deep down, Frank knew covering a story like immigration would keep me focused and save me from defeat. Save me from myself. He told me he had offered to loan me to other bureaus to help out and get a pulse on other immigrant communities.

Plus I spoke Spanish.

Why weren't more immigrants applying for amnesty? Did the U.S. government exaggerate the number of undocumented workers across the country? Or were they just afraid of stepping out of the shadows? The *Journal* was making a commitment to double down and cover the story like no other media company.

Start your journey in El Paso, Frank said, and I almost exploded with joy. Relief. I want you to return to El Paso and play waiter at your parents' restaurant. Talk to customers, friends, people in the community, and write what you know. What you see. Write a first-person account. Explain the nuances, the different layers of the story, like only you can. Think, write like a photographer. Give me details.

Frank liked to challenge us to write stories so eloquent that we would distract the readers in the morning. The goal was to make our readers' cereal soggy—to get them so lost in the story that they would put their spoons down and read rather than eat. He looked at our raw copy and challenged us to find that extra line with fine detail that made the characters fly right off the pages.

I stared at him in disbelief. Startled. Thrilled. I couldn't find the words, nor did I want to make too much of it. I wanted to be cool, a pro. Just an ordinary assignment, kind of like going to Massachusetts and reporting on fishermen smuggling scallops. Like the scallop story, this story would also be pitched as an A-hed, journal jargon for the narrative human-interest feature story smack in the middle of the *Journal*'s front page.

I felt the spark again, just as when I worked at the *El Paso Herald-Post* and was about to go off on assignment and kick the hated rival newspaper's ass. I tried to restrain myself.

Frank, thank you. I won't let you down.

I know you won't, he said.

I got up and left, looking at my colleagues with a new sense of belonging. Suddenly I felt I had every right to be there, that I was more than some charity case, a poster boy for "diversity." I suspected that was all I was to some colleagues. I felt inferior, just a high school dropout with a community college education but without a diploma and who hadn't paid his dues. Now I had something to offer. Something they couldn't produce.

I walked straight to the restroom, where I slowly danced the way Miguel Bosé dances to that song "Que No Hay," slow, very slow, shaking my shoulders, my hips, my butt, raising my hands over my head, my knees and feet tapping to the song in my mind, turning slowly, watching my moves on the mirror in front of me. I was over the moon. The door suddenly opened. I froze, caught in the act. I turned red and tried to compose myself, relieved to see it was the Puerto Rican janitor with a perplexed look on his face.

I smiled sheepishly and walked out with that unfazed look again, grinning inside for the rest of the day. I picked up the usual hoagies for my colleagues. Sometimes the short-order cook behind the counter would look at me and roll his eyes as I fumbled between wheat, rye or white bread, mustard, horseradish or regular, and peppers that had no bite. Not this time: I ordered them the way I was supposed to, without hesitation. What a shot of confidence can do!

I kept looking at the clock, desperate to leave for Tequilas and share the news. When quitting time came, I strutted across Broad Street, winked at the statue of "Billy Penn," who seemed to tilt his ridiculous hat at me. I headed to Tequilas and imagined the faces of my friends when I told them I was headed for El Paso. I acted like I was heading home for good with a big smile on my face.

At Tequilas we had become obsessed with amnesty. David was particularly fixated. Half his kitchen and server staff had been deported during an immigration raid. I would never forget the afternoon he called me at the *Journal* office and bluntly asked me if I had proper work documents. He sounded dead serious. Of course, I said, but I leave them at home, suddenly panicked. This wasn't the border, where you never knew if INS agents were around the corner and they questioned you just because you looked the part. This was Philadelphia, I explained to David. Why did he ask?

Why would I carry my documents with me like I did when I worked in the fields of California? *Chingao.* I work at the *Wall Street Journal*, I reminded him, now on the verge of falling off my chair. I recalled how a few weeks earlier I had been questioned by immigration officials at the El Paso airport about my citizenship and, without my documents at hand, I took out my credit card.

All I need now is my American Express card, I thought, preferably with the *Journal*'s name on it.

Who wants to know if I have the right documents, I asked. *¿Quién, cabrón? ¿La migra?*

Relax, David said reassuringly. I just want to know whether you want a second job, he said very seriously. The INS raided my place. The tips are great.

Now David believed amnesty could bring his workers out of the shadows and keep his business running smoothly. No more interruptions by INS agents.

The four of us friends all had our papers in order.

David got his permanent residency through marriage and vowed never to become a citizen, something I agreed with. This was before Mexico allowed dual citizenship. It would be another twelve years—1998—before

Mexico permitted dual citizenship. In 1987, becoming an American citizen would mean giving up Mexican citizenship. Doing so, David said, would mean a betrayal not just to Mexico but to the other country he worshipped for standing up to the U.S. government: Cuba. Primo was in the States legally on a temporary work visa and had no interest in staying. His future was in Mexico. Ken, of course, was New Mexican and a U.S. citizen by birth. I was a green-card holder, a permanent resident, and hadn't given much thought to U.S. citizenship. Why would I? I lived on the border and crisscrossed both sides. But now, living in Philadelphia and with dreams of returning to Mexico someday as a correspondent, Frank was convincing me of the protection U.S. citizenship would provide in a "foreign" country, even Mexico. I wasn't convinced.

I walked inside Tequilas and told the guys I was leaving Philadelphia. I had had enough of Billy Penn's experiment, which was doomed from the beginning.

David seemed to take it the hardest. He asked me to stay longer, even promising food at a discount and tequila from his secret batch. He felt bad after I told him the hangovers were making my stay in Philadelphia worse. Ken and Primo didn't know what to make of the news. They took long drags on their cigarettes, congratulated me and then played devil's advocate.

I was walking away from a dream job, Primo said.

Don't be hasty, Ken added. Give it more time.

They seemed so genuinely hurt that I felt bad about my joke, and finally confessed: I'm not really leaving. I'm fucking with you. I'll be gone for no more than a week, maybe two. Their smiles returned. I'm covering immigration. The story surrounding the amnesty program was giving me the freedom to travel outside of Philadelphia, and not just to El Paso but maybe Los Angeles, Houston, Chicago and even small towns in Wisconsin where Mexicans had flocked.

Like those Mexicans across the country who were crawling out of the shadows, I was finding my own freedom, away from this stale city of Philadelphia, I told them.

I raised my glass and toasted Reagan's amnesty. They reluctantly joined me.

SECTION II

The Giant IRCA Awakening

6.

Freddy's Café

I was on the plane back to El Paso to work at Freddy's Café, not as a failure, but as a *Wall Street Journal* reporter with questions that needed answering. The trip would turn into a front-page story, a first-person account of why amnesty hadn't become the panacea that immigrant advocates had promised. I would get my hands dirty waiting tables again in the service of my higher calling as a big-time East Coast journalist.

In other words, the *gallo* was back.

On the airplane I dreamed of the grand scene: I'd stroll into Freddy's, greet the clients, strut proudly with my blue blazer, light blue button-down shirt and khakis and hear people say, *Look, that's Herlinda's son. He works at the* Wall Street Journal, *in Philadelphia.*

Of course, they won't know how big of a deal it is, but just the fact that the *Journal* is a newspaper for businessmen and I'm visiting from the Northeast will impress them, I thought. My mother tells me the clients miss me. When she tells them I'm living in Philadelphia, they all say, *Wow*, qué bien. Felicidades, *Doña Linda*.

Dreams of grandeur. *Puras fantasias.*

My parents nearly pushed me into my dad's pickup truck at the airport. They were happy to see me but in a rush. It was almost lunchtime, they reminded me. They needed to get back. They were grateful for my help waiting tables. My mother peered into my eyes, ecstatic, as though I were back from the dead. I explained to them I could have taken a cab. The *Journal* was paying, I said, stressing the words "the *Journal*" and "reimburse." They seemed offended that I even thought about a taxi.

Will a cab bring you a *gordita*? my mother asked, unwrapping a *gordita de chile verde*, freshly made, as I got into the driver's seat.

Not a chance, I said, salivating, the chunks of beef and chile sauce spilling over. My father took the passenger side. My petite mother scooted into the jump seat.

The road from the airport delivered us south onto I-10. From the elevated highway, you could see the borderline and the sprawl of Juárez spreading south to the horizon, where shantytown neighborhoods scaled the foothills of the Juárez mountains. Religious fanatics had painted on the mountainside in letters so enormous they could be seen from El Paso: *LA BIBLIA ES LA VERDAD. LEELA.* The Bible is the truth. Read it.

I remember thinking, What is this? I told my friend Jacobo from Juárez—a frustrated musician now working as a cameraman in Tucson—that we should go up and paint over it. Ironic, I thought: demanding people read the Bible when in Mexico in the early 1980s nearly a fifth of the adult population—17 percent—was illiterate. How about demanding people take back their country at the ballot box?

The highway curved around the bald Franklin Mountains toward downtown. On the south side, trapped between the Union Pacific rail yard and the border, was El Paso's Segundo Barrio, an impoverished neighborhood that seemed indistinguishable from the Juárez neighborhood on the other side. On the north side of the highway, up on a hill, sat the wealthy Kern Place neighborhood of stately homes and trees and green grass—just about the only green in the city. I could see the border and longed for the world of in-between. And at the same time a strange thought came to me: I could see the limits of this place. Unless you had deep pockets, the right connections or stellar education credentials, the climb up was difficult. I had neither. What would I be if I hadn't left?

Eat, because you will need it, my mother said, handing me another *gordita*.

Freddy's had been packed more than usual. Freddy's was more than a family business. It was also a goldmine for stories.

U.S. Border Patrol agents, in their dark green uniforms, muttered every morning over coffee about how the floodgates were really going to open now to Mexicans heading north. Amnesty to millions of Mexicans, they griped, although they sounded excited about the new choppers, guns and boots on the ground they were going to get to "secure" the open doors. They would turn the border into a fortress. I liked listening to them, generating ideas in my head for future articles.

Some of my mother's patrons who were illegal workers—or *ilegales*, as they called themselves—were careful to show up only when Border Patrol, or U.S. Customs agents, weren't around. Likewise the *contrabandistas*, who smuggled everything from Cuban cigars, guavas, mangos and Argentine wines north of the border and headed south with TVs, refrigerators and guns; and the maids who crossed to El Paso every day to clean houses and went home every night to the slums in Anapra on the outskirts of Ciudad Juárez.

There's a lot of confusion about this amnesty program, my mother said. Maybe you can provide answers.

I'm just a reporter, I reminded her. I ask questions.

My mother didn't ask about my job. She was more concerned about my blazer.

Nice jacket, but take it off. And why are you wearing your nice blue shirt?

My mother was wearing her usual polyester pants and the apron favored by Mexican *mayoras*, the best cooks: one that covered her shirt, with pockets in the front and buttons down the back. A pink one was her favorite.

I wasn't wearing the shirt we bought at JCPenney that last Christmas but one I found with my new friend Ken back at Wanamaker's, I bragged to my mother.

More reason you don't want it to get dirty with enchilada sauce, or *caldo de res*, or guacamole. Don't wear that. You should know better.

Sí, mamá. I was trying to impress you, I confessed sheepishly.

As usual, my father said nothing.

I noticed he was still wearing a coin changer around his waist. He was now driving a food truck and operating two others, one with an employee with no work permits and the other with my brother David, who had quit high school to support his pregnant wife. I regretted not teaching him about birth control, but what did I know? The issue was taboo at our home.

My father still missed his days driving tractors, not food trucks, and he would tell me sometimes that selling burritos was not the most manly job, but he liked to be his own boss, not having to answer to anyone.

He just doesn't like to talk, I reminded myself.

I wondered how he and my mother made it without talking to one another.

But just as we pulled into the freeway, he broke the silence and went for the jugular.

Will the amnesty program help unite families like in 1965? he asked. How many families are eligible? How many will be able to apply and be reunited?

Projections are all over the place, I responded. It's unclear at this point. Do you think it's a good idea to reunite close families and leave the extended family members behind? I asked, hoping to extend a rare conversation until we arrived at South El Paso Street, just four blocks from the international bridge. My parents had good business sense, positioning a Mexican restaurant owned by immigrants just a few feet away from hungry pedestrians who crossed into the U.S. to shop, work or visit families.

I was hoping to open a conversation we had never had: Did he have any regrets about immigrating? Was it worth fracturing our own family, near and far?

Not all of my father's brothers and sisters decided to apply for permanent residency or green cards. They didn't mind working temporarily, but they wouldn't uproot their families up north and leave behind their beloved Mexico. Those decisions were made and respected, but although many of us were in *el norte*, we were at the core a divided family, seeing relatives only on holidays, or worse, funerals. Our language was fading and too often they saw us as Mexicans bleached by American ways. *Pochos.*

I don't know, my father said. My relatives are mostly dead or living in the United States, he replied, and looked at my mother, something he usually did when he had run out of words or didn't know what to say.

What do you think, Herlinda?

How would I know? my mother said. He's asking *you.*

It's okay, I interjected. I just wanted to know what's going on to better understand the story.

My mother continued: It's making a lot of families nervous, because so many men already have new families and new wives living in secret. *Muchas mujeres sospechan pero quién sabe.* It's something many Mexican women have always suspected but never been able to prove. My mother didn't overtly include herself but her tone suggested otherwise.

My father looked uncomfortable—annoyed, even.

Are you nervous yourself about your secret life being uncovered? she asked my father.

Here we go again: the same ridiculous accusations, he said. Your son is here. Let the past go.

Papá, thank you for bringing us to the United States and reuniting us as a family, I said, trying to deflect the conversation, something I had grown used to doing as a boy.

Don't worry, *mijo*, my mother said, seeing how I had tensed up. Your father has more pressing things on his mind these days. We're now required to check every employee for documents and make sure they're telling us the truth, that the documents are not fake. That means scrutinizing everyone. Asking our nieces, nephews, our friend El Caballero, a smuggler who went by the nickname "the Gentleman." Imagine that— as if we don't have enough things to worry about.

I asked about our undocumented workforce. How big was it?

My mother chuckled. We don't knowingly know that, she said, repeating a line from employers throughout the country, stressing the word "knowingly."

The law was a sham. It also stated if somebody's documents look legitimate, if they, quote, "appear to be genuine on their face, the employer must accept them and cannot question them or ask for more documentation."

This was the border and fake documents were galore.

Can you imagine your father playing INS agent? my mother asked, with irony in her voice.

Shit, my father responded. *Ni que estuviera loco.* (I'm not crazy.)

The government has been talking big since I was a boy, younger than you. They're not serious. What will they do without us?

My father had an elementary school education, a short attention span and limited English that didn't go far beyond the word "Shit" and "Thank you, mister," depending on the situation. After more than twenty years in the United States, assimilation eluded them—not for lack of trying, but because they were too busy working their butts off, meeting payroll, paying taxes and now playing INS agents. While my mother ran the tiny kitchen and floor at Freddy's, my father handled the finances.

Now he was making sure his employees had documents—an impossible task, he complained, because so many used fake documents.

My father was already intimidated by the confusing and continually shifting slate of enforcement deadlines, various forms and multiple requirements for verifying recently hired and newly hired workers. Few businesses were happy about it, but the law was a special burden for small-business owners like my parents. Not just the paperwork but finding legal workers willing to do tough jobs.

Already, my mother said, her sisters, both labor contractors in central California, were worried about labor shortages. They were in full panic mode, unable to drum up workers to pick tomatoes or hoe sugar beets. Crops were rotting in the fields. Many, especially the women, were talking about leaving for the service industry in states like Colorado. Fearful employers, including my mother's sisters, were afraid of hiring anyone who couldn't prove their residency or citizenship beyond a shadow of a doubt.

The U.S. was in a bind and facing an ugly truth. These workers are irreplaceable, my aunt Hermila told my mother. They were so desperate for money that my aunts began selling letters to workers to show proof of employment. The scam lost them their labor contracting licenses and led to legal problems that would follow them for decades.

America wasn't just hiring workers for cheap wages; employers valued the work ethic that came along with their blood, sweat and tears. They had a willingness to leave it all, their sweat and dreams, in the fields and on the factory floors. Risk it all. Sure, amnesty would pull people out of the shadows, but at what price? Securing the border was now part of the public discourse by politicians. In the aftermath of the killing of DEA agent Camarena, the mood on the border had changed.

People are nervous, my mother explained.

I WALKED INTO the café, following my mother, sure that everyone was noticing the new me, my threads from Wanamaker's, my Bostonian shoes, my new haircut, courtesy of a barbershop near Wharton. My ten-year-old sister, Monica, greeted me with a smile as she took orders over the phone. She was dressed in her usual uniform of blue jeans, a navy shirt and a pair of white Keds. She had her hair carefully combed in a tight ponytail. It was Saturday and she wasn't at school. She spent weekends picking up plates, taking orders and refilling people's glasses with water. She was too young to serve coffee. I hugged her tight. She couldn't stop smiling.

Inside the tiny restaurant with capacity for about fifty people, tables for four covered with avocado-green oilcloth lined both walls of the narrow space. A photo of Mexican revolutionary Pancho Villa and paintings of Mexican food, painted by an El Paso artist, hung on wood-paneled and white walls. A little vase of artificial red roses and gardenias topped each table. My mother made sure that the tan tile floor was spotless and shiny. A candle to San Martín Caballero, the patron saint of entrepreneurs and of good luck, sat on a shelf behind the register with a message: "San Martín, *dame suerte y dinero.*" The restaurant felt smaller than I remembered. It was remarkable that these four walls could feed our family and our aspirations.

The lunchtime clientele, with hats and baseball caps, as well as well-dressed women, many who worked as vendors, were engrossed in conversation, digging into hot plates. I heard the loud chatter of hellos, jokes and politics, people comparing notes about where Border Patrol agents were standing guard that morning and where to pass illegal merchandise. Mornings were about plotting and afternoons were about measuring wins and losses.

I was back on the border, back at Freddy's.

As I walked into the kitchen, dirty dishes were stacked and quickly being washed to accommodate new clients; the stove's four burners were boiling *caldo de res* and some of my mother's signature dishes, *chile verde* for *gorditas* and burritos, rice and beans and, of course, *menudo*. There was little of it left by now, as breakfast time was over and we were transitioning into lunchtime. Our cook, Petrita, backed away from filling a plate with flautas, part of Freddy's lunch special, *comida corrida*, that included *caldo de res*. She said, Freddy, *qué guapo*, and returned to adding cilantro to the soup. I wondered if she said that because of my blue blazer, although I don't think she even noticed it. Ernestina gave me a huge hug—*mi Freddy hermoso*. After the short greetings, I took off my blazer and stuffed my notepad in my back pocket and my black pen in my shirt pocket, my ego a little bruised that everyone didn't look up from their *caldo de res* and gasp in unison at my grand entrance. No one clapped or stood up to shake my hand. Nothing.

My mother watched me. She seemed worried.

You seem like you lost a lot of weight. People don't eat on the East Coast?

I'm on a special diet called *sopa Campbell*, I said, making a bad joke. She looked confused. I didn't try to explain.

Then my mother admonished me: If you are going to interview our customers, think of them as people, not as characters in some story. Some are family, friends, she added as I wrote the words, "Freddy's Café, 1987" outside my notepad.

Of course, *mamá*.

Among the many applying for amnesty, she reminded me, were employees at the restaurant and relatives on both sides of the border. Some remained on the fence, not sure what this would mean for their families back home.

I don't think the gringos get it, she observed. There's no such thing as family reunification because there's no such thing as close or extended family. What does family mean to them? How do you separate them? We're all family. Sooner or later they will come together, here or there. This whole immigration thing is a mess, a farce. Half my family is back in Durango. I rarely see them, but I just hope amnesty will help us come together again, at least the lucky ones. But I doubt it. People are suspicious.

Why? What are they suspicious about?

History, she said. How can any Mexican trust the United States? Americans might wake up and decide to deport everyone, or take another chunk of Mexico.

I looked at the clients, who were divided by shifts. For late breakfast we had a mix, shoppers from Juárez carrying big empty bags. Or regular ones like Tanny Berg, who ordered *huevos rancheros* and black coffee every morning. The lunch crowd were mostly employees from the surrounding blocks who dropped by to savor the *comida corrida*, which had long been a neighborhood favorite. Everyone knew that woman, my mother, could cook Durango-style right down to the spicy chile.

I forgot Philadelphia, took out my reporter's notepad from my back pocket and began taking orders, going table to table. By noon the *menudo*, whose fame had gone viral before social media was a thing, was gone, having fed customers who crossed borders, or zoomed from up north in New Mexico and even Oklahoma.

If you had stayed behind, we could have marketed *menudo* throughout the Southwest, my father reminded me when I asked whether my mother had saved me some.

Are you kidding? I asked. It's all gone?

No, of course I saved you some, my mother said, giving my father a long stare. We emigrated to help them open doors through education, not by running a restaurant.

Influenced by my short stint at the *Wall Street Journal* and the culture of covering capitalists, I defended my father.

Mamá, I think he's right. I'm covering all these companies, giant ones and small ones. It's all about marketing. Your *menudo* can go mainstream like Tastykakes.

Tastyqué? Never mind, get to work, because you're tired and you need to get home and rest. Your brothers can't wait to see you. We have a barbecue lined up for you afterward. I smiled widely. They did miss me.

The regular clients were also happy to see me, engaging me in small talk.

What's it like over there, Freddy? asked Maggie. Mague to my mother, Maggie to me. She ran a photo studio across the street. Cold, right?

Never been through anything so cold like that, I said. There were days I couldn't feel my hands.

You look great, she said. You lost some weight.

I missed my mother's food. I smiled sheepishly. I've been up since four a.m., but I'm so happy to be here that I'm not tired.

I could have talked to Maggie, a pretty woman and longtime customer, for hours. But I knew she wasn't looking for amnesty. She was a U.S. citizen.

What are you doing waiting on tables?

I'm homesick and working on a story about amnesty, I said.

Wow. You're going to write about El Paso?

Yep, and on the front page.

Be good to us. El Paso always gets bad press. Drugs, illegals. Dirty, dusty border town.

No worries, Maggie. I'll be fair, I said, and maybe even sprinkle some unsolicited love.

Hey, Freddy, try that table. Maggie had been eavesdropping. Seen them here lately. They're fixated on amnesty. They might be helpful.

Thanks, I said.

And as I walked away, I asked the standard question: *Caldo* good?

Always great. Delicious, she said. Can I get more lemon and salsa?

Con gusto, I replied. If David could only see me now, I thought.

I fixed my eyes on the new consumers.

I noticed the new waitress. Maria Elia Porras, who crossed the border as Susana. She was now awaiting word on her application for amnesty. She was Mari to us. Couldn't miss the smile and gentle wink.

Hola, Freddy, she said. She confirmed some customers were pondering applying for amnesty, skeptical. Just be nice, she said.

I introduced myself as Herlinda's son, explained that I was working as a journalist for a big paper back east. I'll be your waiter, but I'm also a reporter for the *Wall Street Journal* and I have a few questions if you don't mind.

They seemed apprehensive when I asked if I could take my notepad out. Some looked at me as if I were a bit crazy. Now I regretted trying too hard to be from the Northeast. Maybe the ruse was working, because no one wanted to talk to me.

My mom poked her head in from the kitchen.

He's my son, she said. He just wants to know so he can write it in an influential newspaper and people can know what you think.

They looked at me again with a grin, their nerves at ease. Some even began to raise their hands, hoping I would approach them to take down their quotes. Plenty talked to me only at the urging of my mother, who smiled proudly at her idiotic son's inability to charm sources without her help.

The dining room buzzed with curiosity. Are you also a lawyer? a woman asked me. Some wanted me to explain the law itself.

Just a reporter, I said. Not smart enough to be a lawyer.

Some weren't convinced that amnesty was really a grand opportunity: too good to be true, plus too many rules usually meant more distrust. One man took out some money and offered it in return for my advice. Thanks, I said, but your opinion is more than enough.

Four men shared a table, taking refills on coffee and talking about the law. One wore a cowboy hat and a tattered Western shirt, another a baseball cap. Neither had documents. They were waiting for others to be the first to apply for amnesty.

Some believed the law was a trap, a clever way to round them up and deport them. Others feared that only the rich, or those with connections to the rich, would qualify.

Elias, an *ilegal* from Torreón, Coahuila, was trying to persuade his friend José to be the first to test the law.

José, he said with encouragement in his voice, you have an honest face.

But José, who came from Gomez Palacio, wasn't convinced. I dreamed that I went to the *migra* office, he said. I walked in through the front door and was immediately escorted to the back door, where a van waited for me. The van was already packed with other *ilegales*.

Still, Juan Campo Silva, a wiry man and longtime Freddy's customer from Chihuahua, suggested: "Maybe the *migra* is tired of chasing us." His friends looked at him in disbelief.

No quieren a los ilegales (They don't want us illegals), another piped up. That will never change.

Back then everyone said "illegals." Even the immigrants called themselves *ilegales*. Only the term "wetback" was considered an insult, and Mexicans, to strip it of its power, began adopting the term to describe themselves.

Juan continued: I don't want to get excited only to be left standing at the altar.

After years of viewing immigration to the U.S. as an economic "safety valve"—desperate men, rather than join the military, would migrate north—authorities in Mexico took a dim view of the new law. That May, for instance, police in Juárez were preparing to disperse a group of protesters who were reportedly defacing an international bridge linking Juárez and El Paso. But when the police saw that the protesters were painting a mural of a woman being carried across the Rio Grande on a man's back, they joined the crowd, watching approvingly as the painting progressed.

In the midst of all the graffiti painted on the bridge, a plaintive question was scrawled on the concrete, asking the United States: "You sure you don't need us anymore?"

I SAW THAT GRAFFITI as Billy Calzada and I headed south of the border to Juárez to play hooky. It was just like old times, except I felt Billy's discomfort, like he was nervous I wouldn't be the same. Maybe I wasn't. But I quickly shed whatever big-shot baggage I had brought home with me and settled into the old rhythm with my buddy. We wasted no time getting wasted.

We hit El Noa Noa—the high-ceiling cantina with its neon lights that Juan Gabriel memorialized in his song of the same name—and, my favorite, the Kentucky Club on Avenida Juárez, just blocks from the bridge. At the mahogany bar at the Kentucky, the bartender served us tequila after tequila and pop-top cans of beer, and I could almost hear David scolding me for drinking Cuervo and Sauza (as they were the cheapest tequilas) and Corona, and mentally told him to buzz off. I was in my element and loving it. I can't remember where we slept, in Juárez or in El Paso, but I went MIA for forty-eight hours before Frank finally found me at the *Herald-Post*, hungover and talking to my former editor, Ray Chavez, about getting my old job back.

Frank had been calling Freddy's and my mother's house for two days and no one knew where I was, he said. What had I been doing for two days? Did I have the story or not? I had already been scolded for "inadvertently" charging up an adult movie on the company card—I was really that depressed and inexperienced—when the *Journal* put me up in a Philadelphia hotel when I first arrived; now I had disappeared on my first "correspondent" assignment that Frank had pushed hard to the New York editors. He was counting on me, he said.

How I wasn't fired this time or the last, I still don't know. Frank was saintly in his patience with me.

Sheepishly, I apologized.

I STOPPED NURSING MY heartbreak and got to work, again inspired by my parents' work ethic. I managed to bring it all together: the mishmash color of the border, the diversity of experience, the fear of the unknown, the feeling of helplessness. Whether immigrants were bold or timid, all were subject to the anger or benevolence of the American government. Here, on the border where so many went to commiserate as they gulped down my mother's hearty *caldo de res* or Mexican stew, was where the heart of the immigrant experience began to form. It was the point of departure where immigrants dispersed to all parts of the country. They left to work and assimilate, to have children and build a new life, often filled with sorrow as they reinvented themselves. This was the line of separation where people lived in between. A fragile bridge between cultures, languages and worlds drifting apart.

I nailed the piece and redeemed myself and maybe also helped Frank redeem himself as well, for taking a chance on some Mexican kid who kept getting it wrong until he got it right.

The Freddy's Café article was so well received—it was written with passion and eloquence, one editor said—that six months later the New York editors asked Frank for another.

7.

A Fickle Nation

Once I rediscovered how to be a proper journalist thanks to my mother's help at Freddy's, I settled back into life in Philadelphia. This time the buzz of my calling kept me from falling back into homesickness and heartbreak. My mind reeling, I couldn't help but wonder how long it would take for the pulse of the nation's problems to be felt first in El Paso and then to spread out across the country. El Paso was far into the future, anticipating the problem and all its complexities while still battling demons from the past. I wondered how the rest of the nation was faring, wishing that I was closer to the battleground rather than thousands of miles away in Philadelphia. As I wrestled with these thoughts, Ken simply wanted me to dine somewhere else besides Tequilas.

A block away was one of the most famous chefs in the world, a Frenchman who had recently relocated to Walnut Street, and the place was finer than ever, with white tablecloths and an army of forks flanking the plates, enough to make me squirm. His old restaurant on the corner of Sixteenth and Locust had been a landmark. Ken and Julie were offering—I would say threatening—to take me there if only I could find an unwrinkled shirt. I kept putting them off, worried I wouldn't know how to behave or what to talk about if we ran into one of Ken's attorney friends. So I said no again and again without explaining why.

There's more to Philadelphia than Tequilas, Ken told me.

Really? I asked, half joking. The truth was that I wasn't sure I wanted to know. I'm as happy here at Tequilas as I will ever be, I said.

The unknown of that foreign city was unappealing. But when I was in a good mood, I did notice myself warming up to the place.

I began to walk up Market Street, sometimes Arch Street, all the way to Philadelphia City Hall with more pride as I looked up at the statue of

Billy Penn. The hollow bronze statue weighed 53,000 pounds and stood 500 feet above street level. But I was more fascinated by the symbolic weight of the statue. For a country made of immigrants, those running away from persecution and looking for opportunity, the contradictions began early and were never quite put to rest, beginning with the question of what exactly constituted a citizen. It wasn't until 1790, twenty-four years after the Declaration of Independence was drafted, just a few blocks from where Tequilas now stood—that a law limited the privilege of citizenship to free whites of "good moral character" who had lived in the U.S. for at least two years. Later, that requirement changed to fourteen years. From the beginning, immigration was a contentious issue with some debating that states, not the federal government, had the right to preserve their religion, values and morals by enforcing their own immigration laws.

Except for the surviving Native American populations and African slaves, the United States remained a largely European society, primarily English-speaking. Benjamin Franklin once railed against "swarthy" Germans. So many Germans lived in Philadelphia that Franklin once asked: "Why should Pennsylvania, founded by the English, become a colony of aliens who will shortly be so numerous as to Germanize us instead of our Anglifying them?"

Despite this animosity, America was conflicted, seeming to want it both ways. In times of growth, workers were needed as the country expanded westward. Immigrants poured into Ellis Island, up to 10,000 people a day. By the end of the nineteenth century, an estimated 20 percent of immigrants in the United States hailed from Germany, having fled religious persecution or the repercussions of a failed revolution and looking for economic opportunity—by far the largest of any immigrant group.

Before 1882, American ancestors did come legally because there were no federal laws concerning immigration. In an effort to maintain the "Anglification" of America, starting in 1875, a series of restrictions on immigration were enacted. They included bans on criminals, people with contagious diseases, polygamists, anarchists, beggars and importers of prostitutes. The first ban on a specific ethnicity was the Chinese Exclusion Act of 1882, which was aimed at halting the influx of Chinese railroad workers. The act was later expanded to curb immigration from most Asian countries. The 1917 Immigration Act restricted the immigration of "undesirables" from other countries; these included "idiots, imbeciles, epileptics, alcoholics, poor, criminals, beggars, any person suffering attacks of insanity . . ."

By 1920, anxiety in Protestant America was growing. Immigrants were taking too many U.S. jobs and changing the culture and feel of the nation. They were challenging the Protestant American way of life. In response, laws imposed numerical quotas based on immigrant nationality that favored northern and western European countries. White Protestants constituted the vast majority of the country's decision makers, they worked to ensure that only white Protestants could determine the future course of the country.

The Immigration Act of 1924 included the creation of the U.S. Border Patrol and set quotas on the number of people from certain countries who could legally enter the U.S. It sharply restricted arrivals of Italians and eastern European Jews. Behind the act was a nefarious plan of assimilation through a travel ban of immigrants from Asian countries. At the time—with poverty driving out hundreds of thousands, like the post–World War I Italians or the "undesirables"—the law would shape U.S. immigration policy for nearly three decades.

Domestically, the U.S. government had more than once turned on its own citizens. In 1942, following Japan's attack on Pearl Harbor, President Franklin D. Roosevelt ordered the incarceration of up to 120,000 people of Japanese ancestry into camps across the country. More than 60 percent of them were U.S. citizens. Many years later, Reagan issued an apology to Japanese Americans.

All along and just across the border were the Mexicans. Even as signs popped up across the Southwest stating "No Mexicans," particularly in Texas, the question persisted: Could Americans do without them? Historically, the U.S. government didn't exactly know what to do about Mexicans. It was—often still is—a love-hate relationship.

During the Great Depression, up to two million Mexicans and Mexican Americans were deported or expelled from cities and towns across the U.S. and shipped to Mexico. According to some estimates, more than half of these people were U.S. citizens born in the United States.

Yet somehow Mexicans were held to a different standard than other immigrant groups, one that depended, then and now, on job demand. Along the U.S.-Mexico border, Anglo ranchers viewed the crisscrossing of Mexicans between Mexico and Texas, New Mexico and Arizona as a welcome annual pilgrimage. The workers, most of them landless *peones*, came in search of opportunity. For instance, cousins and uncles in Juárez would cross into far West Texas to pick cotton and return home. No questions asked.

They worked the season, from planting to harvest, then returned to Mexico to spend their money and visit family. This was a time in our history when the relationship between both countries was mutually beneficial. It took into consideration our binationalism, and the economic workflow ebbed to the tune of supply and demand. Back in Mexico, Mexicans made an average of 25 cents a day and lived in the shadow of large hacienda landowners. Tens of thousands made a beeline for California and worked alongside Chinese and Japanese farmworkers.

Between 1915 and 1919 the number of Mexican workers in California's citrus fields increased to more than seven thousand. They made an average of $1.42 per day, the lowest wage of any immigrant group. With the United States' entry into World War I, the country needed workers, and soon the U.S. enacted a temporary provision to allow Mexican workers in to help manufacturing companies throughout the Midwest, railroads across the country, poultry farms in Chicago, asparagus fields in Ohio, shipyards in Virginia and automobile factories in Michigan.

Over time, Mexicans became a growing headache for Protestant Americans. Many American businesses believed a small, manageable number of Mexicans was needed to keep the economy humming and do the backbreaking industrial and agricultural jobs that other Americans refused to do. But the numbers of Mexicans had to be restricted and carefully controlled, otherwise they'd risk changing the makeup of the country forever. Immigration opponents believed that this would lead to the downfall of the United States, a miserable fate that the Roman and Greek Empires had suffered before us.

In difficult times, Mexicans were scapegoated by politicians and targeted for mass deportations. The periods between the 1930s and 1950s fluctuated between massive deportations and demands for Mexican workers.

The fickleness knew no end. U.S. employers, particularly those in the Southwest, opposed restrictions against migration from Mexico. The boys from Mexico worked so hard and were so loyal, ranchers argued even as accusations of mistreatment soared. As the U.S. entered World War II, the cry for Mexican labor increased. Welcoming arms opened again.

Between 1942 and 1965, some five million contracts were awarded to so-called *braceros*, mostly Mexican men who arrived in the United States to help offset the loss of tens of thousands of men who left to fight abroad, first in World War II, then the Korean War. They deepened or created new migratory patterns that stretched from Stockton, California, to

Texas to Maine, from Pittsburgh to Colorado to Ohio, Michigan, Indiana and Illinois, with its giant meatpacking industry. The Bracero Program lasted twenty-two years and became the largest foreign labor program in U.S. history. It was also the defining program that brought me into this country.

Yet, without a doubt, the most dramatic opening came with the 1965 Immigration and Nationality Act, because it took into account millions of immigrants who did not come from Europe. It was the change that Americans had failed to make since white Protestants dictated policy. Building up to this moment, John F. Kennedy called restricted immigration laws "nearly intolerable." Mexicans eagerly hoped for laws that could finally take their families and love of country into account. The administration kept its word as President Lyndon Johnson carried the torch and signed the 1965 act into law at the Statue of Liberty. Although the law maintained per-country limits, it also created preference visa categories that focused on immigrants' skills and relationships with citizens or U.S. residents. The 1965 law unequivocally changed the face of America, as my collegue Joel Simon noted in his book *The Other Americans*.

"This bill says simply that from this day forth, those wishing to immigrate to America shall be admitted on the basis of their skills and their close relationships to those already here. The fairness of this standard is so self-evident that we may well wonder that it has not always been applied," Johnson said.

The bill set numerical restrictions on visas at 170,000 per year, with a per-country-of-origin quota. However, immediate relatives of U.S. citizens and "special immigrants" had no restrictions. The bill became law at a time when the issue of border control was hardly even mentioned. Instead, the reform grew out of parochial concerns expressed by big-city Democrats, a desire of congressional leaders from places like Chicago, New York City, Milwaukee, Cleveland and Buffalo to ensure that any eastern European refugees who arrived in their district received legal status as residents, which would open the door to citizenship and eventually votes to keep their political machines roaring.

At the time, some fifty thousand Mexicans entered the U.S. each year as legal permanent residents, while hundreds of thousands more, including *braceros*, entered on temporary work visas.

The changing face of America unnerved conservative senators, including South Carolina's Strom Thurmond, a notorious segregationist, and West Virginia's Robert Byrd, a former KKK member. Thurmond argued that it was imperative "to preserve one's identity and the identity of one's nation." Byrd argued that unfettered migration from Latin America would fundamentally change the makeup of the U.S. "The day is not far off when the population explosion in Latin American countries will exert great pressures upon those people to emigrate to the United States," he said.

Before the introduction of the 1965 law, no numerical restrictions were placed on Latin American immigrants. The number of entry slots available to Mexico and other Latin American countries was slashed dramatically in 1976 to twenty thousand visas per year in an amendment to the law. But the economic demand and proximity did not change. Mexico was conveniently still just along the southern border, with able bodies ready to do the job. When the Bracero Program ended in 1964, hundreds of thousands lost their temporary legal status but were encouraged by eager U.S. agribusinesses to come across to help harvest the land anyway—a reality I knew all too well as a field boy in California. Over the years, millions became "illegal immigrants."

Latin American and Asian immigrants began to surpass Europeans. Indeed, prior to 1965, the demographics of immigration stood as mostly European; an estimated 68 percent of legal immigrants in the 1950s came from Europe and Canada. However, in the years between 1971 and the late 1980s, immigrants from Hispanic and Latin American countries made up an estimated 45 percent of immigrants, with Mexico accounting for the vast majority. The law did more than just change the ethnic makeup of immigration. It also greatly increased the number of immigrants. Immigration constituted 11 percent of the total U.S. population growth between 1960 and 1970, growing to 33 percent from 1970 to 1980, and to 39 percent from 1980 to 1990.

I knew of these burgeoning numbers from my life on the border. However, sitting in the Northeast, thousands of miles away from the epicenter, it seemed that Mexicans somehow were still flying way under the radar outside of the Southwest. At least, that's what I thought before I discovered Kennett Square. That's when I realized that we weren't alone in the region.

I was driving through Intercourse, Pennsylvania, having been intrigued enough by the name itself to rent a car one weekend and go see what people did there. I don't know what I was really expecting, but I left disappointed. The town was more than an hour out of Philadelphia, a sleepy Amish community of farmers, wagons and women in bonnets, all intermixed with annoying tourists like myself. What was I hoping to see, sex in the streets? The town was quaint and boring.

I was on my way back to Philly when I spotted them in the borough of Kennett Square: men who looked like me, walking on the side of the road, carrying firewood. My heart beat faster. At a stop sign, I rolled down the window and heard music blaring from a car parked in a lot on the corner: Los Bukis singing "Tu Cárcel," a song Primo and I had turned into an anthem of sorts.

A dead giveaway: Mexicans.

I stopped the car, got out and tried to make small talk, even offered them a ride home. They politely refused. The enforcement components of Reagan's amnesty started going into effect in 1987, and they seemed as suspicious of me as I was doubtful of them. One asked if I was part of the secret *migra* force scouting for deportees. I nodded my head and grinned, marveling at his sense of humor, though the serious look on his face didn't change. I walked part of the way to their trailer home with a small group, telling them who I really was, a reporter born in Mexico. They warmed up. And they invited me to a little store called El Sombrero to buy beer and beef, jalapeños and tortillas. We headed for their trailers and we sat around their campfire. Small talk. They worked in nearby mushroom plants. The stench of mushrooms was so strong, I tried holding my breath as much as possible. It was cold and volunteers would take turns tossing wood into the pit. More than the fire, the music kept us warm, although I worried neighbors would grow impatient and call the cops or, worse, INS. The night wore on and the questions began.

They were curious. What did a reporter do?

I listen, I said, and write stories.

How could I protect them? Wouldn't *la migra* pick them up if I wrote a story?

Before I answered, a man named Juan quieted everyone.

Everyone knows we're here. Who are we kidding?

I will do whatever I can to protect you, I said. Beer flowed as they opened up and shared stories.

I headed back to Philadelphia giddy. But in the days that followed I started to doubt myself. What if I hadn't really seen them at all? The memory of the familiar faces of perfect strangers felt like a mirage. It was a testament to the isolation I felt as a Mexican in Philadelphia that I would even doubt my own recollection of other Mexicans. The feeling was strong enough that I rented another car and headed back to Kennett Square.

Finally, I told Frank what I had found and, skeptical at first, he succumbed.

You're sure, he asked.

Yep, I said. Checked it out. I'm very sure.

He thought there was a story there. I did more research and, sure enough, the Pennsylvania mushroom industry's entire workforce at that moment consisted of hundreds of men from Mexico, men who were quietly replacing Puerto Ricans, who years earlier replaced African American and Italian workers. Once Mexicans started coming in the late 1970s and 1980s, the new replacements consisted of a network of men, the vast majority from Guanajuato. They lived in man-camps, often amid the overwhelming fungal smell of the mushroom factories.

The second time I went, it was afternoon, early winter, so the sun would set before 5:00 p.m. I saw rows and rows of playfully painted Victorian homes, snow and white people. I parked the car and waited for a shift change that a man at a convenience store had tipped me off about. The man didn't know whether the men were Mexican, but he was pretty sure they were "Latin," as he put it.

I waited some more and then I saw one, two . . . men who looked like me. I rolled the window down.

Oye, ¿dónde puedo encontrar tortillas de harina? I said, asking a guy where I could buy flour tortillas.

He pointed. *En ésta misma calle, la misma tienda.* (There is a store just up the road.)

At El Sombrero, I found Humberto Rocha, a Mexican American from Horizon City, a satellite of El Paso. We hit it off right away. He ran a small grocery that fronted a big warehouse of Mexican goods that he sold to restaurants and *tienditas* all around the region. He bought his products in Chicago, staked with warehouses that carried everything Mexico.

How did he end up with a Mexican store near Intercourse, Pennsylvania, not far from the Amish? I asked.

Employers ran out of Italians, African Americans. Then they discovered Mexicans and the line had no end. They were mostly men, willing to go anywhere for a job. They weren't even necessarily people; just workers. And like my family, they also knew of someone who knew of someone brave enough to try something new with dollar signs. Best thing was there was a steady and rapid stream of Mexicans, arriving by the hundreds without their families, without plans to set down roots.

The demand for Mexican food is growing everywhere, he said—like I had to be blind not to see it. Convenience stores were packed, especially on pay day. Taquerias were opening up. And now with amnesty, just wait, he added, grinning and predicting, families too.

Maybe you shouldn't be grinning, I thought. Too many could represent a backlash.

One of the men asked if I had time to join him and others for a cookout. They had killed a goat earlier and planned to make *barbacoa* tacos that night. I gladly accepted the generous invitation and soon took my place around a grill outside a trailer house and ate tacos with *chiles toreados*, a dozen men or so gathered over a fire pit. We ended the evening at a dance hall, once popular with Italian workers, now lined with Mexican men, some dancing with the two or three women hanging out, others awkwardly dancing by themselves.

If living in Philadelphia had felt like being a foreigner in another country, finding and confirming the existence of Kennett Square felt like I was turning a corner. Slowly I began to realize that the battleground wasn't necessarily the border anymore. The border was more like the siren sound from a lighthouse, an effort to put *paisanos* on notice that shit was about to hit the fan. I began to feel more relevant. I also began to think that maybe this was why "the mainstream" didn't care too much about us. We were tucked so far into the shadows they didn't even know we were there. And behind all that noise was static American history, an understanding that the Mexican immigrant was certainly not the non-German, Protestant ideal that Benjamin Franklin came to later believe was the American archetype. So if we weren't *that*, then what were we?

Immigrants in Kennett Square dreamed of Texas, California, states that felt more familiar, closer to home.

Homesick dreamers.

I empathized.

Apparently, others did, too. The story hit the front page of the *Journal*.

8.

The Rebuilding of America

Everywhere I went, it seemed Mexico was closer than I thought. Houston, Phoenix, Chicago, followed by small towns like Racine and Lake Geneva, Wisconsin.

I started in Chicago and, as promised, Primo met me there. I stayed at the Drake Hotel. He bunked with friends. He wanted to show me "his" Chicago, where he had cut his teeth as a young grad student in the 1970s, enamored of and deeply embedded in the burgeoning Chicano and labor movements. He took me to Theresa's Lounge, a blues bar on the South Side, home of Junior Wells and Buddy Guy. Thanks to Primo, well-known Mexican scholars like Enrique Semo, Rosa Albina Garavito and Adolfo Gilly, and later, political figures like former candidate for president of Mexico Cuauhtémoc Cárdenas, got an unforgettable taste of Chicago blues at Theresa's.

Primo would come alive at night and hold court among activists and community leaders—African American, Puerto Rican and Mexican—around tables wet with cold beers and spilled tequila. That was the beauty of Primo, the way he could be so mysterious but with the kind of citizen-of-the-world charisma that would make him feel at home with people of different nations or skin colors. He always made it a point to take people dancing the night before big meetings, get people to drop their guard, realize that we're all human, no matter if you're from Chicago, Philadelphia or Mexico City.

The nights would go on forever. There was so much booze, so much tequila, men and women mingling until dawn. Primo would occasionally take one of the few women to the dance floor, a prelude to romance.

The parties, dancing, were nonstop, recalled Susan Gzesh, an immigration lawyer in Chicago. No one owned the dance floor better than Primo.

Chicago was as Mexican in 1982 as it was once Polish, Primo said. And it wasn't just Chicago, but nearby suburbs, including Cicero, once the home base of mobster Al Capone. Ironically, years earlier, some of Capone's mobsters had fled the area and hid in plain sight in Mexico, including Guadalajara and Cuernavaca.

Primo spent much of his time in Pilsen, on vibrant and noisy Eighteenth Street, integrating himself into a community, where he'd see written signs that said "*Se Habla Inglés*." There was nothing of Mexico in the architecture of the three-story brownstones.

But neither the University of Chicago nor his activism would allow Primo to forget about love. On Saint Patrick's Day, after watching the parade and the river dyed green, he and an American woman he was involved with—drunk and feeling the love—decided to get married the next day at City Hall. The marriage lasted just three years. He ended up with a green card. He could now travel back and forth to Mexico without hassle. Whenever we asked about his former wife, Barbara—what she was like, if he could describe her—Primo would demur. There was no way to confirm his story, and I sometimes had my doubts, but this is how he told it: it was a casual marriage that promptly ended, amicably, after she fell in love with an Argentinian physicist and he with a leftist.

I felt like the two Mexicos were converging in the streets of Chicago: an angry but hopeful Mexico, he said.

As I traveled farther into the Midwest, I met fewer activists and more workers. I visited communities to find the pulse and capture the mood swings of a people perplexed by their newest neighbors, workers who were finding it harder to say goodbye to their new surroundings. The presence of Mexicans in the remote places of Iowa, Nebraska, Wisconsin and Michigan wasn't necessarily new. Brave, bold people long before them had begun the tradition. The only difference now was that their numbers were growing faster.

At the end of World War I, writes historian Eduardo Moralez, labor shortages prompted representatives from agricultural and industrial companies in the Great Lakes region to send recruiters to Texas towns and cities, where they promised to pay wages, room and board, as well as the cost of transportation for workers and their families. The 1920 census recorded 686 Mexicans living in northern Indiana. By 1924 the trickle of ethnic Mexican migrants in Indiana turned into a cascade when approximately four thousand Mexicans from Michigan who had been working in agriculture arrived to take jobs in the steel mills of Gary and

East Chicago. The 1930 census recorded a total of 8,769 people identified as "Mexicans" living in these two cities.

During the early years of the Great Depression—when jobs were scarce and foreign workers unwanted—massive deportations removed thousands of ethnic Mexicans from the Great Lakes area. The Depression deepened suspicion and resentment toward Mexicans. Just as previous waves of Irish and German immigrants became scapegoats during economic hardship, Mexicans faced the same struggle. By the close of 1932, town and state officials, together with private businesses, had "repatriated" more than thirty-two thousand ethnic Mexicans from Illinois, Indiana, Michigan and Ohio.

Uncle Eutemio, or "Güero" to us because of his light skin, remembers dreaming of his chance to head north to Chicago, California. He remembers watching deported men getting off buses, sad and desolate. He learned quickly. When you go to the United States, he told me, think of it as temporary. A place to work. You get in and get out.

Yet the pull of agricultural and factory jobs nevertheless drew Mexicans back to the Midwest in the intervening decades.

I saw that states like Iowa and Wisconsin were caught off guard by the changes sweeping their communities. Back then, the size of the population of undocumented workers was as many as five million. I was now following a silent pilgrimage of immigrants deeper into the heartland of America, immigrants often referred to as the sleeping giant with the potential to reshape the most powerful nation. Jobs went beyond milking cows or picking apples. Wisconsin, with its lakeside resorts, had long been a thriving weekend getaway from the Chicago area. This was, in part, due to the vision of the son of a poor Irish immigrant turned millionaire by the name of William J. Newman.

Newman's father had emigrated from County Cork, Ireland, in 1880. Young William was born in Montreal and later moved to Chicago, where he built his fortune. He started as a newsboy but moved to construction, eventually erecting many historic buildings in Chicago, Philadelphia, New York City and half a dozen other American cities. Newman was too busy to take a vacation but dreamed of weekends in scenic Wisconsin. Believing others wanted an escape, too, he picked a location with a perfect view and built a retreat. He brought in engineers and workers from Chicago to build a dam where Dell Creek entered the Wisconsin River and flooded the valley, creating a thousand acres of shoreline. His resort would feature a beach, a golf course, hiking and horseback riding trails, a trout pond and an amusement park, according to the

Wisconsin Historical Society. But someone needed to clean the stables, wash the dishes and tend to the farm that provided fresh vegetables, milk, butter and eggs for the guests at the Dell View Hotel.

He hired Irish, Polish and German immigrants. Eventually the work-force in the resort area of Wisconsin evolved to include mostly Mexican immigrants, many of them remnants of the railroad industry seeking new opportunities. They gave the service industry a try.

Newman never saw his dream fully realized. He was forced to give up the property during the Great Depression and in 1932 the federal government went after him for tax evasion, claiming he owed $1 million in back taxes. Newman's lawyer was disbarred and eventually convicted of preparing false tax returns. After World War II, Americans once again longed for leisurely weekends and had the money to spend on vacations. But by then Newman had sold his resort to an investment group that would benefit from growing tourism at the lakeside resort.

I know this because Newman was the great-grandfather of Angela Maria Kocherga, a blond, green-eyed beauty who I had met during one of my trips home to El Paso. She was at Freddy's one Sunday morning with a group of my friends and I couldn't take my eyes off her. I tried unsuccessfully to approach her but she politely rebuffed me. I kept thinking about her, though.

I headed out on the road in a rental car to small-town Wisconsin, first Kenosha, then Madison, and on my return to Lake Geneva and Racine. Madison's dairy industry was employing Mexicans; in Racine, Mexicans were working in the service industry and in agriculture outside of town. Whatever culture shock I felt in Philly couldn't compare to Racine.

The city of about eighty-five thousand on the shores of Lake Michigan, just seventy-five miles north of Chicago, had only recently seen an influx of brown people. Census figures before 1960 list Racine's Hispanic population as "N/A." By 1980, Hispanics accounted for more than 6 percent of city residents. That didn't sound like much to me, but it was apparently enough to rattle some locals, who referred to the newcomers as "illegals" or "illegal aliens." That latter name—borrowed from the language of the U.S. government—really bothered me. Aliens? Geez, they were just Mexican people, not extraterrestrials from Mars.

I pulled into Racine's clean but empty downtown in the middle of the day to report on the changes, the pretty shores of Lake Michigan nearby. I stopped at a local downtown hotel, the type of local place where I could get some flavor for the area. It was late. I asked the clerk, an old, rosy-cheeked white man, for a room.

Where are you from? he asked, but not with the usual friendly tone of a clerk making small talk with a guest. He sounded suspicious.

I'm from the border, I told him. He raised his eyebrows. Okay, I thought, maybe he doesn't know where the border is. I added: I live in Philadelphia, where the U.S. Constitution was drafted, home to the Liberty Bell, Benjamin Franklin, I said, realizing that I was trying too hard now.

Do you have your papers? he asked.

I thought I heard him wrong. What papers? I asked. I have my credit card, American Express. I work for the *Wall Street Journal*.

Do you have proof? he asked.

That was about the point in the conversation that I walked out, half-pissed, half in shock. I don't know if it was the first, but it felt like the first time I had experienced overt discrimination—from someone other than a Border Patrol agent—for being brown. I silently cursed him, mustered what little dignity I still had and found a room elsewhere.

In the morning I met a young Mexican guy and asked how in the world anyone from Mexico could function in towns so cold, temperature- and culture-wise, and suspicious. I really wanted to ask about discrimination, but weather was always an icebreaker.

You get used to everything when you're away from home, the man said, the cold weather, discrimination, everything. *Sí, hay mucha discriminación*, he said. *Pero hay buenos trabajos y aquí estamos.* There is a lot of prejudice but there are good jobs here, so here we are.

During the trip I interviewed residents about their new neighbors, and the tension was palpable. Some didn't know what to make of me. I spoke English. Perhaps I was Italian. I'm just a reporter, ma'am, sir, I'd remind them. Just tell me your story. What do you make of the newcomers? Of immigration reform? Of amnesty?

But the conversations then took on different nuances. Their honesty made me feel as uncomfortable as they were about "the others" around them.

Left-leaning Madison, Wisconsin, was about the only place where I stopped that was not just welcoming to immigrants but willing to protect them—one of the nation's first so-called "sanctuary cities." Residents seemed to recognize and be grateful for the help provided by mostly Central American immigrants in the dairy industry and, more recently, in the city's service industry and on campuses.

Driving through Wisconsin, I thought about George, a white man I had met in the fields of California's San Joaquin Valley. I never knew where he was from, just that he was a Vietnam War veteran in his late forties or early fifties, an occasional fieldworker who changed my perspective on the world. He could have been a member of Wisconsin's white working class, for all I knew. For weeks he helped me load bins on tractors at the edge of a tomato field. In the field a roaring, massive farm machine harvested the red-ripe fruit onto a conveyor belt, where Mexican women, standing on a platform over the belt, sorted with nimble fingers hundreds, maybe thousands of tomatoes an hour into those bins. Every once in a while the machine would break down, the field would grow quiet and George and I would listen to Neil Diamond and talk. I was in my early teens and every word he uttered made an impression. I was on the verge of dropping out of high school, the biggest cliché for the offspring of farmworkers: more than 60 percent of us didn't graduate.

A wiry man with a small paunch and sad eyes and wearing an Oakland A's baseball cap, George became my mentor. That summer he gave me answers to questions I had never even thought to ask and set me on a personal journey that continues today. During our breaks we'd take our gloves off and sit atop the bins in the sudden stillness. He taught me soulful songs like "Sweet Caroline" and "I Am . . . I Said," hinting at a hidden pain he wasn't ready to share. Neil Diamond was the closest thing I had heard in English to José Alfredo Jimenez, so mournful, so melodramatic. I asked him about the war a few times but he would never open up. These were stories he wouldn't tell me, he would say, for fear that I, too, would grow bitter. Instead he would change the subject to women and check out the sorters from afar. I grew embarrassed. He watched the ladies—covered from head to toe except for their eyes to keep out the sun and dust and grime—and he would encourage me. Get it while you can, Alfredo, he'd say. Then he'd zero in on my cousin Carmen, who was still in her teens.

I know she's your cousin, Alfredo, but that girl is the most beautiful woman I have ever seen. Look at those eyes, her lips.

George, Jesus, she's my cousin, I protested.

And he would just laugh.

He joked that the lessons of life weren't free. He asked me to teach him basic Spanish because someday he wanted to head south and begin again. Mexico, maybe. A second chance.

Sure, I said, but only if I can go with you and show you the Mexico I once knew. I'd remind him I wasn't a U.S. citizen and had no intention of ever pledging allegiance.

Mexico is home, I explained.

You were only a child then, he replied. A romantic fool—foolish. He laughed off my nostalgia and we talked about life. His view was that sex, music, wine and food were the only things worth living for—which was something an inexperienced fifteen-year-old like me wasn't used to hearing. I didn't know what sex meant, other than the closest thing to paradise before you passed, with no return, through the gates of hell. You could go to hell for that, I'd been told. Maybe because of what he saw in Vietnam, George would say, Alfredo, do what makes you happy, 'cause it's all gone and done in a matter of seconds. Something about his secretiveness on the subject reminded me of my uncle Jesse, who had also fought in Vietnam and never talked about it. He was the labor contractor and knew George.

Follow your passion, George would say. He wasn't happy loading tomato bins, but it was a temporary job, enough to pay the bills.

I told him I believed in fighting for justice, for equal rights for workers, just like my mother did out there in the fields. The power of the *huelga*, using her term for strike.

You need to take care of the things you can take care of, George said. Justice is too complicated and can leave scars, broken hearts. Then he grew quiet. America is not a grateful nation, he told me. Americans had already killed two Kennedys and Martin Luther King. He warned me I would always be an outsider, even as Mexicans kept coming. Numbers didn't matter. If I, if my family, didn't commit to being American—not just paying taxes but voting and becoming players in the system—we would always be in the fields. He was bitter about America's role in Vietnam. He had fought alongside Mexicans and Mexican Americans who served in the U.S. war effort and their efforts had been overlooked.

Mexicans are a forgiving people, I said, quoting my mother, who liked to remind me that history had given us the most practice in forgiving others. We've been repeatedly humiliated by the United States.

I told George that my mother stressed the importance of keeping an open hand to individual whites, the Anglos. As long as we kept our dignity and they had a touch of humility, we could remain friends, my mother believed.

That's weakness, George admonished me. Americans respect strength, not weakness. Americans don't like to sacrifice. I'm here to raise a little money and then I'm out of here. I'm checking out. *Fin*. Americans will complain and strive for the next best thing, but they don't look to the past. Americans dream of big thoughts for tomorrow. That's where you come in. You're building the country today, but at what cost? So you can keep your faith, humility, integrity and dignity intact? In the end you'll be fucked over by Americans unless you become American. Maybe then you can level the playing field. Don't play second fiddle to anyone, Alfredo.

This country needs your optimism, not your bitterness, he concluded.

His words reverberated in my mind for years.

Sometimes George didn't say much at all. He read books. He shared one, *The Art of Positive Thinking*, which opened my eyes to reading. I became a fan of Larry McMurtry's *The Last Picture Show* and *All My Friends Are Going to Be Strangers*, the story of Danny Deck, a promising young writer who drifts from his native Texas to California and back, looking for people to hold on to.

I didn't see George again after the summer. He promised to keep in touch but never did. Years went by and I would ask after him, but no one knew a thing. Someone said he had headed south of the border and found a new start and a new name, which was never disclosed. My uncle Jesse didn't even know where he was and soon forgot him. Everyone did.

George came and went like a ghost. How many more Americans felt like George, especially here in the Midwest, abandoned by their own country? Americans torn apart by war, illusions, disillusion. Americans looking for their own identity and threatened by someone like me, a son of Mexican farmworkers. But also Americans who, like George, believed in second chances and new beginnings. Americans who, like George, encouraged people like me to remain hopeful. As jaded as he was, he was also strong, determined, romantic, optimistic, an American through and through. And I longed to be like him.

9.

Farewell, Philadelphia

The biting winds seemed to strike an invisible shield around me. When I returned to Philadelphia, I didn't even notice winter—my second there. I was finding my skip, zigzagging from my apartment, through the University of Pennsylvania campus and strutting across Rittenhouse Square, up and down Locust. The change was everywhere, starting with me.

I'd accept Ken's invitations to receptions at his apartment with a view of Schuylkill River, mingling with his lawyer friends and a few reporters, including Julie and colleagues from the *Philadelphia Inquirer*, who seemed to win Pulitzers every year. I felt awkward but was learning the art of small talk, smiling, holding a wineglass and pretending to be really interested. Wearing Ken's hand-me-downs also gave me an extra boost of confidence, especially the trendy ties he let me have. I was wearing his tweed jacket and a skinny pink tie before they were all the rage in his social circles. I could now carry on a conversation on a range of topics, from the latest stock trading scandal to marketing strategies used to lure Hispanic consumers. I had met Isaac Lasky, the marketing guru behind Campbell Soup's Hispanic advertising, who knew just about every number and projection. Isaac was a Mexican Jew from Polanco and I was fascinated with how he had ended up in Michigan and his interest in the fastest-growing minority group in the United States.

Numbers, he replied. U.S. demographics were shifting substantially: the U.S. Hispanic population would double with each decade, and later quadruple.

He asked—not without disdain—how a Mexican immigrant who had dropped out of high school could ever end up at the *Wall Street Journal*.

Opportunity, I shot back.

What I didn't add but wanted to was that the Mexico City elite just couldn't accept that a poor *pocho* like me could really make it, could they? Well, America really was different from Mexico, I wanted to tell him.

While Ken roped me into his fancy cocktails, Primo urged the three of us to join him at the Monte Carlo, a smoky salsa ballroom where he'd take center stage, taking turns with adoring female dancers with dresses so tight they seemed glued to their bodies, twirling, hips pulsating, taking three steps for every four beats of music. The place was packed with Puerto Ricans and other Latin Americans: Ecuadorans, Uruguayans, Colombians and always at least one Mexican, Primo. He had rhythm in his skinny frame, feet moving to the *son Cubano,* the cha-cha-cha and the mambo. At times he'd take his handkerchief and wipe the sweat off of his forehead without losing a step. Ken was the only one brave enough to join him—always with his signature confidence, of course. Obviously he didn't have the pulse, pace or tempo of Primo. But who was I to criticize? At least he was brave enough to be on the dance floor.

David and I hid behind couples and the thick layer of smoke, tapping our feet discreetly, hoping no one asked us to dance—and whenever they did, we'd smile politely and say no. When they insisted, we'd nod our heads and look the other way.

David thought that was a bad strategy.

They may think we're a couple, he said.

I'm okay with that, I countered. Dancing would be more embarrassing.

Once Primo came after us to dance and in doing so chased us out of the Monte Carlo, literally running around the ballroom until David and I found the exit and ran out. We walked through Center City, gawking at the changes around us. The city looked cleaner, more orderly and inviting. Center City was in the midst of a revitalization campaign to push out crack dealers, prostitutes and their pimps. The area was so downtrodden that restaurant owners had formed a campaign to clean up the streets. David took his task a bit too seriously. One night he had just left the restaurant with cash from that night's earnings in hand and got in his VW van to drive home. As he drove out he noticed clusters of prostitutes and pimps roaming the empty streets, cars moving slowly, drivers looking for a quickie. David believed Center City had more to offer than vice.

He called the police and stayed inside his VW for an hour until the cop arrived. When the policeman arrived the pimps and prostitutes went up to the police officer, greeted him, and laughed as though they were friends. Disgusted, David got out of his VW and went straight to the cop and angrily confronted him, demanding an explanation. The cop pushed back, asking David, Who the fuck are you to be questioning me like that? David responded, I'm just a business owner, trying to make a living and keep the place clean, keep America's promise alive. Amid the finger-pointing and screaming, the cop threatened to put David in jail. David said go ahead. Follow me to your headquarters, and the cop did. David was hoping he would see one of the good cops he knew who had been part of the neighborhood committee. To his surprise, no one was there. David was cited for being belligerent. He was dragged off from the headquarters and taken to jail. He barely passed a Breathalyzer and was thrown into a cell. After three hours he was allowed to call Annette and told her to take his phonebook and call some of his most loyal restaurant customers, including state legislators, a police captain, an attorney, and city councilman Angel Ortiz. Before dawn, the police chief showed up and promptly issued David an apology and said he couldn't be processed for another fifteen hours until his turn came up before a judge. The chief said he could stay inside his office and wait until his turn. David said no, he wanted to go back to his cell, wait his turn and be processed as any citizen just doing his duty to report drug dealers, prostitutes and pimps and ended up in jail, while the illicit activity was still in the streets.

That would be a great story to tell the media once I'm freed, he told the chief. Twelve hours later, David was released and a group of politicians waited for him. The police chief apologized even more profoundly. That's okay, David responded, but you have twenty-four hours to clean up Center City, or I will go public.

Also, David added, can I get my cash back? It's missing.

That night, a cop showed up with the missing earnings, returned them to David and drove off.

America's possibilities loomed large, even as the nation grew uncomfortable with those crawling out of the shadows. These were the stories I increasingly wrote about. I wanted to know what was becoming of the United States. My Freddy's Café story turned out to be a valuable way of humanizing numbers and projections. Some 3.1 million undocumented workers were legalized under IRCA, cementing a permanent presence of Mexicans countrywide with unclear consequences. Immigration reform had one again served its pressing political priority: correcting problems of the past. No one, however, was preparing the country for its future.

The United States was undergoing the so-called Great Moderation, a period of robust economic growth starting in the early 1980s that would last for more than twenty-five years. And even then the size of the Mexican immigrant population—the labor force that helped anchor this growth—barely kept up with the economy. In hindsight I failed to look deeply enough to truly understand the tensions and consequences that many of us could not even fathom at the time. We were strangers to one another.

DESPITE MY RISING COMFORT level, I couldn't wait to say goodbye to Philadelphia. If this were graduate school, as Ray once told me, I felt ready to graduate from the Campbell's beat and make a bigger difference by working on stories about these changes, this great immigration wave of *mis paisanos*. I just had to get back to Mexico and the borderlands, which to me was the most intriguing and complex part of my two homelands, Mexico and the United States. In Philadelphia, Frank had groomed me to become a better reporter, learn to develop big story ideas, dig for relevance, the "nut graf"—that paragraph that gets to the point in two sentences or less—the kicker quote at the end, all crucial stepping-stones that Frank was generously laying before me. The more opportunities I had to write the stories I really cared about, the more I knew what I wanted to do with my life. I wanted to find a new beginning in Mexico, like the one George and I had once talked about back in California.

After my forays into once-voiceless immigrant communities, Frank began to assign me to even more stories with Dianne Solis for the Houston bureau. I was a huge admirer of George Getschow, the bureau chief there. He was a finalist in 1984 for a Pulitzer for his series "Dirty Work," which uncovered the horrors of slave labor camps in the Southwest. And more importantly for me, he was the author of that story I had clipped out back when I was a student newspaper reporter. George's piece about Napizaro, Michoacán, was legendary and had struck a personal note. I read the story countless times and almost memorized the lead word for word: "An astonishingly effective U.S. trade program is operating in this rural hamlet of 1,200 people—but Uncle Sam knows nothing about it. He wouldn't like it if he did."

The story was, in part, about the impact of remittances from the United States to the Mexican community of Napizaro, thanks to the town's main export: its men. More than three-quarters of Napizaro's heads of household were working in the United States. Getschow was connecting the dots across binational communities the way I dreamed about. He revealed "invisible" communities in the U.S. and showed American readers what these workers at the bottom of the economic ladder had sacrificed, what they had left behind and the impact of their migration on their host and home communities.

I was in El Paso working on an immigration story when Frank called me with big news. Getschow wanted to meet me personally about a job in Dallas, where he was now the bureau cheif. Frank had gotten word that the *Dallas Morning News* was courting me. He asked me about it and I confirmed. He said he didn't want to lose me. If the Philadelphia bureau couldn't keep me, he would see to it that the *Wall Street Journal* would.

I'd like you to meet with George in Dallas, preferably at DFW airport, he said.

I made arrangements to do the "job interview" during an extended layover between El Paso and Philadelphia. Frank gave me George's number and asked me to call him to coordinate.

I did so nervously. I called him and he said something to the effect of Hey, Alfredo, look forward to meeting. Call me from your gate and I'll meet you there.

How will I know how to find you? I asked. This was before Facebook and I had no idea what he looked like.

I'll find you, he said, and abruptly hung up.

When I called him from DFW, I gave him my gate number, and within thirty minutes I heard a tall, wiry man with wavy, stringy blond hair shouting at the top of his lungs: Alfredo Corchado! Alfredo Corchado! He had an easy smile and steely blue eyes.

George? I said. I was taken aback. He was wearing blue jeans, a matching jean shirt and boots. I was embarrassed by what I wore, an unusual suit and tie, obviously overdressed for the interview.

Hey, great to meet you, he said. Then he immediately took a seat and got to the point. He said he wanted me in Dallas to help the bureau cover the border, immigration and a changing America. It all sounded like music to my ears.

I'm your reporter, I said.

In the back of my mind, I was really thinking, Where have you been all my life? I was so nervous, I quickly ran out of things to say, other than to say how honored I was to meet him, and confessed I had carried a copy of his Michoacán story with me to Philadelphia. I told him the impact it had on me, especially as a Mexican immigrant studying at a college right on the border. It was encouraging to see the interest that America was taking in us, and it was enlightening to understand so many subtle nuances of the ripple effects on two countries. He said he would help train me and prepare me to write stories just like the one from Michoacán. His offer gave me chills. I couldn't believe I might really get that chance.

Deep down, I dreamed of becoming a foreign correspondent, telling stories about families like mine. That seed had been planted years earlier by my guidance counselor, who convinced me that El Paso Community College could provide me an opportunity to become more than a hairdresser, an idea I got from watching *Shampoo*. Warren Beatty hardly worked and got all the girls. In retrospect it was a stupid idea, but I was grasping and had no role models, other than union leaders Cesar Chavez and Dolores Huerta, whom my parents worshipped. The counselor said I showed curiosity for the world. Maybe I should consider diplomacy or become a foreign correspondent, a spy. I could work anywhere in the world.

You mean I could work in Mexico, reconnect with my roots and get paid to do it? Earn dollars working for a U.S. paper in my homeland?

Yes, he said.

I could hardly believe it.

The idea still made me a little nervous. I was more *pocho* by now, speaking more Spanglish than Spanish. I wanted the Spanish language to flow off my tongue again, the same language that had soothed me as a boy and encouraged me to dream as a young man growing up in the fields of California.

I wanted to speak Spanish as fluently as the woman I was falling in love with back in El Paso. I kept going home to El Paso, both to report and in hopes of seeing her. Angela wouldn't go on a date with me but never said no to hanging out in Juárez. She was a mix of Ukrainian, Irish, English and eastern European heritage, born in Mexico City and raised in Guadalajara before moving to the Texas-Mexico border.

Like me, she was also a journalist, a graduate of the University of Texas at Austin.

I thought I could convince her that our common interests would create a strong foundation for something more . . . *maybe*, if she would just give me a chance.

In Juárez, I once took her to El Noa Noa, the bar featured in Juan Gabriel's hit song. She said he was corny, that her music taste trended toward Depeche Mode, U2 and David Bowie. Yet no one danced *El Noa Noa* quite like Angela. She'd break into a sexy sweat.

Angela believed Juan Gabriel and David Bowie could coexist, and eventually I, too, began to think coexistence was possible. I found reasons to be optimistic. With every taco, enchilada and fajita they discovered, Americans could one day embrace us, too. They would also understand this whole coexistence thing. And maybe it could be like a dance rather than some awkward dinner sitting among strangers.

The good news was that it looked like I'd be heading back to Texas for good, rejoining the world of the in-between. The DFW interview was a hit and the *Journal* offered me a job in Dallas. I would say goodbye to Philadelphia. I would no longer see Billy Penn's shadow over a city that was only just beginning to feel like home—or, at least, a city where I could belong to.

SECTION III

Malinche's Children

10.

Marriage of Convenience

My last evening in Philadelphia, colleagues from the *Philadelphia Inquirer* threw a party for me. They asked me to invite *Journal* people and I did. Frank showed up briefly and handed me spurs for an old pair of Texas boots that I wore from time to time. He handed me a white baseball cap with *WSJ* on it that I still have. Julie's hair was unusually puffed up and Donald the doorman wore a stylish black turtleneck. They were accompanied by Trisha from the advertising department, who seemed genuinely sad when I mentioned that I was moving to Dallas.

This would have never worked out—I'm too much of a Cowboys fan, I said, trying to lighten the mood, which only seemed to darken when Ken presented me with a Philadelphia Eagles jersey.

My plan was to leave late that night, jump in a rental car and drive as far southeast as possible. Ken, David and Primo were the saddest of them all and delayed me with goodbyes that felt more like a wake, as if we would never see one another again. By the time I turned the ignition on, it was 2:00 a.m. I drove all the way to somewhere in Virginia and made it to a rest stop for a quick nap. I couldn't wait to get to Texas. I woke up and drove all the way to Nashville. Lying on a hotel bed, flipping through the channels with a remote control the size of a brick, I clicked into a documentary on Philadelphia. I felt a tiny pang of remorse, so much so that I called David back at Tequilas. The three had gathered, he said, and expected me to turn up any second and tell them this was just another sick joke. Again, I promised to stay in touch and urged them to visit me in Texas, or for sure Mexico City, one day. I was so sure that was where I'd end up. It's not the end, I said, trying to convince myself more than anyone else.

When I saw the Texas state line, with the car radio blasting *norteño* music, all of the sadness seemed to wash away. I started punching the air and screaming Yeah! Yeah! I drove straight into rush-hour traffic in Dallas with a huge smile on my face.

It turned out that while the job in Dallas was closer to home, it was still more of the same business news. Mexico felt so close yet so far away. George Getschow made good on his promise. He helped me break a story on the real reasons San Antonio mayor Henry Cisneros was not seeking higher office—the married father of three had fallen for another woman. The story disappointed many friends and sources who questioned why a Hispanic reporter would reveal dirt on a Hispanic politician.

You should be proud, Alfredo, Getschow said. You pissed off everyone without anyone questioning the facts. That's great. He'd break into laughter.

Soon after, Getschow left to write a book. I began to drown.

More than a year into my stint there, I sat down with the acting bureau chief in Dallas to discuss my future. I said working in Mexico was still my goal and inquired whether the *Wall Street Journal* would be open to the possibility.

Yes, the bureau chief replied. But you're looking at several years down the road, maybe five or more years before we'd even consider you. You need more seasoning as a reporter and you need to improve your writing.

I wasn't sure whether his answer reflected my own performance at the *Journal* or if it was just part of the newsroom dynamics. But I was too ambitious and impatient to mull over his words or even consider delaying another second from what I had long wanted to do. I had never felt so sure about anything in my life, so I reached out and shook his hand and told him I'd finish the stories I had begun and, once done, would take my skinny brown ass and return to the border.

My mentor, Ray Chavez, was now the city editor at the *El Paso Herald-Post*. Ray promised me the freedom to pick my own stories. The newspaper certainly wasn't the *Journal* and resources were limited, but my passion and heart overruled any logic. I would give it a shot. Besides, my interest in Angela continued to grow. She and I were the best of colleagues and would talk for hours about ways to tell stories that resonated with readers and viewers beyond the border. Even though she merely considered me a friend, I was convinced time was on my side.

I wanted to be around my family and reunite with my parents, especially my father, whose health was failing. He was showing signs of memory loss, and he was drinking too much. He went to Juárez one day and simply vanished. It wasn't until days later that my family found him in a jail. He didn't recognize his own sons who picked him up. I wanted to be closer to him.

My friends, led by rabble-rouser Moises Bujanda, were still hell-bent on changing El Paso, and my mother's café was their war room. Freddy's had become an international forum for change, a magnet for politicians from both sides of the border, statewide and nationwide. Every other Sunday, the city's power brokers would gather at my parents' tiny café, then go first to South El Paso Street, just blocks from the international bridge, and later to Alameda Street, near Bowie High School. These politicians would preach about a vision of inclusiveness and empowerment. Border residents were searching for their own answers to questions about the region's worth and survival in a rapidly changing world.

I wanted to be a part of that answer; with my return, I could show that the brain drain could be reversible. I was eager to write the narrative of a community that knew no borders. And with my *compa*, Billy Calzada, by my side again, the world felt like it was ours to discover. The stories we could cover would be rich and complex and revealing. Of course, I had my doubts. In the months leading up to my departure, I had buried myself in Thomas Wolfe's book *You Can't Go Home Again*, which I had begun reading on that Septa bus in Philadelphia. I finished the novel during traffic jams on I-30 North in Dallas, where cars, pickup trucks and semitrailers would snarl for long stretches at a time. The more I read, the more nervous I got. Was I going home too soon, moving back in with my parents without my own room? And how could I ever top the *Wall Street Journal*? Anything else felt like a step down. But I needed my own place. Breaking the Mexican code that children didn't move out until they married, I told my parents I would get an apartment on my own. It turned out they couldn't care less, as long as I was coming home.

Once in El Paso, nostalgia quickly evaporated as reality set in. Billy and I realized that journalism was already in serious decline. I would never return to Mexico, at least not with the *Herald-Post*, which was cutting costs and not expanding. I spent fewer than three years at the *Herald-Post*, a shell of that vibrant newspaper I had once been a part of. Any travel that involved a hotel stay took much convincing, like pulling teeth.

While I couldn't travel, my editors believed that my experience at the *Journal* qualified me to become a columnist. I began writing a weekly column on free trade, a concept I wanted to fully explore to understand these historic shifts between our countries. With all the hyperbole generated by talk of a North American Free Trade Agreement between the United States, Canada and Mexico, it seemed that the so-called Chicago boys—the brain trust in the economics department of the University of Chicago that went after Primo and other Ivy Leagues elsewhere—had finally found a cure to decades of economic ills in Mexico and the border.

Pundits and presidents said the new pact would improve our lives, create the largest trading bloc in the world, improve wages and reduce poverty levels in Mexico, end illegal immigration, generate millions of new, high-paying jobs and usher us into the twenty-first century. It sounded like an awful lot of promises. Or a miracle.

I had the hometown boy's view: I knew little about policy, but it felt, at least for those of us on the border, that we were no longer the problem but part of a solution for both countries. El Paso was a dead-end working-class town with few compelling jobs to offer college graduates. NAFTA promised to make the city a hub of trade overflowing with white-collar jobs in supply-chain management and logistics. And where else but here? El Pasoans knew trade better than anyone. Trade ran through our veins. Our lives were about exchanging goods with Mexico, and sometimes smuggling illicit ones. All you had to do was watch the Paso del Norte International Bridge for an hour to see it in action—the constant flow of people and products back and forth. We also traded drinks, food, music and love. We were NAFTA before the term became one to hate or embrace.

I was enthusiastic about being a columnist and seeing my picture alongside my name. Yet some readers thought I took myself a bit too seriously. That was around the time when friends and foes alike started calling me "Free Trade Freddy." It seemed like many of us had bought the sales pitch from sleek politicians, even when answers were vague. One evening on my way home, I stopped at the Whataburger on Paisano Street not far from my apartment overlooking downtown El Paso and ordered the standard burger with jalapeños. The checkout guy recognized me from my column and asked me to sign my name on a Whataburger bag in exchange for extra jalapeños.

A huevo, compa, I said.

Is it true free trade will rescue us from these shitty jobs? he asked. He thought I was an oracle and he asked what career he should follow in this new world.

I sat there in my car, idling, challenged. I mulled over his question for a while and realized I didn't really understand what the economic outcome would be, or the consequences, even as they played out in my own family.

My aunt Chala and three of her four daughters had once worked as seamstresses in El Paso. For four decades the industry had provided steady jobs that helped support families, ensuring economic stability. My father and brother David would drive their catering trucks right up to their factories and wait for hungry clients, most of them women, to grab every bean, green and red chile burrito my mother had prepared that morning.

Tía Chala retired in 1980, but her daughters worked for more than a decade longer—until this thing called globalization came in and took away their jobs and shipped them across the border into Ciudad Juárez, where wages were a dollar or two per hour. More than thirty-five thousand seamstresses' jobs were lost in El Paso, thanks to NAFTA.

Yes, part of me was excited about NAFTA, a treaty that justified our existence on the border. Once we were seen as potential traitors to both countries, for being so close to one another that at any moment we could actually stray. We were bilingual and bicultural. Outsiders saw us either as *pochos* on one side or spics on the other. But we saw each other across the border as part of the same region, the same *familia*, sharing the same problems but also looking to the future from the same horizon. Now here we were, with the potential to move our two countries into a new era of peaceful coexistence, a coexistence where we could prosper as a result of our differences rather than suffer because of them. I hadn't been sure how to respond to the Whataburger cashier, so all I'd said was it can't get any worse. Which was really the Mexican definition of *Hay que echarle ganas, compa*.

But will things get better? he persisted.

I hope so was all I could say. Keep reading. We'll find the answers together, I added, driving off in my white Camaro with the T-top, the California plates since replaced by those with the Lone Star logo.

In El Paso, sources for my column ranged from academics to border business leaders, most of them salivating over the big NAFTA payoff. I kept in touch with my Philadelphia friends, although we had still never met as a group again. But they still served as bellwethers to help me sense the country's new moods, its growing complexities. Ken visited me once. It was the early nineties and I was in "Free Trade Freddy" mode. Ken wanted to see the border and find out if it was how he remembered it when he and his father had come to pick up "illegals." After dinner in Juárez and more tequilas than he was accustomed to, he grew frustrated by the long lines at the international crossing and started to pull out his legal credentials until I screamed at him from the driver's front seat and told him to get his ass down.

He needed to call a girl he had met and had been dating off and on.

I looked into his face of anguish.

Welcome to the border. This is fucking real love, I said sarcastically as Wham!'s "Careless Whisper" filled the darkness along I-10. On the way to Scenic Drive, I challenged Ken to find the dividing line between two countries. In a time before smartphones, Ken couldn't care less. He just wanted to get back to a telephone to call his girl named Laura, a law graduate, even though it was 3:00 a.m. her time.

David, Ken and Primo were the internationalists with their fancy worldviews about Cuba, Uruguay and Mexico. I lived on the border and was part of both countries. When David and Primo talked about the wealthiest nation ripping apart third world countries to sustain its own way of life, I thought about creating opportunity for us here at the *frontera*. Our economic and cultural existence was justified, because for years we didn't think we were good enough.

The tectonic plates of the North American economy had been shifting even before Reagan became president. In November of 1979 he launched his presidential campaign by sharing his vision of a new North American community, a continental "common market" among three nations. The former California governor called for a "North American accord" to create an environment for people and commerce to flow freely. His vision was met with stiff resistance by Mexican and Canadian leaders, fearing a union would only accentuate U.S. dominance over its weaker neighbors.

"The key to our own future security may lie in both Mexico and Canada becoming much stronger countries than they are today," said candidate Reagan, dressed in a gray suit and burgundy tie, his hand touching a globe and pointing to North America. ". . . It is time we stop thinking of our nearest neighbors as foreigners . . . A developing closeness between the United States, Mexico and Canada would serve notice on friend and foe alike that we are prepared for a long haul, looking outward again and confident of our future; that together we're going to create jobs, to generate new fortunes of wealth for many and provide a legacy for the children of each of our countries."

Looking to the past and future, Reagan envisioned a time—perhaps one hundred years on—when we can dare to "dream that at some future date a map of the world might show the North American continent as one in which the people's commerce of its three strong countries flow more freely across their present borders than they do today." Reagan found in Mexico a friendlier neighbor than in years past, when Mexican leaders once proclaimed to admire the United States' enemies, including Cuba and Nicaragua. Reagan had as an ally Miguel de la Madrid, a Harvard-trained technocrat who also had a vision to open Mexico to the world. Mexico had long nurtured protectionist trade policies that dated back to President Lázaro Cárdenas's nationalization of the oil industry in the 1930s. The government—always dominated by one party, the PRI—tightly restricted foreign investment and controlled the exchange rate to protect the country's industrial sector. The practices worked for Mexico, with the economy growing at an average of 2.7 percent between 1936 and 1973, with some periods more bullish than other, reaching as much as 6.7 percent, before descending into a tailspin.

In the mid-1980s, a worldwide energy crisis crippled economies globally and the Mexican government declared bankruptcy. Mexico's economy was now teetering on a depression. A debt crisis in 1982 saw Mexico default on its foreign debt obligations. De la Madrid, who came into office in 1982, was under pressure from the United States. He rewrote the country's prescription for its economic health: trade liberalization, more foreign investment and lower trade barriers. In 1986, Mexico agreed to join the GATT, the 1948 General Agreement on Trade and Tariffs. Mexico began pushing toward deeper economic integration with the United States and its neoliberal model—phrases that seemed to suggest the reshaping of human life as we knew it.

U.S. experts talked about the accord in terms of incremental moves modeled after the 1952 European Common Market. The United States had to compete with the European Union and powerful emerging Asian economies, and what better way than through a North American common market? As Mexico's economic fortunes slid, proponents of free trade and a new era of liberalism, believed Mexico could take a page from the Four Asian Tigers—Hong Kong, Singapore, South Korea and Taiwan—which since the late 1950s had transformed economically via rapid industrialization and had maintained high growth rates. NAFTA offered a golden opportunity to northern Mexican states' *maquiladora* industry of assembly plants. Companies could pay Mexican workers a fraction of what American factory workers made and quickly export cheaper goods to the U.S. For opening trade and adopting strict monetary and budgetary policies, the United States "rewarded" Mexico by lifting trade barriers. NAFTA was the ultimate consolation prize. Mexico reluctantly accepted, amid concerns of being swallowed by its wealthy northern neighbor.

A few of my sources were downright skeptical of NAFTA—none more so than Primo, whom I called from time to time to get a pulse from Philadelphia on Mexico. Anytime I believed Mexico was about to take off on that trip to the first world, as President Carlos Salinas de Gortari promised, Primo would stress caution and ground me. The popular phrase "economic integration" was booming even louder, suggesting that both countries were heading into a marriage of convenience. It was a marriage based on trade, cold and loveless, moving blindly into the future. Primo called it a shotgun wedding between the United States and Mexico.

He was so suspicious of free trade that he visited me in El Paso as part of a border tour. I tried unsuccessfully to hide my nickname, Free Trade Freddy, but he had already heard it from a union leader in El Paso before we even saw each other.

Free Trade Freddy? he asked.

Just the term made Primo cringe. He also had a secret to share. Back in Philadelphia, I remembered seeing Primo whispering into a telephone and afterward looking lost in thought for what would seem like hours, transformed into a human chimney, taking deep drags on his cigarette. He would never tell me what he had been talking about or who he had been talking with, even when I heard references to Chicago, Mexico, Nebraska, Iowa and the Mexican state of Querétaro.

How do you know so much? I asked. I'm a reporter. I need to know. Tell me. What's your secret?

Jaime Serra Puche. He's the person I've been talking to, Primo said over beers at the Tap Bar and Restaurant, a local dive with some of the best nachos in downtown El Paso.

No shit, I thought. Serra Puche was the top trade negotiator under Salinas de Gortari and later the finance minister under President Ernesto Zedillo. He also happened to be Primo's college pal. In fact, Serra Puche had just reached out to Primo to help him set up a private debate between top U.S. union members opposed to NAFTA. As head of the American Friends Service Committee's U.S.-Mexico Border Program, Primo was working with unions and farmers throughout the border, along with activist and later journalist and author David Brooks from New York City. They promoted some of the first exchanges among Mexican, U.S. and Canadian unions, farmers, environmentalists and immigrant rights advocates as trade deals became the thing between Mexico and the United States. All saw themselves as affected by what they called the elite agenda of economic integration.

What we were trying to do, especially Primo, was insist you can engage in the critique of the elite agenda, but not by scapegoating Mexico, or making Mexico the enemy, recalled Brooks. It was important to have a social, binational, even tri-national response. Have a seat at the table.

Primo back-channeled key meetings between the two countries. Once in Washington, Primo arranged for Serra Puche to meet inside a hotel with key union leaders, with only a chalkboard. The heads of the union tried to convince Serra Puche that NAFTA was a bad deal that would benefit only the wealthy top transnational companies at the expense of workers on both sides of the border. No way American workers could compete with Mexican wages. Serra Puche recalled he countered that the North American region would become the most competitive in the world.

Three hours later, no one had given in one centimeter, Primo recalled. But all agreed that they needed to communicate more and keep the channels open. To celebrate their civil debate, the three agreed to toast with tequila.

I warned Jaime that any agreement without a labor pact would be disastrous for workers on both sides of the border, Primo recalled. But by then NAFTA was literally on the fast track for approval and it was clear Mexico didn't care about worker rights for Mexicans, much less raising meager wages that amounted to about three dollars per day. Cheap wages were Mexico's strength.

Primo also brought three African American delegations to Mexico City, which included civil rights leaders, artists, scholars, businesspeople, labor and community organizers and elected officials. His goal was to personally introduce different players and stakeholders, people who could suffer and benefit from NAFTA. With Serra Puche's help, Primo set up a meeting with Salinas de Gortari as well as radical teachers and students, helping players from both sides become more active on a trade agreement that had practically ignored the perspectives and participation of the African American community. As a result of these delegations, in 1993 the mayor of Mexico City, Manuel Camacho Solís, invited Coretta Scott King and Andrew Young, former mayor of Atlanta, to the dedication of a statue of Martin Luther King Jr. The statue, in the fancy Polanco neighborhood, faced one built years before honoring Abraham Lincoln.

A U.S. jobs boom would lure even more Mexican workers into the United States, meaning that many more would be living in the shadows—workers without rights, easily exploitable, vulnerable to the whims of the

United States. That was what globalization was all about, Primo lectured me. Making money on the backs of the poor.

This is exactly what is happening, Primo said. I don't have to tell you that. Signs are everywhere on both sides of the border.

I remember the worry lines on his forehead deepening whenever we got on the subject at Freddy's.

Mama, Papa, this is Primo, I said introducing them at Freddy's one day. He and two other friends helped me survive Philadelphia.

Primo humbly introduced himself to my parents as just another immigrant from the state of Michoacán.

My father had a soft spot for Michoacán and its straw hats. I knew a lot of people in California from Michoacán, he told Primo. Good workers. They don't give up easily. Great pickers.

They were so grateful to him for helping me get through my homesickness that my mother offered him an extra serving of *flautas* with extra guacamole and insisted he join us for *menudo* the next morning.

Con gusto, señora.

Think of the time the Bracero Program ended, the reason why you're even here, Primo continued later. The program ended but the demand did not. Back then the *maquiladora* program took off in Mexico as assembly factories boomed in Juárez. They were supposed to employ all the Mexicans headed home after the Bracero Program ended. But wages and working conditions were dismal.

We're all headed for *maquila* wages, he added.

I initially dismissed his words as East Coast liberal, do-gooder talk, the kind I had grown accustomed to back in Philadelphia. On the border we were hungry for opportunity. Just about any bone would do to free us from third world wages and failing conditions that characterized the poverty of our city. On the outskirts of El Paso lay *colonias* without water or electricity. We also wanted to become part of the U.S. mainstream. More cross-border business had to mean a better life, right?

I took Primo on a ride along the border and showed him what our Border Patrol chief Silvestre Reyes had done. He had sealed the border with Operation Blockade, later renamed Operation Hold the Line, I said.

A Mexican American did this?

Yeah, with family in Mexico, I said. Crime has dropped. The border is so safe that Reyes's popularity is growing. He might run for office.

A la madre, he said. *Esto está cabrón.* The nativist streak will explode. Imagine what a red-blooded American would do!

Yeah, Pat Buchanan, I responded.

During Buchanan's campaigns he mocked Republican elites, denounced free trade and globalization, antagonized minorities and promised to build a "Buchanan fence" along the Mexican border. His nostalgia for the era of mostly white America fueled racist divisions smoldering beneath the surface. He lost the Republican nomination in 1992 and ran again, assuring that his livid supporters and issues would eventually prevail. Someone had to take their country back from the foreign invasion.

We're headed for the clash of civilizations, Primo said, alluding to a theory by Samuel P. Huntington, a political scientist at Harvard. Huntington had whipped the country into a frenzy, first with his theory, followed by his book *The Clash of Civilizations and the Remaking of World Order* and later, *Who Are We*. He issued dire warnings that the changing demographics in the United States would lead to a cultural war of civilizations between Anglo-Protestants and newer immigrants, particularly Latinos. Catholics. Muslims.

"While Muslims pose the immediate problem to Europe," he wrote, "Mexicans pose the problem for the United States."

Huntington expanded on his views, denouncing the "Hispanization" of the United States and claiming that many Mexican Americans didn't identify with the United States and acted "contemptuous of American culture."

He posited that cultural identities were shaping the patterns of cohesion, disintegration and conflict in the post–Cold War world. In other words, Mexican migration was ruining the United States, threatening its Protestant origins.

"The large and continuing influx of Hispanics threatens the pre-eminence of white Anglo-Protestant culture and the place of English as the only national language," he wrote. "White nationalist movements are a possible and plausible response to these trends."

Primo was so disconcerted that the former wannabe priest and Quaker-influenced human rights activist urgently wanted to open communication between peoples of two countries that could see beyond religion, race, culture. To that end, he was forming a little-known labor movement to help organize workers and farmers across Mexico and the U.S. against powerful corporate interests gradually consolidating around trade. Primo worried that the poor on both sides would become even more vulnerable.

Meanwhile, physical boundaries began to divide "us" from "them." The governments of both countries had long talked about building fences. In 1915, Sonoran governor José María Maytorena ordered the construction of a fence to separate the two cities of Nogales. Four months later, local Mexicans tore down the fence. The so-called tortilla curtain, a raggedy chain-link fence, was raised in the late 1970s. The U.S. government had just authorized the U.S. Army Corps of Engineers to replace the fence that separated Nogales, Sonora, from Nogales, Arizona, with a fence built of rusty landing mats from the Vietnam and Persian Gulf Wars.

Just weeks after signing NAFTA, President Bill Clinton gave the go-ahead to the upgraded fence. Border residents had mixed emotions regarding the Clintons, I told Primo. My mother and I recalled that during Bill Clinton's presidential campaign, Hillary Clinton visited El Paso and even stopped at Freddy's Café for *menudo*. After being told she was eating cow stomach soup with *pozole* corn and red chile—oregano, lemon, onions and cilantro were optional—she politely pushed the plate away and didn't take another bite. But they did leave us a hefty tip.

Primo broke into laughter. *En serio?* Really? So much for the Hispanic vote. How do you get the Hispanic vote without eating *menudo?*

The rumblings throughout the United States were fault lines cracking across Mexico, a country used to earthquakes. This one was bigger, stronger. Trade and amnesty were about to finally break Mexico in half. Across Mexico, mayors of small towns were seeing the most troubling trend they'd seen in their lifetimes: women, too, were making a beeline for the United States and were not going home anymore.

Over the years, my hometown of San Luis de Cordero had become a haven for old men and women holding the community together in the face of waves of migration to the U.S. If the women leave, I remember my uncle Antonio telling me, we're done. Close the town down. Put up a sign that reads: "Lost to the United States."

My uncle, with a deep resemblance to his father, Arcadio Jiménez, with pale skin, short and stout, once ran the town as mayor. He knew what he was talking about. The women are the anchors and now they're leaving for good, *mijo.* He called me "my son" and saw me as a future family patriarch. As such, he wanted me to know certain things. Since the men first started leaving for *el norte* under the Bracero Program, there was always the expectation that they would come home. They always did come home for holidays—migration in those days was circular, thanks to the work visas the Bracero Program offered and crafty smugglers, many of them neighbors. Yet even then there was a deeper hope that one day, once their men earned their money and made a name for themselves, they would come home for good. Maybe they'd own a ranch, grow corn and raise their families and then watch their children grow up.

My *tío* always hoped Mexico would do well enough to retain the next generation. But he was starting to lose hope. First the men left. Then the women. Then the families. The muscle and the soul of the town disappeared somewhere north. He had a point. How could Mexico's small-time farms compete against highly subsidized U.S. agribusiness giants like Cargill and Archer Daniels Midland under NAFTA? He feared the human networks would strengthen. The glue up north would become that much more powerful. All at the cost of Mexico.

He would be the mayor of what now? he asked, a question I posed to Primo as we drove along the banks of the Rio Grande in my Camaro with the T-top off to the spot where Paisano Drive nearly kisses the river. On the access road, I pulled into the parking lot of the La Hacienda café, where I would go to hang out with Angela on weekends and where El Paso pioneer Simeon Hart's flour mill once stood. Just beyond the river were flat-roofed, brightly painted houses with Mexican addresses. But there were also four stone markers arranged around a parched fountain, including one to commemorate the spot where conquistador Juan de Oñate first forded the Rio Grande at El Paso del Norte, the lowest snow-free pass through the Rocky Mountains. I was inadvertently standing in the place where Texas began and Mexico ended. Before me, right on the edge of the Rio Grande, was ground zero for a deepening wound between both countries: a long line of Border Patrol vehicles growing longer by the day with agents staring into Mexico.

Taking in the beauty and the history, Primo ruined the moment by confiding, "This is a Molotov cocktail," referring to the odd irony: free trade and amnesty. Reagan's campaign slogan—"Let's make America great again"—represented a vision of uniting the continent that ironically would ignite tensions. Primo and David Brooks came to the conclusion that midwestern factory towns would never survive with Mexican workers willing to do the same job for an eighth of the price.

As always, the more time I spent with Primo, the more I looked at things differently. The way he talked, I wondered if this whole economic integration thing was more like rape, the submission of the working class to greedy capitalists. The new La Malinche, a reference to the Nahua Indian who once served as an interpreter, adviser and mistress for the Spanish conquistador Hernán Cortés. We were now the bastard children of this loveless marriage. People caught in the middle. We were La Malinche's descendants, our origins traced to Quetzalcoatl, the mythical plumed serpent that rises up, symbolizing rebirth after death. Upon us was a new dawn, yet we were still straddling a hundred-year gap, with one foot in the twenty-first century and the other stuck in the unrealized ideals of the Mexican Revolution. I mean, what choice did Mexico have when the most powerful country in the world wanted to do business? Just say no? This was the United States rewriting the narrative and announcing to the world, starting with its two overly polite neighbors, Canada and Mexico, how to do business now. We all had to get over protectionism and embrace globalization.

That's one way to look at it, Primo said, looking terrified. *Esto se va a poner de la fregada, Don Alfredo,* words that more or less meant a powder keg was about to explode. Write that in your fucking column.

I knew he was serious. While he occasionally used the word "fuck," he rarely if ever used it when it came to, let alone in reference to my beloved column that increasingly was becoming my own obituary. Free trade wasn't a simple, neat package, the cure-all for El Paso and its historic economic disparity. But as usual Primo sounded like a conspiracy theorist, sure that Mexico was on the verge of selling whatever was left of its conflicted territory to the United States, the powerful giant that would smash it up, take it apart and overrun it with blandness.

But dull and boring didn't sound all that bad to me. Dull and boring sounded like predictability, first world conveniences, a fertile ground for economic prosperity. And what's wrong with that? I asked. What's wrong with zoning codes and rule of law? Look at San Francisco, San Diego, those beautiful cities in California, or Santa Fe, New Mexico. Could these cities have retained their charm if they were still part of Mexico? Or would there be *colonias* brewing around the city, those endless slums like those in the outlying areas of Ciudad Juárez and Tijuana?

Alfredo, you don't know your history. Read. Read a lot more. Read before you speak. Think.

How am I wrong?

No country just for the virtue of being the rich and powerful one should impose its will on the poorer, weaker ones, Primo scolded me. Mexico knows that all too well. Stand up for your country. Read about the Niños Héroes.

He was referring to the legend of the young cadets who defended the Castillo de Chapultepec, the nineteenth-century castle in Mexico City, from invading U.S. forces. One even wrapped himself with the Mexican flag and jumped to his death rather than be captured by the Yanquis.

What side are you on? Where's your homeland?

Depends on the moment, I'd say. Depends on where I am.

Who do you root for when Mexico and the United States play soccer?

For whoever is losing.

I pushed the conversation aside, because at times I really had no clue how to answer.

Let me know when you figure it out.

Does our friendship depend on the answer?

No, we'll always have Philadelphia.

Deep down, Primo wasn't buying any of this so-called integration.

I never wrote that column about Primo's powder-keg theory, because shortly after his visit I left the *Herald-Post* for the *Dallas Morning News*.

11.

Homeward Bound

The drive from Dallas's cool M streets to Arlington was a series of frustrating construction delays, a slow dive into dreaded suburbia, but also a renewal of sorts. I was generally unaware of the traffic jams, singing aloud to the Cranberries blaring "Linger," feeling like I was wrapped around Angela's little finger. We were still just friends, although I hadn't stopped trying to win her heart. She was in El Paso and I was in Dallas—still not in the same town but at least we were in the same state.

I had left the *Herald-Post* and taken a job as a so-called Mid-Cities reporter in Arlington for the *Dallas Morning News*, covering city council meetings on Tuesdays and the construction of the Ballpark Stadium for the Texas Rangers, a team partly owned by George W. Bush, and sneaking off to the Foley's Red Apple sales on Fridays or for a scoop of frozen yogurt across the street from the *News* bureau.

Sure, reporting out of Mexico was my ultimate goal, but what was wrong with getting a taste of Middle America by covering baseball and the melodrama of city council? What was more American than that?

Then Primo called one evening as I was singing my lungs out to the radio, making my way out of Arlington as traffic snarled on I-30. Primo had asked David for a loan so that he could go back to Mexico for what he initially thought would be a sabbatical. Instead, he told me he had found himself thrust into the middle of something bigger.

You need to be in Mexico, he exhorted me. A revolution is under way.

He would know of such things.

NAFTA had rallied the masses to revolt, he said, almost giddy.

He and David had witnessed firsthand the seeds of unrest months before, but they didn't know quite what was brewing at the time. Just months before the Zapatista indigenous uprising in the southernmost state of Chiapas that began on January 1, 1994—the day NAFTA took effect—the two men privately hosted leftist leaders from Mexico inside Tequilas restaurant. David and waiters used tablecloths to cover the windows from Peeping Toms to ensure the meetings were kept confidential. They wouldn't even tell me about them. The men in the room talked about the rise of a worldwide workers' union. One of the union members turned out to be a longtime ally of the Zapatista movement.

Primo and David felt at the center of things, even if only as hosts. They helped organize meetings between union representatives from Mexico City and the United States. As far as the Zapatista uprising, neither had a clue that what was being discussed at Tequilas would soon become global news. The Zapatista revolt was led by some of Mexico's most oppressed people, indigenous Mayan communities. They were represented in their guerrilla rebellion by ski-masked Subcomandante Marcos, whose friend, the union leader, ate and drank at Tequilas. They organized to protest the new economic order. And it turns out they had a fan base. Farmers in Nebraska, friends of Primo's, applauded the uprising, and stood by their smaller and poorer counterparts in Chiapas. The uprising became Primo's sign to return home, not just for a sabbatical but maybe for good. He had always dreamed of a people's revolution.

This is the moment, he told me. The urgency in his voice got me worked up as I was struck in traffic.

Mexico is where it's at, he said. Forget city council. Come write about the revolution. Weren't you inspired by John Reed? He was referring to the American journalist from Portland, Oregon, buried in Moscow, who wrote *Ten Days That Shook the World*, a book about the people's uprising and the rise of Lenin.

Didn't you see the movie *Reds* a million times, he asked, making me regret that I shared this fun fact during one of our tequila-soaked evenings back in Philadelphia.

Twenty-three, to be exact, I reminded him. I'll see you soon. Next year in D.F.

Mexico doesn't have a year, he said. It's happening now.

Primo had received a personal letter from Subcomandante Marcos that was published in *La Jornada,* Mexico City's left-leaning publication, which also became Marcos's diary for his poetic diatribes. He read me part of the letter in which Marcos begins "Señor Primitivo Rodríguez Oceguera" and continues with a title, "El México que queremos," or "The Mexico We Want."

Marcos wrote about Heriberto, an impoverished, toothless three-year-old, and his own nightmares about "not about finding the remedy against poverty" but instead—in so many words—watching impotently as Mexico put lipstick on a pig. In his own rhythmic song, he wrote that NAFTA threatened everything under the sun between the Río Bravo and the Río Suchiate, at Mexico's southern border.

And just like that, Primo made me forget about the sales at Foley's, the frozen yogurt and the growing camaraderie with the Arlington bureau. My destiny wasn't in North Texas but south of the border. This was, after all, what we had talked about back in Philadelphia.

I pressed the *Dallas Morning News* to make good on its promise to base me in Mexico City. The editors were still reluctant, so I trotted out a veiled threat: the *Arizona Republic* was courting me. Maybe I should just decamp, and they'd let me cover Mexico, NAFTA and the border. That got their attention. The *Morning News* agreed to send me south, as part of an expansion into Latin America and a commitment to covering Mexico's democratic opening. Mexico was ripe with political assassinations and uncertainties, including a presidential candidate who was challenging the PRI from within to be more open to democracy. The country was in turmoil. The *Morning News* would double the size of the Mexico City bureau to two journalists and eventually grow it to a team of nearly a dozen, giving the newspaper the largest bureau of any U.S. media outlet in Mexico. The *Morning News* also opened another office in Monterrey, in the northern state of Nuevo León, signs of the importance of NAFTA to Texas.

By the end of 1994, I was moving into a historic neighborhood fit for Frida Kahlo in the heart of Coyoacán, a quiet, leafy neighborhood. I felt like I had made it. I was surrounded by bright colonial homes, some of them two stories high, painted with rich colors that seemed inspired by the red meat of a watermelon, the deep green of an avocado, the soft yellow tones of a guava and the skins of velvety purple figs. My favorite homes were painted deep blue, a dark enough shade that reminded me of the southwestern skies over the desert landscape as day turned into night. I lived in a fortress-like home, surrounded by neighbors, including Serra Puche, Primo's old friend and now—for at least a few weeks—the new secretary of the treasury, and one of the key NAFTA architects. I'd walk by his mansion on my way to Las Lupitas, my new foodie hangout with the best *champurrado*—a thick hot chocolate drink made with corn flour, cocoa, cinnamon and clove—and quesadillas slathered with refried beans.

I was fond of the owner, a native of Chihuahua. We talked politics in Mexico and possibilities yet to be explored. Down the street was one of Carlos Salinas de Gortari's homes, and that of his predecessor, Miguel de la Madrid Hurtado.

Enormous palm trees towered over the rooflines of clay-orange *tejas*. The streets were ancient cobblestone that led to historic plazas where children jumped in puddles of water left by gardeners as they watered flowers, many of them the bougainvillea that my mother loved. This neighborhood was the heart of Mexico City in the *corazón* of the country itself. Accordion music lent a romantic air to the place. Coyoacán had played host to many great loves, from Hernán Cortés, the Spanish conquistador, and his mistress, La Malinche, to muralist Diego Rivera and his beloved Frida Kahlo, as well as her onetime lover Leon Trotsky. The Russian spent the last years of his life in Coyoacán, feeding his pet rabbit. Coyoacán seemed frozen in time while much of Mexico was changing drastically, in tune with changes in the U.S. policies that would forever alter our two societies. The scourge and blessings of globalization were upon us.

My first assignment was covering the "revolution" that had beckoned the Zapatista uprising. I flew to San Cristóbal de las Casas, in Mexico's green and mountainous southern Chiapas state. It wasn't an auspicious beginning: the overcrowded "communal" taxi forced many of us to sit on top of one another as we drove toward the small towns where *zapatismo* had its stronghold. Unfortunately we crashed on the way and I lurched into the windshield, glass shards slicing my face. I arrived bloody, dazed and with a loose tooth, the big-time correspondent already fucking up.

This was a transformative time. I'd eat tacos on the streets and shop discreetly at the new Wal-Mart on weekends, afraid that protesters would publicly shame me and thousands more for shopping at a chain that threatened hundreds if not thousands of smaller stores. One night I bought a Fisher brand television set, which still works, and gave the cabdriver extra cash to sneak it into the *vocho*, a Volkswagen Beetle, away from the angry mobs.

Many Mexicans were shocked to see their country, long a protectionist and nationalist haven for anything anti-gringo, now being invaded by foreigners who infringed on their own way of life and jobs. Those mom-and-pop stores caved to capitalism, which defaced their culture and forced them to shut down their family *changaros* in order to make room for U.S. food franchises. Street vendors selling tacos were threatened by

McDonald's. My fruit lady at the Coyoacán market worried her fruit would rot or customers would stop coming, preferring Wal-Marts and their trendy indoor space to her humble corner at the market.

But living in Mexico wasn't just about reporting the story. After all, Mexico was also *my* story. I savored the moment when my parents first visited me in my own home in Mexico City. I spoiled my mother in Coyoacán and later in San Miguel de Allende and Dolores Hidalgo, where the remains of singer-songwriter José Alfredo Jiménez lay. She potted beautiful jacarandas, roses and bougainvilleas to decorate my new home—her own way of reconnecting with the country she had left decades ago and, like me, vowed to someday return to. Now her hands dug into the Mexican earth for pleasure, for aesthetics—not to prove herself worthy to the ranchers in central California but to delight in her homeland.

With each bite of decadent mole from Oaxaca, *tamales de plátano* and *buñuelos* drenched in chocolate, I wished that each savory moment could erase the years that my mother broke her back and heart on the fields of California and in the kitchen at Freddy's Café. Once, her tights burned onto her skin when scalding soup was spilled all over her at the restaurant. She was rushed to the hospital by a customer but was soon back at the restaurant kitchen. Freddy's could never really stay afloat if my mother wasn't there. She *was* Freddy's. Longing to be the son to make her smile, I was proud to bring her home and treat her to every delight she longed for. Eventually she became my daily minder as I checked in just to hear her say, I'm living Mexico through you. Love Mexico like I do.

Mexico City became a beacon for all those who had left, including David back in Philadelphia. He was itching to visit. One afternoon he finally traveled to the city and dropped into my new office in Coyoacán. A picture that I have of us looking young and lean showed how much weight we both had gained.

Junk food is bad for you, David, a food snob, warned me.

Yeah? I'm also addicted to every *churro* and *elote* around.

Elotes and *churros* aren't so bad as what's coming next. *Esto se va a poner más cabrón es NAFTA.*

He was referring to the proliferation of McDonald's, a chain he detested. These are the seeds of diabetes, obesity. And he was right. It wouldn't take long before Mexico rivaled its northern neighbor as the fattest nation in the world, a top consumer of soft drinks and a leader in childhood and adult rates of diabetes and obesity.

Another time Ken showed up. His stock was growing and he was cashing in on his binational roots. His clients stretched from

Philadelphia to Mexico City, where he worked as much as half of his time. Representing the Mexican national railway was the cornerstone of his business. He also represented American and Mexican companies in the inevitable disputes and lawsuits. We'd hang out in Mexico City on his expense account, living large. His clients invited him to posh weddings in Tepotztlán, Cuernavaca and Cancún.

One night he woke me up to tell me the obvious: There's so much money here, *chacho*. This country is loaded.

No shit, I said. That's why so many of the poor leave. Economic disparities.

Just 10 percent of the population, the wealthiest, controlled Mexico. Tensions were high and the bureau was growing with Lonnie as the new freelancer and Javier as our driver. Things were looking up in journalism. Mexico City was even experimenting with U.S.-style lunch breaks, one hour, tops—something I quietly applauded, as three-hour lunches laced with tequila had a habit of ruining a reporter's entire day. Great, the American way of life is here, I'd tell my colleagues at the Mexico bureau. Get to the point, I would remind my lunch guests as I practiced the new meal culture by asking at once for both the first and second courses along with the check. Please. The waiters often responded with a stunned look.

Don't even think of tequila, I reminded Primo, whom I had invited over as my guest one afternoon to talk about the latest plan he was working on: granting Mexicans in the United States the right to vote in Mexican elections.

My admonition caught Primo off guard. After all, I had returned to Mexico, where Mexicans worked to live, not the other way around, he reminded me. Didn't I want to get away from the United States?

But weren't we supposed to bring some of our own way of life, too, to make Mexico more accountable, more efficient? I'd remind him.

Ever polite, Primo simply changed the subject.

The whole business of being a foreign correspondent had a whiff of imperialism, even for a native Mexican like myself. Even with a *nopal* stamped on my forehead, I saw Mexico through the lens of an American, questioning what was wrong with my native country, its system, values, priorities, and why the exodus north of men and women went on and on. The many layers one had to go through to get to the truth seemed like an endless hall of smoke and mirrors.

My day would start with Radio Red, the booming sound of José Gutiérrez Vivó, a hard-charging journalist clamoring for truth, seeking accountability before the term was trendy. When in the city, I'd walk to Lupitas to read three or four newspapers I carried under my arms. I'd sit at a table near the window and witness some of Televisa's soap opera stars walk down the plaza. Or I'd see a former president, former cabinet secretaries, the wealthiest of the rich, walking their pets. I'd read the top stories in the country's oldest newspaper, *El Universal*, left-leaning *La Jornada* and the upstart *Reforma*, closely scrutinizing columnists for any hint of truth, always elusive. I was just a plane ride away from the latest natural disaster in Cancún or Puerto Vallarta or Manzanillo or from the latest tragedy—Mexicans dying from exhaustion in a cramped eighteen-wheeler—and watching as their coffins arrived in a tiny town of Michoacán.

As a Mexican American journalist living in Mexico City, I wasn't alone. My own newspaper began an even bigger expansion that required recruiting a team of stringers that stretched out across the country, based in cities and states that had more relevance to readers back in North Texas. I spent much of my week driving through rural Mexico, covering stories of immigration or looking for interesting features. At every place I visited, I reached out to reporters and inquired if they were interested in being part of a team, and the vast majority said yes.

NAFTA had opened the doors to dozens of other American correspondents with pressing questions about a new complex relationship on full display. Never had there been such interest in Mexico. We constituted a new generation of reporters who knew both countries by heart and were well versed in the nuances and subtleties of each culture. Paul de la Garza from the *Chicago Tribune*, Richard Chacón of the *Boston Globe*, Ricardo Sandoval from the *San Jose Mercury News*—these three were so assimilated they'd carefully sniff the wine corks and ask about droughts in the areas where the vineyards were located. I joined Dianne Solis and later José de Córdoba, my former colleagues at the *Journal*, with a sprinkling of freelancers like Sam Quinones and Franc Contreras, and later David Sedeño and Ricardo Chavira. Of course, photojournalist Keith Dannemiller and Dudley Althaus, the dean of the correspondents, who blazed new trails at the *Houston Chronicle*, greeted us one and all.

Angela's opportunity to join the list of foreign correspondents in Mexico City loomed closer. We'd talk nightly. She was now in Dallas. She wanted to walk Avenida Francisco Sosa and enjoy a leisurely lunch at the San Angel Inn like the rest of Mexico City's movers and shakers, to stroll in casually like we always belonged. I'd tell her in the time of globalization, all was possible. She should come home and make

Mexico better, enjoy weekends in Tepoztlán or Cuernavaca. She could tell stories and build bridges.

She'd listen as her dogs, Natasha, Nell and Zorro, barked in the background on her tree-lined street in Dallas near Glencoe Park. She'd give it up in a second to be in Coyoacán, she said. She made occasional trips to visit me and I showed her what was becoming of Mexico, which filled her with envy. When I wanted to really lure her, I'd use Jalisco as bait. She couldn't refuse, especially Guadalajara. We marveled at the city's glamorous historic center dotted with colonial plazas and the *jardín* filled with families strolling, mariachis in their *charro* outfits playing trumpets and strumming *guitarrónes*. We passed by wide avenues and landmarks such as the neoclassical Teatro Degollado, an elegant cathedral with twin gold spires, and the Palacio del Gobierno with its stunning murals by José Clemente Orozco. This wasn't just any city. This was Guadalajara, Angela's childhood home and every immigrant's nostalgic dream.

Like the United States, many states in Mexico are so culturally distinct that they can feel like their own small countries. Jalisco is one of them. The state borders tropical Colima and Michoacán to the south and mining mecca Zacatecas to the north, and boasts miles of Pacific Ocean coastline to the west. Like California, Jalisco is a cultural powerhouse and a political and economic bellwether for Mexico. In the state's central highlands, the deep-blue hue of Jalisco's agave fields stretches to the horizon like a vast ocean between the tequila-producing towns of Amatitlán, Atotonilco, Los Altos de Jalisco, Arandas and the town actually named Tequila.

Angela and I traveled to Lake Chapala and Ajijic, places she knew well from her childhood, home to so many Americans by then that I began a habit of looking for George from California in every park and street. Could George be somewhere here, too, aching for that new start he pined for in the fields after having endured the horrors of war? I imagined him living somewhere in some fishing village along the Pacific Coast, away from curious people like me, or maybe San Miguel de Allende. He was probably dead by now, but I still looked everywhere, hoping to catch at least a glimpse of him. George's dream was now my reality.

We walked and drove through a dizzying array of lights flashing in numerous roundabouts of Guadalajara, or *glorietas*, and ate *carnitas* at El Abajeño with mariachis serenading her with "La Malagueña" and "Granada." These were songs she once listened to as a child with her beautiful mother, known affectionately as Bebe, and their elegant grandmother nicknamed Gaga by Angela and her siblings. Her grandmother had moved to Mexico with her second husband. Angela's mother would later follow. Up on Vallarta Avenue, a sadness would come over Angela. Like my memories of San Luis de Cordero, Angela's idyllic childhood in Guadalajara presented an almost painful nostalgia. She explained that she had no desire to look back beyond happy childhood memories and didn't like to remember what it was like leaving Mexico behind.

As a child, she didn't know what discrimination meant and especially that it could happen on either side of the border. Leaving Mexico as a child had been one of the hardest things for Angela. She and her siblings were excited that they would be moving back to the United States, the country of Barbie dolls, Milky Way candy bars and Saturday-morning cartoons in English. Gaga was leaving Guadalajara to marry a Texas rancher with a vast property right on the border in Hidalgo County. He would get a nickname from the grandchildren while in Guadalajara: Gogo. A few months after the wedding, Angela's mother decided it was time to return to the United States, too.

But the border was a confusing place for Angela, as it was neither the U.S. nor Mexico. The kids in her school spoke a strange mix of Spanish and English she would later learn was "Spanglish." Some looked Mexican but didn't speak a word of Spanish. And her classmates did not know what to make of her, either. They'd call her a *bolilla* on the playground or in the halls. The only *bolillos* she knew were the crusty rolls she loved in Guadalajara smeared with frijoles. She would come to understand that *bolilla* was a reference to white bread—that is, white people. At first she felt foreign in this strange borderland but later, with its blurring cultures, language and binational people, it would become the place where she felt most at home.

Our friendship only deepened because of our mutual goals, love of journalism and life on the border. We supported one another as we tried to lay claim to what was once our Mexico. Angela began her career as a public radio reporter at a community station in El Paso, followed by a stint as a reporter at the same CBS television affiliate station that had fired me not long before because the anchorwoman told me she didn't think I had much of a future as a journalist.

I'd remind her how her upbringing gave her a view of Mexico unlike any other.

Take advantage of who you are and tell stories, I'd say. Every now and then I'd take her hand on those walks through Guadalajara and squeeze it tightly. Sometimes she wouldn't let go. Once I even stole a kiss.

Where else but on the border could we have met? We were brought together by a geography and destiny in a region that was much more than a borderline defining two countries. Angela had a term for us, those with one foot in each country.

We're "combination people," she'd tell me. A blend of two homelands and cultures, equally comfortable on both sides.

I didn't understand what she meant but figured it was something akin to *norteamericano*, a North American, something I longed to become, someone from both countries.

Things slowly came together for us. Angela had paid her dues and finally got the chance to work in Mexico. A. H. Belo Corporation, the oldest media company in Texas and the company that hired Angela, was growing, buying up TV stations across Texas and the rest of the country. Marty Haag, the visionary leading the broadcast empire, realized a Mexico bureau was a must, especially for Texas, where family and business ties were undeniable. Angela moved to Mexico City, where she filed stories nationwide as bureau chief of Belo's television division. For much of that time she worked with videographer Ernesto Torres, who also had a burning desire to return to Mexico, his parents' homeland. Angela and Ernesto shared an office with the *Dallas Morning News*'s Mexico bureau staff.

We finally had a chance, I thought. We were back in Mexico, both of us. The United States was just across a muddy river. We didn't realize we were really in the middle of an earthquake shaking both countries.

12.

Tequila Midnight in Guadalajara

I followed the smoke inside the Tequilas bar in Guadalajara because I knew it would lead me to David, Ken and Primo. I didn't smoke. I was here to become David's tequila taster, in search of the perfect spirit. We had been constantly talking about getting together again as a group. Perhaps for a wedding, or a funeral. We were as morbid as we were hopeful. But no one died, no one got married. In the black-and-white photos of us at the Tequilas cantina that night, I'm wearing jeans and a blue shirt. Ken is wearing a vest. David's shirt is open at the top, exposing a bear-like hairy chest, and Primo is wearing his trademark beret. He was caught by surprise because his eyebrows are raised.

We were summoned by David to this bar, this night, to celebrate what had been a lifelong quest. He had spent several months meeting the "dons" of tequila—Don Julio and Don Felipe—and he believed he knew now where he was going to find the best agave: in Los Altos, the high-lands of Jalisco, where the soil produced a more complex taste that was easier on the palate. He had connected with people who owned plenty of agave fields and believed in preserving traditions—not selling out to the big corporations that were contracting all over the state and buying up fields to boost their industrial-scale production of tequila, which was growing in popularity.

David had quietly spent the last ten years following his lifelong passion, researching and interviewing *jimadores*, tequila makers, especially those from the Jalisco highlands, all in his quest to make the perfect, artisanal tequila. He thought he was closer to figuring it out.

The timing was crucial. Mexico's cultural identity was increasingly threatened by globalization and the entry of so many U.S. products.

David's own research showed the disruption in the marketplace was an opportune time. He was talking to some of the top experts in the region. For the trip, he had set up several meetings with top tequila distilleries in Guadalajara. He had invited me to come along, meet my idols, too, Don Julio Gonzalez and Don Felipe Camarena of El Tesoro de Don Felipe.

He spoke passionately of his mission to produce his own unique batch of tequila, the right combination, something between *blanco* or *reposado* and *anejo*. He studied the stages of a tequila's agave maturation process, convinced the secret lay there. He was driven by pride in his culture, in tequila's history. He was convinced the spirit's origins were not fully known. The more he studied, the more he suspected tequila went beyond that conventional story repeated over generations.

Still, with the rise of Mexican restaurants and thanks to Jimmy Buffett, as well as the frozen margarita, the Tequila Sunrise, demand exploded, making Jose Cuervo and Sauza into even bigger brands. But then, in 1989, players like Patrón and El Tesoro de Don Felipe changed the game, proving that Americans would pay a higher price for prestige and fancy bottles. Since then, imports of pure agave tequila surged, with the greatest leap coming in the super-premium division. Sales of high-end tequilas increased by 700 percent in the past fifteen years.

Ireland had its whiskey. France, Spain, Italy, Argentina, Chile and even South Africa boasted fine wines. Shit, even Cuban rum was being smuggled to the U.S. through Mexico in defiance of the embargo. So why were Mexicans portrayed as drunken bums under a cactus tree, a half-empty bottle of tequila next to their cartoonish figures? That image peeved us on both sides of the border, relegating tequila to the depths of a cheap drink that made you hallucinate weird shit and do stupid things.

David was dogged about authenticity. He wanted to understand the present by digging into the past. He wanted to find tequila's true origins and rewrite the narrative of Mexico's iconic drink. He believed the drink was cloaked in elegance, much like Mexico itself. We just had to rewrite the story through tequila. He thought he was close, homing in on the recipe and production techniques.

I think customers will pay the right price if we produce the best quality, he said.

David was convinced a more sophisticated, knowledgeable clientele would pay more for quality tequila. If customers were paying $15 for enchiladas, they would pay the same for tequila.

KEN WAS STILL TO climb higher up the ladder of success as he continued working at the white-shoe law firm of Schnader. He now wore Canali suits even as he did pro bono work. In a profession measured by billable hours, Ken learned quickly that hard work and long hours were rewarded. At the height of his success, he took a hefty pay cut and became a federal prosecutor. Although temporarily put back on a tight budget, Ken relished the opportunity to become a real trial lawyer working on corruption, tax and white-collar criminal cases. Now, in 1997, his name went on the letterhead of Trujillo Rodriguez & Richards, LLC, a high-end law firm with a penthouse office in Rittenhouse Square; one partner a Jewish American and fellow Penn Law grad. He was well on his way to his first million, winning and settling a series of big plaintiff cases against big corporations, from tobacco to auto companies, fighting on behalf of the little guy. He was itching for his first Porsche, commuting back and forth between Philadelphia, Mexico, Cuba, to represent wealthy clients.

I was proud that Ken had learned the art of pacing his tequila back in Philadelphia. He had learned that when the four of us were together, the nights would be long and few would be longer than tonight. He was poised, well-dressed, looking like a dandy, an elitist, a cross between Guadalajara's chic Colonia Americana neighborhood and Rittenhouse Square. He and David were cashing in on their bicultural roots, if money was the measuring stick. At times I'd witnessed ugly signs of things to come. The competition between them was palpable. Ken touted his Ivy League smarts, his education, his rags-to-riches story. David wanted to prove that sheer determination was the key, no matter what. I was their bridge, but a tenuous one at best.

It still wasn't easy being Ken's friend. At times he seemed to compartmentalize his existence. On one of his earlier visits to Mexico City, he stunned me by asking me to be his best man, which I sheepishly accepted. Just weeks after we saw him in Guadalajara, he would marry Laura Luna, a University of New Mexico Law School graduate. Ken met her on a trip to Albuquerque to be with his father, who was next in line for a kidney transplant. Ken's uncle Bill had set him up on a blind date. Dancing to Los Lobos's version of "La Bamba" at the American Legion Post 13, Ken fell hard. Straitlaced, uptight Ken finally lost control. I had never seen him so sappy and raw. It was almost impossible to crack Ken's façade, but Laura had done it, and apparently so had I. Yes, we were close, but of the four of us, Ken seemed the most distant, rarely dropping what I saw as a front. He knew many people and had many acquaintances, yet he didn't really seem close to anyone. Not knowing what else to say, and flattered that he had chosen me to be his best man, I accepted. We celebrated his upcoming wedding, drinking till dawn in my house in Coyoacán, listening to Alejandro Sanz's "Corazón Partío" and dancing in our boxers.

Primo was still working both sides. He and friends in Chicago, Raul Ross and Chuy Garcia, were determined to build a north-to-south network by gradually changing the constitution and allowing Mexicans abroad to vote in presidential elections, Primo had returned with the right binational credentials. More than a decade abroad taught him the importance of uniting his two Mexicos, *él de aquí y él de allá*, north of the border and south. He knew the struggles up close and personal. He helped lead a union of the Mexican mushroom workers I'd met in Kennett Square, marching with them to Harrisburg, the capital of Pennsylvania. He got David to put the apron away and get involved, and even got Cuauhtémoc Cárdenas, the presidential leftist icon, to stand in solidarity with the mushroom workers, calling for improved working conditions. A Spanish-language publication misspelled two names: "Pensilvania" and "Zuro" instead of "Suro." Primo is missing in the photo.

For a man who had been gone from Mexico for seventeen years and had been successful at organizing workers on both sides of the border, his welcome home was underwhelming. Like me, he faced an unfor-giving country still resentful we had left in the first place. Primo was invited back by his longtime pal Sergio Aguayo to help with Alianza Cívica, an NGO with the goal of empowering Mexicans to strengthen civil society by voting. Primo soon suspected something else was afoot in the country. The PRI, as corrupt as it may be, was synonymous with stability. Was the U.S. government now supporting organizations such as Alianza Cívica as a way to keep the left out of power? What role did the U.S. government play in Mexico's democratic opening?

The *New York Times* and *La Jornada* published stories that essentially underscored Primo's suspicions. One story was reported by David Brooks, Primo's longtime friend and now a reporter at *La Jornada*. The story suggested the CIA, through the National Endowment for Democracy, was secretly trying to build a democracy that would align with U.S. interests in the region. The CIA supported groups like Alianza Cívica to influence Mexican voters in the interest of stability. Imagine that: a foreign government influencing a sovereign country.

For now, Primo kept his suspicions to himself, but the seed was planted.

THE RESTAURANT WAS A typical downtown cantina, with brick walls, very dark, a few couples dancing on a small dance floor. We gathered around a long table of brown leather-backed chairs. We toasted the dawn of democracy, political empowerment for Mexicans on both sides of the border.

We toasted David, on the brink of achieving his tequila dream.

In typical David fashion, we were not alone that night in Guadalajara. As usual, David's entourage showed up: childhood friends and a handful of students from the Philadelphia University of the Arts. Taking the photographers to the agave fields wasn't just to take pictures of stunning landscapes but part of David's long-term strategy to humanize the workers. Humanize Mexico. Change its narrative and watch the new image reverberate on both sides of the border. The photographers passed around images of that day, shots of *jimadores* carving out pineapple-size hearts that contained the *aguamiel* from which the tequila would be made. The experience also piqued his curiosity in photography.

The photographers included John Carlano and Hidemi Yokota, a former student who had just flown in from his home in Japan with cameras and bottles of eye drops to keep himself awake. At times he'd doze off, only to be awakened by the ranting of a poet—Primo—captivated by a woman by the name of Hilary Parsons Dick. She was a graduate student of the University of Pennsylvania, studying the growing immigrant ties between Mexico and the United States, from either the agave fields or nearby in the central state of Guanajuato where mushroom workers were making a beeline for Kennett Square.

Despite the reason we were all called to be there—tequila—with every drink Hilary turned into the main attraction. We all, with the exception of Ken, fell a little bit in love. Primo might have lost his head the fastest, though: trumping all our meager efforts to talk to her, after enough tequila and plenty of dancing, Primo found a seat beside her and began to recite a poem off the cuff, dedicated to her. He was rapping before rapping was a big thing in Mexico.

No joke: it went on for hours.

Hilary listened intently, instantly charmed. Primo must have been more than thirty years older than Hilary, but damn if he didn't have charisma and a way with words.

We came to call that poem—and we began to refer to that night as—"*Ésta es la noche.*"

> *Una joven nota de arena*
> *bañó los ávidos ritmos*
> *de mi piel sedienta*
> *eras tú,*
> *tú enigma*
> *tú inasible torbellino*
> *mujer merengue salsa espuma*

I was intrigued for other reasons. Hilary was heading up a ground-breaking study of the binational ties developing between Kennett Square and the small town of Moroleón in rural Mexico. Both sides of her family had originated from mining towns in Wales and Scotland and later moved to the slate and coal mining hills of Maryland and West Virginia. She was moved by the traumatic migration stories of her own family, particularly her mother, and zeroed in on Mexican migration as her interest at the university. Now she was poised to spend a year of fieldwork in the central state of Guanajuato, studying the impact of immigration in the post-amnesty period.

The trip underscored what her two mentors, Jorge Durand and Douglas Massey, were warning both countries about. This migration of Mexicans was fast, furious and unpredictable, something I was witnessing across the countryside. More worrisome was that the natural circular pattern of people coming back and forth—something they had done since before the Bracero Program—had been disrupted, maybe for good.

Salinas de Gortari had famously promised that, with NAFTA, goods, not people, would be exported to the United States. With no labor accords, Primo feared, the exodus north would never end.

Prior to IRCA, Mexican immigrants didn't settle in the United States as they were doing now. Between 1965 and 1986, according to studies by the University of Pennsylvania, about 27.9 million undocumented Mexicans entered the United States and 23.3 million returned to Mexico, a net gain of just 4.6 million people, suggesting that most of the laborers followed seasonal crops, nearly always with the desire to go home.

I had traveled throughout Mexico and witnessed the emptying of the countryside. I saw the tales of two cities in one region of Guanajuato.

One was lively, with women, children and old men roaming the streets and sitting in the town square, with businesses humming thanks to remittances sent from men in Canada working under a guest-worker program. They returned with the seasons, just like my father had many years before. A mile or two away, another town of similar size was dying.

The locals talked about their relatives having left not just for Illinois, Texas or California but for states they never heard of, with names they couldn't even pronounce. They showed me letters with postmarks from places like Nebraska, Iowa, Minnesota, Maine and even Vermont. Yes, wage disparity was a huge factor, but that wasn't the complete narrative. Few seemed happy with their decision, especially because coming back wasn't so easy anymore. At times as they packed and said goodbye, they seemed to be headed for a wake.

I woke up the morning after in Guadalajara and couldn't escape a realization that was slowly creeping in: that another Mexico was growing in the United States. This other Mexico was trapped, on the cusp of the unknown.

Unlike our generation, Mexico was now in the rearview window.

I was missing half the story.

13.

Trapped in the U.S., No Going Back

I was inside a bar in San Luis Potosí, a state emptying out to Texas, particularly the Dallas–Fort Worth area. People couldn't make it on less than $3 a day, which meant they could eat only beans and tortillas, and meat every now and then.

I was looking through my notepad when two suspicious characters with pointy cowboy hats and piercing eyes broke into applause.

Who are they? I asked the bartender, as images of lawmakers in D.C. filled the television screen.

Coyotes, he said. The price to smuggle *mojados* across has just doubled. Do you need me to connect you?

No, just curious.

I went up to them and introduced myself. Can I ask you a few questions?

Sure, just don't use our names.

What are you celebrating?

The harder it is to cross, the more we can charge, said one.

By 1996, Clinton had signed draconian immigration reform that subjected many more undocumented immigrants, including legal permanent residents, to detention and deportation. Congress also announced new frameworks for cooperation between the federal, state and local governments.

These guys were toasting to U.S. congressional leaders, particularly Senator Phil Gramm, Republican of Texas, and the unintentional consequences they had unleashed by getting firm on immigration. Increased profits lay ahead for *coyotes*. The new policy was a boon for smugglers.

In the United States, Mexicans, of course, had become the latest convenient political *piñatas*.

Operation Blockade in 1993 in El Paso had spread to similar operations on the West Coast with Operation Gatekeeper in San Diego. In Arizona, Operation Safeguard didn't receive the necessary resources, resulting in the funneling of desperate migrants into the remote desert, where temperatures often soar to 120 degrees in the summer. The number of those who died on the journey north began rising.

The governors of Texas, California and even Florida threatened lawsuits unless the Clinton administration took action to halt illegal immigration. They complained of billions of dollars in state welfare funds being drained and claimed that immigrants were taking jobs and committing crimes, crowding hospital emergency rooms and overwhelming public schools with their "anchor babies," children born in the U.S. Up until the 1995 midterm elections, when Democrats lost both houses and Clinton was forced to negotiate with the Republicans, Clinton had never really made illegal immigration a top priority, but widespread public frustration could not be ignored. On the advice of his new conservative adviser, Dick Morris, the president found a way to narrow the political gap with his opponents: immigration. Clinton was already frustrated that many of his initiatives were being blocked by Republicans. He handed over immigration policies to his foes, who couldn't wait to rally public opinion against NAFTA. This wasn't, as Reagan once said, an open continent.

Clinton essentially caved to Republican pressure during his State of the Union Address in 1995, when he said: "All Americans, not only in the states most heavily affected, but in every place in this country, are rightly disturbed by the large numbers of illegal aliens entering our country. The jobs they hold might otherwise be held by citizens or legal immigrants. The public services they use impose burdens on our taxpayers. That's why our administration has moved aggressively to secure our borders more by hiring a record number of new border guards, by deporting twice as many criminal aliens as ever before, by cracking down on illegal hiring, by barring welfare benefits to illegal aliens."

In a subsequent radio address, Clinton said, "We are a nation of immigrants, but we're also a nation of laws. It is wrong and ultimately self-defeating for a nation of immigrants to permit the kind of abuse of our immigration laws we have seen in recent years."

In his eight years in office, Clinton deported more than 12 million people—more than President Ronald Reagan and George W. Bush and more than twice the nearly five million people later deported under President Barack Obama, according to the Migration Policy Institute.

By the mid-1990s, two-thirds of the booming Latino population nationwide, reaching 31 million, was of Mexican origin. Predictions stated that by 2050, 25 percent of U.S. residents would identify as Hispanic or Latino, surpassing earlier projections.

Of the 3.1 million immigrants granted amnesty, 85 percent were Mexican workers already in the country. Promises to block the border and prevent new waves of immigrants failed. In the thirteen years since the passage of IRCA, the number of Mexicans legally and illegally moving into the United States jumped to an average of 340,000 annually, up from about 100,000. These were all signs of a robust U.S. economy and economic strife in Mexico as Mexicans saw the peso plunge and their livelihoods decay. IRCA was pushing immigrants into nearly every corner of the country.

The generations coming in were settling down quicker, having children, celebrating baptisms, seeing their kids off to school, having *quinceñeras* for the girls, then college, marriage—a lifetime of celebrations. They were part of a massive demographic transformation, fueled by the greatest infusion of new blood since the flood of European immigrants of the last century.

The trend hardly went unnoticed. Some in cable news made a living off trumped-up fear. Immigration, always a political hot-button issue, was now 24-7, dominated by the anchor turned fearmonger Lou Dobbs on CNN's *Moneyline*, who was punching back nightly. Decrying illegal immigration as an invasion, he screamed for a border fence to stop drugs and "illegal aliens" who were spreading diseases.

I remember sitting in my hotel room in Dallas, where I was visiting editors about the issue, watching the screamers on cable news, including Fox News, peddling stories disguised as journalism, short on facts, some of them twisted, baiting disenfranchised viewers with raw meat. And it seemed to be working because ratings were through the roof.

The call for more hardened, militarized borders wasn't in response to terrorism but in part to Mexico's drug smuggling to meet an insatiable U.S. demand. The displacement of millions of Mexicans after the implementation of NAFTA sent sectors of the Mexican economy into a tailspin. The treaty that was aimed at eliminating trade barriers and generating so much investment across North America led, in part, to drowning Mexico.

Mexican small-business owners were bankrupted by the likes of Wal-Mart, Sam's Club and food franchises. The massive migration that ensued reflected the darker side of the Clinton doctrine of open trade and a jobs boom. With no guest-worker program that could have provided a legal pipeline of Mexican labor, the labor came anyway. Walls, more boots on the ground, more patrolling and new surveillance technologies were meant to take control of the border. The big U.S. contradiction was playing out on the border.

Instead of keeping immigrants out of the U.S., I told my editors, the U.S. government was unwittingly keeping them in. I made my case successfully and asked for a temporary relocation to the United States, which was approved.

Son, I think this story is bigger than one person, said Kerry Gunnels in his Texas twang. He rarely called me by my name. Maybe it was a Texas thing, but I liked his interest and support, and felt comfortable with his familial term for me. The others agreed.

They assigned a handful of reporters across the United States to the story. NAFTA and IRCA were causing tremors on both sides of the border. Investigate the changing face of America, we were told.

I started with my family.

The human pipeline was no longer limited between San Luis de Cordero and Texas or California. My family began to disperse to places like Oklahoma, Kansas and especially Colorado. The women now had options to do something other than the backbreaking work my mother and so many of our aunts did. The men and women didn't just want to irrigate fields, or stoop under the burning sun of the San Joaquin Valley or pray for the rain to go away so they could return to hoeing sugar beets.

Colorado in particular offered jobs in the service and hospitality industry, processing, mechanized plants and new educational opportunities for the children. Among those who fled California was my cousin Ruben. As an illegal immigrant he was bringing in roughly $20,000 per year at a maintenance plant near Mendota. That was with overtime, working more than sixty hours a week. Once he was legalized under a provision of IRCA known as the Special Agricultural Workers Program, or SAW, Ruben's fortunes took off.

In 1986, he applied for legalization, able to easily prove he had worked for more than ninety days that year harvesting fruits, vegetables and other perishable crops. With documents in hand, Ruben headed for Commerce City, Colorado, as a new group of Mexican workers quickly replaced him back in California, all undocumented, some of them friends and relatives. They too had succumbed to U.S. labor demands.

California had its moments, he told me one evening when he stopped in El Paso before crossing the border on his way to Durango for the annual Christmas break, along with a flood of men and women in trucks carrying gifts.

California opened doors for so many, he said. But Colorado was more welcoming, economically, at least.

Historically, Colorado made sense. In the town square of San Luis de Cordero hangs a faded plaque commemorating those who went north with an ancient map of the Camino Real route that the Spanish conquistador Juan de Oñate took, crossing the Rio Grande in 1598, moving through El Paso up to New Mexico and beyond to Colorado.

Colorado felt like destiny, Ruben said.

I think there will be pushback, I cautioned. Too many Mexicans, too fast.

California, he said, had turned unwelcoming and cheap. Look at Proposition 187. They don't want us anymore. But don't always be the reporter and enjoy the time with your cousin, he half joked.

Deep down, Mexico was baffled and indignant. The relationship with the United States was ever complex. A politically, economically stable neighbor wasn't enough anymore. For a decade now Mexico had been doing exactly what the U.S. had asked, opening its economy, adopting stable monetary policies, even moving toward an open and too often messy democracy. One Mexican diplomat noted that when the economy takes a nosedive, Americans "blame everything that goes wrong there on the Mexicans," referring to a backlash in the 1990s when fears of uncertainty fueled states, beginning with California, to pass harsh laws against unsanctioned immigrants.

In 1994, California had passed Proposition 187, a sweeping anti-immigration law, known as the "Save Our State" initiative. Governor Pete Wilson didn't draft the measure, nor did he place it on the ballot. But, facing an uphill reelection bid, and 20 points down in the polls, Wilson seized on the provocative initiative. Through what critics called a racist campaign, the Republican governor tapped into the fears and bigotry of Californians to rescue his flailing candidacy. He alienated Latino voters, and Mexico, by stumping for propositions that targeted affirmative action and a range of government services, including public schooling for illegal immigrant children and bilingual education. His actions further distanced Latinos, and their conservative values, from the Republican Party. The controversial ballot initiatives suggested that white voters were uncomfortable with the racial and ethnic changes under way in the state.

Some Republicans, led by Texas governor George W. Bush, tried to save the party. Bush aggressively courted Mexican Americans across

California, often speaking in Spanish, trying to distance Republicans from Wilson.

The federal courts ultimately blocked the law on the grounds that California was overstepping federal immigration authority. But the damage was done, proving that inflammatory rhetoric toward immigrants could be a winning formula.

Mexico took notice, as did Latino groups. California, which alone was home for 50 percent of all foreign-born people in the country, pushed back. Proposition 187, plus the enactment of tough new welfare and immigration laws, led to record levels of immigrants to become citizens to retain their public benefits. Nearly 1.1 million immigrants nationwide became citizens, shattering the record that was set the previous year, in which 445,853 were naturalized, and turned the state more or less permanently blue, making life for Republicans difficult. Gradually, California would become the first large state to enter the uncharted territory of "majority-minority" status, meaning that no racial or ethnic group accounted for a majority of the population. For the first time in the state's 150-year history, the white, non-Hispanic population fell below 50 percent, driven largely by the growth of the Latino population in the state, given the high birth rate within that group.

A new generation of Latino leaders was swept into office, led by Cruz Bustamante in 1995 as the speaker of the state assembly, the first Mexican American elected to a statewide job since the nineteenth century. The Democrat from California's Central Valley, where I grew up, won by a one-million-vote margin.

Carlos González Gutiérrez, a Mexican diplomat, kept up with the drama unfolding back in California from his tiny, dreary office in Mexico City's Polanco neighborhood, an IBM computer and a radio at his side. Carlos looked like a typical Mexican government official is supposed to look in a suit and tie, except he had a captivating smile that drew you in. So friendly. He was quietly plotting a new relationship with the United States, seeing with a measure of satisfaction the outcome he first began to envision during the term of Salinas de Gortari, back when he dared the next generation of Mexicans to think globally. It wasn't necessarily a brand-new idea. Cuauhtémoc Cárdenas had set a new precedent during the campaign. The son of Mexico's revered nationalist president Lázaro Cárdenas took his campaign into U.S. territory. He lobbied immigrants to vote for him either by returning to Mexico or by talking to families back home.

The lesson didn't go unnoticed by Salinas, who conferred with his foreign minister, Fernando Solana, and ordered him to come up with a plan to work with Mexican immigrants abroad. They even came up with a name and called it Program for Mexican Communities Abroad, which later became IME, Instituto de los Mexicanos en el Exterior, part of a fundamental change in Mexican foreign diplomacy. Carlos, who had worked for five years at the Mexican consulate in Los Angeles, was suddenly recalled to help run the program. This could be the bridge his professor at the University of Southern California tried lecturing him about, he recalled.

He had his chance now with Zedillo, Salinas's successor. In Dallas, President Ernesto Zedillo had already hinted of bigger things to come: "You are Mexicans, Mexicans who live north of the border," words I heard back in Philadelphia, words I now wrote in my notepad as I watched him, intrigued by the mere recognition of Mexicans living in the United States. Mexican leaders were normally cautious, because any mention of the diaspora could be construed as Mexico meddling in U.S. domestic affairs.

Now, ten years after Carlos had completed his master's thesis at USC, real life was playing out before him as the radio blared the latest story coming out of California. He replayed his days back in 1987 when he was an international student, thanks to a scholarship offered by USC. His professor, Abraham Lowenthal, took him aside on his first day and told him the issue that would have the biggest impact on U.S.-Mexico relations for the next forty years wasn't the Mexican currency or even the price of oil. Those will always fluctuate. The future was Mexico's diaspora in the United States. Transnational politics. Mexico needed to form a political lobbying group, not unlike the American Jewish organizations with links to Israel that help influence U.S. foreign policy.

Carlos didn't know much about Jews, or Mexicans in the United States for that matter, other than the fact that Mexicans had been migrating legally and illegally for generations. Lowenthal sat down with his new pupil and described a world unknown to Carlos, one in which Mexicans abroad were laying down the railroad tracks of a foreign policy that was just now developing. He assigned him tomes to read and study, and told him to look at the Jewish model. Like Mexico, Israel was always at the whim of the latest White House resident.

The diaspora was Mexico's most valuable tool to influence change within the United States, just as in Israel. Of course, Israel's diaspora was like a diamond, whereas Mexico's was a stone, a work in progress that needed to be refined.

He continued working at the Mexican consulate, watching closely how human dynamics between the United States and Mexico were changing in the wake of NAFTA. Thousands of immigrants were forming even more social clubs across the United States, much like their predecessors from Ireland, Germany and Italy—clubs named after the immigrants' hometowns and states to help ensure that compatriots maintained cultural and economic ties to home. The new consequences went beyond sending remittances and funding church activities or town fiestas.

Immigrants now wanted to be political actors back in Mexico. That decision came with detractors who accused them of trying to impose on Mexico U.S.-style democracy, complete with transparency and accountability. I remember visiting one immigrant from Southern California who had opened a chain of taquerias and had now returned to his hometown in San Luis Potosí as mayor. I was flabbergasted at the line of people waiting to see him and talk about their problems, waiting for a miracle. Others saw immigrants as arrogant. But they knew their homeland could do better.

Carlos saw them as future ambassadors. He returned to Mexico after serving a first tour of duty at the consulate in Los Angeles; it made him fiery, at times angry at the mistreatment of Mexicans he witnessed in California as punching bags for politicians. I met him through another source and we quickly connected over fried quesadillas in Coyoacán, not far from our respective offices. We were about the same age, both timid, but we broke the ice when he told me he had Durango roots through his father, who was from the town of Guanaceví, not far from where I was born. Good, I thought, he wasn't just a *chilango* boy from the capital. He wasn't some blond hack from Polanco sounding off proudly in English, showing off his American accent to demonstrate that his English was better than mine.

He spoke in Spanish and didn't correct me when I mangled my words. Yet I felt uneasy when at times he spoke of "the immigrant" as though he were describing me. The one who left but always vowed to return. The one who yearned to be back with every Javier Solis song; who once picked grapes and oranges to the music of Juan Gabriel. *That's me, goddamn it*, I felt like telling him. But I didn't. I'm a reporter, after all. I was convinced he would be the source to help me navigate my two worlds closing in. He could help put a face to the economic integration. And humanize NAFTA.

He spoke about his experiences in Southern California, but also about his worries of what could happen if the Mexican government didn't do more to help their countrymen back in the United States. He was now heading up the office to bridge the gap between the Mexican government and Mexican Americans, increasingly gaining political clout, as proven in California. He called them "voices of moderation" to temper relations between the U.S. and Mexico. He was now the curator of a new project that would impact millions of Mexicans on both sides of the border. He pushed the hometown association model nationwide. He wrote long memos to his superior, Javier Treviño, in the hopes they would be passed on to the president himself. They were.

In 1997, at a speech before the National Council of La Raza in Chicago, Zedillo finally uttered the words that shook both countries: "I have proudly affirmed that the Mexican nation extends beyond the territory enclosed by its borders." Behind the scenes was none other than Primo, who now working for Zedillo. He had helped write the first draft of the speech.

Hearing those words, Carlos now had the green light to reach out to rising political actors in California and across the United States. He helped organize a meeting in the Mexican presidential mansion known as Los Pinos. Among the more than two dozen invited U.S. elected officials and community leaders—all with family ties to Mexico—was Denise Moreno Ducheny, from the Logan neighborhood of San Diego and a state senator who had been working on building binational ties with top Mexican leaders.

Carlos gave me a heads-up about the upcoming historic meeting in Los Pinos.

Years later, Moreno remembered the day she sat across from Zedillo. The group came with a specific demand: Amend the constitution to restore citizenship to Mexican Americans who had taken an oath of allegiance to the United States and renounced loyalty to any other country. (I was among them: on my editor Frank's urging, I got my U.S. citizenship in 1988 and automatically gave up my Mexican citizenship.) The effort would facilitate voter registration by Mexicans, who still felt a sense of betrayal by participating in the U.S. political process. Moreno was now the first Latina on the state's budget committee. She knew Mexican immigrants were vulnerable. Their welfare status and the education of their children were now at stake in a state filled with hatred toward immigrants. They needed to vote. With dual nationality, Moreno told Zedillo, Mexican immigrants could more readily become U.S. citizens and still own property in Mexico, participate in Mexican elections and immerse themselves in U.S. politics. Not unlike the rights of Americans living abroad.

President Zedillo looked at the group of twenty or so leaders mostly from California, Texas and Illinois. As a native of Mexicali and a Yale graduate, he knew the people gathered before him, and knew their political potential. He called them "the grandchildren of Mexico," a term that brought Moreno close to tears. She had experienced racism in California, a feeling of not belonging to either country, certainly not to the United States during Wilson's Proposition 187 campaign. Television ads blared, showing the "invasion" of Mexicans running away from the Border Patrol. She certainly did not belong to Mexico and its elitist, classist system. Hell, if she wasn't a U.S. citizen, she wouldn't be sitting in front of Zedillo at the moment. She'd likely be a servant somewhere in Mexico. Rejected in both countries because of her background, a mother with roots in Chihuahua and Durango and a father with roots in Minnesota, Virginia and Ireland, Moreno was now talking face-to-face with the president of Mexico and he was telling her—them—that, yes, Mexico needed them. They should no longer live in isolation from one another.

She felt that much more empowered, because Hispanics were awakening politically, at least in California. Yes, other Latinos had been welcomed in Los Pinos, but at no other time had Mexican American leaders walked inside the powerful place and looked at the Mexican leader *de tú a tú*. Zedillo was making a turnabout in Mexican foreign policy, telling the group that they needed to protect themselves from the attacks of Americans that were sure to come.

It was very emotional, recalled Moreno. It was like a pin could drop in the room for everybody. It was an emotional kind of moment. That's what I remember about it. You understood this was a seminal moment in history in some fashion, and it was important for us to be received that way. The timing was important. Remember we grew up . . . during a period when that connection to Mexico wasn't there . . . and now we understood that the strength of us as Mexican Americans can be strengthened by the strength of Mexico as a nation.

The relationship, however, was a double-edged sword. As Mexican immigrants awakened politically, they also became less tolerant of the deficiencies in Mexico, where they recognized and spoke out against endemic corruption, voter fraud and misguided policies that kept people in poverty and forced entire communities to flee to the U.S.

I met Carlos at his favorite eatery, Los Arcos, to tell him I was leaving Mexico for a few months and needed to make contacts with immigrant representatives. He said he had a Rolodex back in the office and he'd connect me to immigrant groups that stretched from Omaha to Des Moines. From Charlotte to Atlanta, there were people who were now becoming dual citizens. Zedillo was making good on his promise.

We may end up becoming *norteamericanos*, people really of a continent, I obsessed, thinking of Angela and those combination people.

I called my parents after that meeting and told them that, thanks to Zedillo, they could be citizens of two countries.

Mamá, corazón, it's time, I said.

What happened? my mother said, alarmed.

Time for you and Dad to become U.S. citizens. Vote.

No, she said. We're returning to Mexico. I don't know about your father, but I know I am.

You don't have to anymore. You're not betraying anyone, any nation. Plus, you never know when this country will turn on you. Protect yourself. Become a U.S. citizen.

We had long lived on the fringes of the United States, even as the family offspring grew. Despite the monthly mortgage payment my parents made, they somehow managed to convince themselves that they would somehow return to Mexico, with or without us. Their final home was Mexico. The mortgage payment made them, at times, feel guilty. Mexico was where they needed to invest, my mother would tell me.

You don't have to feel guilty anymore. We don't have to choose anymore, I said.

Bueno, she said, reluctantly at first and then excited, as though she could become a real player now and no longer sit on the sidelines.

She was especially happy for my father. He could now officially feel this was his country.

I just hope that during the citizenship interview he knows the difference between the *Mayflower* and sunflowers, she added, a running joke in the family. My mother served as his personal tutor. When they drove into Juárez along Avenida Lincoln, my mother would hint: Think about the president who freed the slaves. Abraham Lincoln. When you eat at Chicos Tacos, across from Jefferson High School, think of Thomas Jefferson. To remember Al Gore, think of your weakness, alcohol.

SECTION IV

Uneasy Neighbors

14.

Heartache Heartland

Angela and I set off in a rental car across the United States to become more familiar with a changing country. We were officially an item. I thought I had it all figured out. On New Year's Eve in Dallas, I took out a ring I had picked out back in El Paso. She looked at it, surprised. She didn't say no. She just said she needed more time.

We raced across the Midwest, giving us much-needed time together and doing what we both loved: journalism.

As it had when I first found Mexicans in rural Pennsylvania, the sound of accordion-laced Mexican *conjunto* music blaring from car radios in "white" towns still surprised me, but never like the first time. Our journey commenced in Oregon, and weeks later we resumed the trip in Nebraska, Iowa, Connecticut, rural Pennsylvania, North Carolina, Georgia, Tennessee and finally Texas. The ghosts of history seemed to loom as we saw reminders of a shaky past and hints of an even more uncertain future: the newcomers were no longer single men but families barreling forward with the intention of setting down roots. Vendors peddling tortillas and tacos on the green open roads echoed my memories of California.

Oregon reminded me of the San Joaquin Valley, I told Angela as we drove passed *tienditas* and *tortillerias*. We spotted small cafés promoting *comidas corridas*, or affordable three-course lunches for people on the run, remnants of Mexican culture that had made it to the north. We stumbled upon small Mexicos under construction. Mexicans unofficially named the town of Hillsboro, Oregon, "Palomas" in honor of their hometown in Michoacán.

It's the California story all over again, she said. Well, I guess it's more accurate to call it the American story, because it replicates itself across every state.

I remembered my mother's words: *We're not alone anymore. They're all here*.

Mexicans were leaving their mark on one-stoplight towns from the strawberry valleys of McMinnville, Oregon, to the tobacco fields of Apex, North Carolina. But it wasn't an easy integration. The resistance toward new Mexican immigrants often came more from other fellow immigrants who worried their presence would drive wages down and reinforce negative stereotypes of being brown.

The tensions in some communities were palpable for other reasons. Angela and I got the feeling that the Mexicans were tolerated but not exactly welcomed. They cared for children and seniors; did the backbreaking work of picking fruits and vegetables; landscaped; worked tough restaurant jobs cooking, cleaning tables, washing dishes—and they did it all with sweet smiles and on the cheap. These were, after all, jobs that white and black Americans didn't want. But the darker side of immigration wasn't very far off: like the Italian, Irish and Chinese mafias before them, Mexican criminal organizations were expertly exploiting immigrant networks nationwide to move marijuana, Colombian cocaine and heroin. The vast majority of Mexican immigrants were humble, hardworking people just trying to make a better life for their families; those bad apples exacerbated the tensions toward integration.

My so-called binational correspondent's job wasn't so fancy after all. It revolved around two things, both long-standing vices for Americans: America's insatiable demand for drugs and undocumented workers and cheap labor in the throes of a changing global economy. Mexicans were the enablers for America's charade.

SOME TOWNS FELT FORCED to put out the welcome mat. In Marshalltown, Iowa, a town settled by German and Dutch immigrants, Mexicans brought their skills to the slaughterhouses, fueling a resurgence in what had been a dying industry. But locals also complained about the increase in methamphetamine and opiate use and gang activity. Unsure about these allegations, I called my colleague Tracey Eaton, who was back in Mexico City. He had long covered organized crime, which he essentially compared to a cancer overtaking not just the inner working of the government but its civil society still in diapers. The U.S. and its demand were at the heart of corruption permeating throughout Mexico. His response made me feel like an idiot.

Duh, he said. Where did you think drugs were headed, Alfredo? The U.S. is full of addicts. Mexicans and their corruption were feeding the monster, meeting an insatiable demand for the secret stash they carried, in part, via new immigration routes opening before them. Organized crime thrives and preys on immigrant communities. This time these were Mexicans working unwittingly on behalf of cartels, whose power was shifting back in Mexico with trade liberalization policies and even amnesty.

The more cargo crisscrossed the border, the higher the probability that drugs were hidden inside. But both sides, the United States and Mexico, looked the other way, touting binational cooperation. The conversation was not going to be about illicit drugs permeating across the United States, unless new political optics called for a punching bag. All the while, big seizures were prominently televised, written about by colleagues like Tracey, who remained skeptical.

The corruption of Mexican authorities, Tracey said, was out of control. Indeed, studies showed cartels were paying more than $460 million in annual bribes, up from $3 million ten years earlier, in 1983, before NAFTA.

Two shifts were under way that created the perfect story. One had to do with the fact that the Mexican government went after the "old guard," legendary figures like Miguel Ángel Félix Gallardo, a former cop in Sinaloa; Rafael Caro Quintero; and Joaquín "El Chapo" Guzmán. The strategy was to splash their names and antics in the media for the world to see, prove that Mexico, with the cooperation of the United States, was doing its job and serious about putting the bad guys in jail. But a new generation of more aggressive and violent men—groups heading up the Tijuana and Juárez cartels—began to replace more calculating leaders. A growing, sophisticated farm-to-arm supply chain began fueling America's surging heroin appetite, causing heroin to surpass cocaine and meth gradually to become the nation's number one drug threat for the first time.

As U.S. demand grew, the flow of heroin—a once-taboo drug now easier to score in some cities than crack or pot—was changing, too. The U.S. government hadn't quite caught up to the shift. After decades of "successfully" battling Colombian criminal organizations, the DEA was just beginning to realize that what the Colombians had done was subcontract the trafficking of coke to the Mexicans. The idea was that they would get the heat off their back and lower the risk of extradition. Mexican criminal organizations picked up the distribution expertly; the Mexican diaspora was vastly bigger, better connected and spread out nationwide. Cocaine trafficking began to enrich Mexicans, who became more savvy, reading what the U.S. market wanted. As drugs flowed north, cash and high-powered firearms flowed south.

Tracey reminded me that Mexican drug trafficking organizations had broadened distribution beyond the old big-city heroin centers like Chicago and New York. Now, they were targeting unlikely places such as Marshalltown, Iowa. Midsize midwestern cities were becoming the epicenter of the heroin problem, with addicts buying and overdosing in unsettling numbers. Crack dealers ranged across a far wider landscape, almost invisible to law enforcement.

They arranged deals by cell phone and carried small amounts to avoid detection and prosecution if caught, as later detailed by my colleague Sam Quinones in his reporting for the *Los Angeles Times* and later in his book *Dreamland: The True Tale of America's Opiate Epidemic*, a tidal wave of addiction that began with pills like Oxycontin. This crisis was precipitated by pharmaceutical salespeople and doctors who billed Oxycontin as a risk-free wonder drug and by an enterprising network of traffickers from a small village in Mexico who delivered black-tar heroin to pill addicts in midsize cities and suburbs across the U.S.

Angela and I got a hint of the growing backlash building into a dam overflowing with resentment aimed at Mexico. Back in Philadelphia, some of the most loyal Tequilas customers were DEA agents who loved the food. David also noticed drug dealers at his restaurant and took no chances. He sent waiters to make bathroom raids, make sure the place was clean. He wanted no problems with the feds. The bigger the Mexican immigrant communities grew, the bigger the resentment. All that change had added more fuel to the charged political climate.

We covered hundreds of miles and I saw vestiges of my father in the eyes of the latest generation of immigrant dreamers. Workers now and then remained as indispensable as in my father's generation. The most loyal workforce for U.S. employers was made up of Mexicans. Christmas trees in Wisconsin and Oregon? Sure. Hotels, spas, restaurants and golf courses in Colorado and Nevada? Why not. Meatpacking in Nebraska and Iowa? Poultry processing plants in Illinois? The Mexicans, of course, would do just about anything. And their hosts loved their work ethic.

But these were different times. America was not at war.

Rather, the country's economic model was changing and Mexico was in even greater economic despair. Mexicans no longer viewed the United States as the only escape valve. Some gave in to the growing temptation of easy, dirty money working for cartels. The more Mexico's PRI party opened politically, the more it crumbled, growing old and irrelevant. A quiet chaos was building, one that few initially cared to take seriously. Express kidnappings were a threat in Mexico City. In the countryside, traveling by car in Mexico became increasingly risky. Criminals dressed in military garb set up false checkpoints to shake down travelers—or root out rivals. Fear and suspicion grew, because in truth you could never know who was really in charge in parts of Mexico. But as this darkness began to creep across the country, all eyes remained on the new U.S-Mexico cooperation and Mexico's heroic march toward first world status, even as suspicion lay right beneath the surface.

In a large part because of the weak Mexican economy and growing dangers back in their homeland, coupled with tightening border security in the U.S. that made it tougher to go back and forth, Mexicans were slowly setting down roots in their new American communities. They strengthened fledgling networks that had long existed by further connecting communities across borders. The Americans seemed in awe of their work ethic but nothing else.

I was more acutely aware than before about how I was being perceived as I reported, judged or critiqued. Yet I watched Angela, at times with envy, as she effortlessly belonged to two countries without hesitation. Borders don't define us, she'd say with conviction. And she wasn't talking about the physical two-thousand-mile U.S.-Mexico border but our very own: the emotional, psychological scars that we carry inside. Our internal walls.

Once, when we were in Lake Geneva, Wisconsin, it was Fish Fry Friday at Anthony's, a legendary eatery. The tradition started as a Catholic religious observance but was quickly adopted by Wisconsinites. Angela noticed how I'd turn into a frog and retreat, uncomfortable around the largely white Anglo community. Her people were unfamiliar to me, especially her uncle Bill, a conservative Republican, a sophisticated man full of confidence, sure of himself and his opinions, with fine tastes, including wines, who wore a navy blue Brooks Brothers blazer with a pocket square.

It didn't help that he once asked if I did yard work for a living.

He couldn't fathom the idea that his beloved niece, a Newman, would bring a Mexican all the way to Lake Geneva to meet her uncle. Lake Geneva was a place where Mexicans worked as gardeners in the homes of the upper class.

I once worked as a farmworker, but that was many years ago, I responded.

I didn't know what else to say. He had a dry sense of humor.

Aren't you a reporter? Angela asked when I later said how uncomfortable I felt around him and others. I thought you could talk to anyone.

This is different, I said, groping for excuses. I don't have a notepad.

We're all just people, she said, as I looked for my comfort zone, desperately wishing for David, Ken and Primo. Bring down your barrier. Interact, she'd tell me. Pretend they're Mexicans. Charm them.

I had no clue how to begin. I'd grow silent and realize I wasn't as worldly as I had thought. It seemed that I still wasn't all that different from the man I was when I first arrived in Philadelphia. I had lived mostly in El Paso and Mexico City, not exactly a slice of Middle America. Our worlds remained vastly apart.

In Chicago, Angela and I would stroll along the Magnificent Mile as she reminisced about taking these very strolls alongside her mother many years before, so mesmerized by the twinkling Christmas decorations that they'd forget the cold.

I'd stare at the buildings that her great-grandfather William had laid the foundation for with the sweat of immigrants who built entire cities from the ground up.

When I looked at Angela, her pouty mouth and deep-green eyes, America didn't seem so scary after all, especially when she led the way. She's right. We should ease into things, I'd tell myself whenever I grew needy. She had a talent of changing the conversation to journalism and work.

We drove through the Southeast, which was experimenting with the biggest increase in Latino migration. We ended up in Dalton, Georgia, the "carpet capital of the world," where steam rose from factories alongside railroad tracks. Mexicans, the new workforce, had arrived. And the influx of immigrants meant Georgians were confronting a foreign culture posing new challenges such as finding money for bilingual education.

A former U.S. congressman, Harlan Erwin Mitchell, was leading a crusade to ensure all children received bilingual education, even if it meant importing teachers from Mexico. The Mexican immigrants were the new Americans, who, like immigrants before them, would forge a future for their families and the country they called home.

To do otherwise, he said, would be self-defeating. The workers had families and their children were the future.

BUT OTHERS WERE NOT as compassionate or welcoming, especially in Pennsylvania, a state that had become a part of me. The temperature was balmy and the winds swept through as I drove from the Philadelphia airport to Kennett Square, a place I hadn't visited in nearly a decade.

I visited Jane Perrone, who had begun a movement to discourage Mexican immigrants from moving into her neighborhood. She walked the streets with other neighbors and put yellow ribbons on doorknobs as a symbol of solidarity against the foreigners.

Once tolerant of the men living in the shadows, residents were no longer as accepting when new families began to pop up everywhere. IRCA legalized some three thousand immigrants in Chester County alone, many of them Mexicans from Kennett Square. And they weren't going anywhere. Instead, for the men and women from Guanajuato and Michoacán, Kennett Square's small-town atmosphere was the closest thing to home.

An unsettling feeling swept across the close-knit, blue-blooded families from one of America's most historic towns, also founded by William Penn. Some were downright mad that these men had the gall to strike the mushroom houses and demand better pay, just as my mother had done all those years ago in California alongside Cesar Chavez.

Callers to local radio talk shows urged newcomers to leave. Anger lingered.

Ms. Perrone felt the same.

Until.

Appalled at the rage she helped stir, guilt set in. The transformation began late at night. That's when she began to remember her past.

She'd sit alone in her bedroom and wonder about what she had done, what she had awoken with this movement to rid the town of newcomers from Mexico. She recalled her own family of Italian descent and realized that the arrival of the Mexicans represented nothing more than another phase in the timeless cycle of immigration.

That was why, when Mexicans moved into a new development called Buena Vista Townhomes, she approached her old neighbors and did the unthinkable. This was the land of Penn—imperfect as he was, he preached tolerance. They had to learn to be tolerant. They agreed to give them a chance.

Ms. Perrone and members of the Four Seasons Garden Club did something that shook the Mexican newcomers. Perrone and her neighbors greeted them with shovels and hoes to help them plant flower gardens. They also planted a tiny pine tree to be decorated with ornaments. They grew past their prejudices and instead built a garden, raising a sign that read: *"Bienvenidos Nuevos Vecinos."*

IN PHILADELPHIA, NEW GENERATIONS of young men from Mexico's interior replaced workers from Mexico City and Guadalajara. The earlier immigrants had moved on to other ventures, like opening their own restaurants and running their own food trucks. Tequilas became the magnet for workers from a small town called San Mateo located at the foot of Mexico's active Popocatépetl volcano. Ash falls on the town with every eruption.

Free trade, immigration reform and Mexico's growing urbanization were destroying a way of life in San Mateo Ozolco, a town of roughly thirteen hundred. The countryside was emptying out, forcing corn farmers who could no longer compete with subsidized corn from the United States to leave. NAFTA had devastated the countryside, driving nearly two million subsistence farmers out of business, even as agricultural exports to the United States tripled. The Mexican government had no retraining or reinvention plan for them. The strategy was simple: Promote cheap wages. Many did what came naturally—the very thing generations before had done. They picked up and headed north. They had to seek other opportunities, reinvent themselves if at all possible. Some, like David years ago, found reinvention on the streets of Philadelphia.

Headed for New Jersey, Efren, one of the immigrants from San Mateo, saw a sign that read "Philadelphia," a word that reminded him of his favorite cream cheese back in his home state of Puebla. The men opted for the familiar and changed their travel plans from Jersey to Philadelphia and walked the streets until they ran into the restaurant with the sign that read "Tequilas."

The man from Puebla introduced himself to David and immediately landed a job. Then more came. Among them was Mario, Efren's cousin. Mario Perez remembers walking around Center City with a Spanish-to-English translation book. Restaurant owners and chefs would peer through the windows. Mario feared for his life. One man wearing a chef's outfit appeared to be whispering to them, making hand gestures, jerking his head for them to approach him.

I wasn't sure whether he wanted to rob us or call the Border Patrol on us, recalled Mario. But then a dishwasher from the Dominican Republic joined them and served as a translator.

Are you from Ecuador? he asked.

No, we're from Mexico, Mario said.

The chef's eyes lit up. Puebla? he asked.

Yes, Mario responded.

The Dominican explained that the chef, who was from Paris, was ecstatic because Poblanos were now finding their way to Philadelphia. The Poblanos had earned a grand reputation for their strong work ethic in New York City. The chef wasn't being rude, the Dominican explained. He just wanted to recruit them and anyone else they knew. The restaurant was Le Bec-Fin, once rated one of America's finest French restaurants. This was the place, I told Mario, that Ken once took me to for lunch back in 1987 and I couldn't figure out what to order, much less understand the menu with phrases in French. Growing worried that I would cave in to homesickness and one day pick up and leave, Ken believed I needed to face my fears. Hang out where the elite ate.

But a French place? I asked. I barely knew how to order a hoagie or a Philadelphia cheesesteak.

And I was really afraid of the prices.

Yet I listened with intense fascination as Ken walked me through the entire menu, telling me how lucky we were to be sitting there, because reservations were so difficult for anyone. You had to know someone and slip the host $50 or $100 to remember you the next time. This was the place where I didn't wear my JCPenney blazer but upgraded to one actually picked out by Ken at Wanamaker's. Ken explained that we were at a bistro owned and founded by Georges Perrier, one of the world's most famous chefs. He had opened the place in 1970 and named the restaurant after the French colloquialism for "fine palate."

Ken picked up the tab that day, which I tried to object to, even when I knew there was no way I could afford it—not even half. I don't remember whether it was creamy rabbit or scallops, I told Mario. All I know is I left still hungry, and how so much more I wanted to be Ken, so poised.

I probably washed your dishes that day, Mario joked. Although I soon left for Tequilas.

Well, then you have certainly washed many of my dishes, I quipped. Mario, like others, was captivated by David's story. A Mexican immigrant who was building an empire from the ground up, working six, sometimes seven days a week; driving a deep-red VW van to pick up fruit, vegetables and meat; burning CDs for the latest music late into the night; and constantly changing the menu to stay ahead of the competition.

We all want to be David. To us he's not just the American dream but the Mexican dream, Mario said.

Another Poblano I met, Mario's friend, identified himself only as Pedro. He was now a waiter and hadn't returned to Mexico in nearly five years, opting to endure Philadelphia's frigid winters and humid summers rather than risk the border again. To combat his loneliness, Pedro encouraged nearly three dozen of his friends from Puebla to join him. Most had been corn farmers. His welcome wagon extended to his hometown's soccer team, all of whom had jobs waiting as waiters, busboys and dishwashers in Philadelphia's fashionable restaurants, increasingly the heartbeat of Center City's downtown economy, moving up and down from Boston to Connecticut, New York, Maryland and the nation's first capital. Playing soccer on Sundays.

Nightly, when the city shut down, the only sounds were the grunts from the Puebla men as they hauled that night's food garbage to the dumps outside. I followed them, pen and notepad in hand, alongside a photojournalist, Erich Schlegel. When their work was done, Erich followed them as they pedaled their bikes past Independence Hall, silhouetted before dawn against a moonlit statue of George Washington and the Liberty Bell, on their way to a modest apartment shared by eleven people.

Sometimes, as I ride my bike, Pedro told me with a sheepish grin, pedaling hard to catch up on sleep before he'd start over again, I have to pinch myself to make sure this is real.

15.

Havana Calling, Santana's Guitar

It had been a particularly good month traveling, reporting from the United States—so good that a colleague and I agreed to swap home offices. He'd spend a few months at my place in Coyoacán, practice his Spanish, learn the intricacies of a country in the throes of political and economic change. In turn, I would take over his apartment in Georgetown, source with Washington insiders, walk through Rock Creek Park and take the train from Dupont Circle to Metro Center to work at the *News'* Washington bureau.

Fair exchange, I thought. Plus, I would be closer to Philadelphia, spend weekends with Ken and David.

The growth in the number of Mexicans in the United States remained my priority, as was Cuba. The *Dallas Morning News* was lobbying the Cuban and U.S. governments for a bureau in Havana, and my coverage in Washington included talking with Latin American experts and policy makers on the Hill, at Foggy Bottom and at the White House.

I spent days in the U.S. capital, corralling congressional aides and their bosses in the corridors of power, pacing the maze of the State Department or grabbing a drink with the Pentagon's Ana María Salazar, with roots in Sonora, or Maria Echaveste, one of President Clinton's top advisers, with family ties in Jalisco. We met at the Oval Room restaurant bar, across from the White House, where she worked just feet away from the president. I asked the obvious question: What's the status of this marriage between our two countries?

Off the record? It fluctuates. On the record, never better.

I visited the headquarters of the CIA to get a better sense of what was happening along the U.S.-Mexico border, where drug violence was spiking.

A few days later I had a surprise visitor from the Cuban special interest office in Washington who showed up at the bureau. I was just in the neighborhood, Corchado, the bureaucrat said. They always called me by my last name. Time for a drink?

Of course, I said, and we headed to the National Press Club for happy hour.

The Cuban government will issue you a special visa, he told me.

I had no clue what that involved, but my host said I should go to Havana and do more reporting from there. Most recently, I visited Cuba to cover Pope Juan Paul's visit. For weeks I roamed lazily across the island, falling in love with its people. I didn't need much of an excuse to return.

I was again constantly surprised how well Cubans in their *guayaberas* treated me, giving me a long-term journalist's visa to avoid the tedious paperwork associated with media credentials. The Cuban spooks often picked me up at the airport as though I was some kind of dignitary. They talked about the need for Mexicans and Cubans to stand in solidarity in the fight against the imperialist U.S., which they said was starving Cubans through the embargo, jamming the airwaves and preparing for imminent invasion. They stole half of Mexico's territory. Sooner or later they would take everything—even Cuba.

The way they spoke reminded me of Primo, and I wondered whether this whole time I was wrong. Was Primo a Cuban spy? Not Mexican? Was Cuba the source of his information? Maybe that was why David and Primo whispered to each other. Maybe that explained Primo's beret.

Or maybe I was just paranoid, an uneasy feeling resulting from the fact that I'm Mexican American, and the Cubans, like the Mexicans, saw that as a bridge between countries, across deserts and the Caribbean. We could become a politically powerful bloc to counter the ultraconservative Cuban Americans, so the thinking went. We needed to stick together, the Cuban official said, much like Fidel and Che bonded with Lázaro Cárdenas after the former president welcomed exiles to Mexico as guests, a gesture for which Cuba would be eternally grateful. I'd look at them and couldn't believe they were being so obvious, recruiting me to be their spy, a double agent. Surely they couldn't think I knew so much that I had to be a CIA spy!

They plied me with mojito daiquiris and even tried tequila, but by then I had become a snob like David and almost fell out of my chair when they presented me with a bottle of Cuervo. I don't mean to be ungrateful, but that stuff is lethal, I complained. That definitely should be part of the blockade. Everyone laughed.

No other detail was overlooked. At a restaurant, the owner came over to tell me they had just planted chiles in a small garden so that whenever *el Mexicano*—me—visited, I could add spice to the delicious chicken they served.

Thank you, I told the owner.

We trust you, Corchado, one Cuban told me. We trust that you trust us, too.

Tensions between the U.S. and Cuba were unusually high. U.S.-Cuba ties during the Clinton administration had gotten more complicated, frayed at times, with the hardening of the embargo and after Cuban MiGs shot down two planes piloted by members of the Cuban-American exile group Brothers to the Rescue, killing four people. One afternoon we sat outside the courtyard of *El Nacional* when one of the Cubans bluntly asked whether I could share with them through their emissaries whatever information I had from my meetings back in Washington. Pictures?

You want me to be your spy?

A friend, they responded, a friend to stand with us like Mexico has done all these years.

Whatever secrets I have, or confirm, I will publish them in the newspaper. That's how it works. I'm a reporter, not a spy.

They didn't seem to buy that explanation and asked why I spent so much time at the CIA and State Department, and with key Cuban insiders on Capitol Hill, like Rep. Jeff Flake, R-Arizona.

Doing my job, I said, shocked they knew my activities so well.

I also like to shower a lot, especially when it's humid, I added sarcastically. It's a habit I picked up in the fields of California.

Corchado, don't get defensive.

I relayed the information to my editor, Ricardo Chavira, a former correspondent for *Time* magazine who had also covered Cuba. He laughed. The Cubans are second to none when it comes to human intelligence, especially building new networks and schmoozing with old ones. Just dance with them, he said.

One night back in Philadelphia I was telling David the story, and he just stared at me. He doubted me. David was still obsessed with Cuba.

Cabrón, tell me the truth. Are you a spy for the imperialist?

That doesn't deserve a response, I said. Fuck you.

You have secrets?

Read the newspaper.

Güey, I said, thinking of a way to change the subject, they were so desperate to impress me, they took out a bottle of Cuervo. Can you believe that? Fucking *Cuervo*.

That finally got his attention. David slammed his hand atop Table 21. The mere mention of Cuervo got him all worked up. Let's go to Cuba, he said.

And so we did, several times. The Cubans took to his suave personality and liberal, anti-embargo views. They listened with fascination as David talked about the virtues of good tequila and how no one could win a revolution without the proper spirits.

A bad hangover can kill the effort.

He talked through the night with a new friend, Marta Rojas, an author and a personal friend of Fidel's, of the perils of globalization and defending the Mexican culture. Marta was so charmed by David that she included him in a future book.

That night she took us to a salsa bar, Café Cantante, across the street from the Monument to the Revolution, which pays homage to José Martí, Che Guevara and Camilo Cienfuegos with the quote *"Vas bien Fidel"* ("You're doing fine, Fidel").

Another time we were invited by a friend from Philadelphia to attend a reception with Fidel and religious leaders, but we forgot to bring along the actual invitation. We took a 1957 Chevy convertible with a driver who doubted we'd even get close to the gates of the residence where the event was being held.

El comandante is there, the driver said, making the hand gesture of a beard to refer to Fidel. You won't get close. Each time a Cuban bodyguard asked who we were, I'd say I was a reporter and my friend sold tacos. *¿Mexicanos?* he asked. *Con nopal en la frente*, I responded. It helped that we had been drinking seven-year rum and Herradura tequila, a bottle that David brought as a gift to Marta.

Shockingly, the guard smiled and let us in, ordering the next group to open the gates. David's lifelong wish, the one he shared back from those nights in Philadelphia when he romanticized about socialism, was on the verge of becoming real. Next thing we knew, David and I were just feet from Castro. I was worried about two things: First, Castro's bodyguards would tackle us and take us to prison, and the U.S. government would have to negotiate our release. We'd rot in jail. Or, second: David would have a massive orgasm right there on the spot. To the best of my knowledge that didn't happen, but he did come close.

I wiped the smirk off his face by inviting him to meet Rolando Bezos, a revolutionary who had fought alongside Castro and claimed to be a distant uncle of the stepfather of Amazon's Jeff Bezos. The family, like many Cubans, was disenchanted with the revolution, and invited us to a goodbye dinner for a young friend headed for Miami. In the background was Los Van Van and Carlos Varela playing "Como Los Peces," a lovely song about disillusion that was now a national anthem for young Cubans escaping the grip of Fidel's socialist-capitalist ideals. At the Karl Marx auditorium young Cubans danced to heavy metal music and talked about the ultimate symbol of freedom: McDonald's. David was heartbroken.

I'd often revisit successful *paladares*, small eateries run by families, only to learn they had been shut down by the government or couldn't live under the latest bureaucracy, which grew with any sign of success.

Some flee by sea, I told David, as we drove along the waterfront known as the Malecón, water splashing, children giggling, couples holding hands and rain clouds forming amid a red sunset. Others cross through deserts.

Cabrón, let's ask Carlos to do a concert right here. *Estaría chingón. Imagínate*. Raise awareness of the migration crisis on an international level.

Santana again? Carlos Santana was more than a customer at Tequilas. David and Santana were friends. The legion of customers at Tequilas had sparked new friendships. David's new best friends ranged from politicians, Hollywood stars like Lily Tomlin and literary heavyweights like the Uruguayan writer Eduardo Galeano to sports team owners and figures including Franco Harris, the famous Pittsburgh Steelers football player, and Fernando Valenzuela, the Los Angeles Dodgers pitcher from Sonora, who'd stop by and stay for hours. The founders of the Pew Research Center would also stop in. None became closer to David than musician Santana, a friendship I viewed with some trepidation. In the early nineties, Santana became my replacement at Table 21.

David and Primo met Santana at a Puerto Rican art exhibit in Philadelphia showcasing Santana's album covers. David invited him to the restaurant. He said yes. A budding friendship ensued. Santana became a regular, popping in from time to time whenever he visited Philadelphia for a gig. They had Jalisco and perhaps more in common. One night David's mother, who now lived in Philadelphia, came to Tequilas, met Santana, and proceeded to talk about their native state of Jalisco, tracing back their family's lineage. As the conversation progressed,

David's mother suddenly looked at them and said, You two may be related, noting names, relatives back in Jalisco.

They became convinced they were long-lost brothers.

Carlos and I looked at each other and realized that, beyond the friendship, there was probably more that brought us together. David recalled the story of their meeting. Maybe there was more, Primo and I thought. Santana met the Mexican in David that he never saw in his native Jalisco. David saw in Santana the brother he never knew he had, and the Mexican he wanted to be or the one he was in the process of becoming, accepted as an American. David, defensively, denied any comparison.

Ni madre, he said.

But, Primo pointed out, I also met Santana and he never invited me out. I'm trying to convince Carlos to play in Cuba, he said.

Órale. Genial—meaningless words that I had learned from Mexico's pompous *trendoids* who uttered such crap when they had nothing meaningful to say.

One night he called me so excited that for a moment I thought he had unlocked the secret to his lifelong obsession: finding the right ingredients for his perfect tequila. Maybe he found the actual spirit? Nah. Instead, he had just left a ritzy hotel facing Rittenhouse Square, where Santana was staying. Santana invited him for a *caminero*, tequila, one for the road. Santana took out a demo tape that he carried for his upcoming album. David sat back and listened as Santana, the author of "Black Magic Woman," was jamming his guitar in front of him, playing songs yet unknown to the public: "Maria, Maria," "Put Your Lights On" and "Smooth." David was particularly fascinated with "Migra, Migra," a protest song against the Border Patrol, reciting the lyrics over the phone as he drove home and reliving their evening.

How much did you drink? I asked, sounding like a jealous, possessive girlfriend.

Too much, he said. That's why I have the windows rolled down.

He lived in Merion, part of Philadelphia's main line, about a twenty-minute drive from Center City.

Watch your ass, I said. Cops are everywhere, and you fit the profile. Mexican inside a van. Midnight, crossing the Schuylkill River. But I'm glad you found a new friend—I said, a bit surly.

Quién te quiere, cabrón, he interrupted me as he screamed *Migra, Migra pinche Migra, déjame en paz* . . .

An employer who depended on a formidable workforce from Mexico, David had a dislike for the Border Patrol.

Weeks later the song was part of the album *Supernatural*, which went fifteen times platinum in the United States and won eight Grammy Awards, including Album of the Year, as well as Latin Grammy Awards, including Record of the Year. It included the song "Corazón Espinado," which Santana recorded with Maná, Mexico's top band from Guadalajara.

Carlos is coming over to the house tonight, David called to tell me another time. He's in town for a sold-out concert, but I have a ticket with special access for you. We'll go for the concert first and then dinner. Come over.

I obediently took the train north to Philadelphia and met Santana and his band at David's three-story home. David invited Santana to the room we dubbed La Cueva, the man cave for drinks and midnight confessions. This was where David and I would retreat after a night at Tequilas and confess secret pains of the heart. I had my own chair. David had his. In between, we'd talk about Mexico City, Guadalajara, the daily drama, Washington, D.C., and what was on everyone's mind, the budding love-hate relationship between Texan rancher George W. Bush and Mexican rancher Vicente Fox.

That night, after a potluck dinner that included *flautas* and *cochinita pibil*, a traditional Yucatán-style slow-roasted, marinated pork dish, Santana walked inside the house and nonchalantly took my seat in La Cueva as though he owned it.

I grimaced but I kept my cool and told him how I loved his new album and how before I became a journalist I really wanted to be a songwriter, following in Juan Gabriel's footsteps. The parallels between music and writing—I couldn't separate the two.

He looked at me, dipping his chips into guacamole. He quietly, almost in a whisper, remarked how blessed he felt. He was guided by the Virgincita de Guadalupe, who is always near me. He said nothing else.

Órale, I responded.

16.

The Fallout

I was living in Washington full time now as a correspondent, slowly bridging the gap between Mexico and the United States via stories and interviews, witnessing the growth of the Mexican immigrant community now increasingly spreading into New Jersey and Delaware. I was also witnessing the demise of a friendship.

Shortly after my move to Washington, David and Ken made the ultimate mistake. They tried going into business together. One afternoon on his way to Tequilas after work, Ken took the usual route, walking on Locust Street, when he saw a sign: "For Sale." One of Rittenhouse Square's top pieces of real estate was on the market. Corner of Locust and Sixteenth Street.

Ken almost ran to Tequilas. He shuffled in and didn't even greet the nightly crowd. Instead he cornered David.

Want to be part of America's mainstream? Here was the spot, he reasoned. Here is how you carve yourself into the heart of America, right where the nation started, on one of the most elegant, historic streets of the country. Make a statement. Ken recalled telling David: You've outgrown Tequilas.

This wasn't just any building but an iconic four-story brownstone designed by an architect whose work included St. Mark's Church. The former owners included William J. Duane, who assisted his father in publishing the newspaper *Aurora*, and Benjamin Franklin's grandson. The *Aurora* was known for taking on the causes of Thomas Jefferson and railing against the Federalists. Duane was also a politician who in 1833 served as Treasury Secretary under Andrew Jackson before running for president. In the living room with high ceilings was a magnificent chandelier, an original Baccarat, a gift to Duane from Napoleon's brother,

Joseph Bonaparte, the former king of Spain. The second owner was William D. Dulles, a prominent Philadelphia lawyer and later relative of John Foster Dulles, secretary of state under Eisehower.

Most recently, the building had been home to several restaurants for the Rittenhouse Square crowd, ranging from the Cajun Magnolia Café and earlier La Panetière, where George Perrier had trained before opening Le Bec-Fin. The building entered the national spotlight when it was the featured location in the 2000 movie *Unbreakable*, a thriller written, produced and directed by M. Night Shyamalan, starring Bruce Willis and Samuel L. Jackson.

David had been talking about moving for a while, complaining he couldn't manage the crowd anymore. Tequilas was now part of the fabric of the city, which was well on its way to a dramatic renaissance. To stay current, he constantly changed the menu to introduce the latest dishes from his homeland, with biographical descriptions to educate his clientele in everything from mole's pre-Hispanic origins to the immense variety of heirloom corn. At times I thought he went too far. Once I ordered nachos, which he no longer carried. He was now dead serious in saying publicly that he saw Tex-Mex food as the enemy of Mexican cuisine.

Esas son chingaderas Tex-Mex, he scolded me about my nachos request. *No chingues*.

I wasn't so sure how to defend that, other than to remind him that Tex-Mex was not so different from what we were becoming at Table 21, something else that wasn't solely Mexican anymore. But I backed down. The last war between the United States and Mexico started in Texas, and Mexico ended up losing half its territory.

David had leased the original Tequilas for fifteen years, but because he didn't own it he couldn't find a bank willing to finance the purchase of an entire building that included the restaurant. He needed to move to a bigger location, but the one Ken talked about made no sense. This wasn't just a restaurant but an entire four-story historic brownstone building with three floors of offices above. He qualified for a bank loan to finance the restaurant but not the entire property. Too pricey. David balked at the idea. He would need financial help.

Ken offered.

Let's do this together, he proposed.

And with that, we were doomed. David and Ken, a recent Mexican immigrant and a Mexican American removed by generations, wouldn't end well, I feared.

Ken was doing well for himself, economically and personally. He and Laura had married in a wedding that was a tribute to their state of enchantment, in a pueblo-style Presbyterian church in Taos. The wedding was topped off with a tongue-in-cheek salute to Ken's Española roots. Instead of limos, the new couple hired a parade of lowriders to transport the wedding party. No detail was missed except by me: on the day of the wedding I slept in and forgot the morning donuts for the wedding party. Ken had made me his best man, for better or worse. That afternoon I rode in the backseat of a convertible 1969 Impala lowrider in Española, with an array of friends, among them his preppy law school buddies from UPenn, who were still nursing hangovers. I was still pissed that I forgot the donuts that day. David and Angela gave me shit about the donuts as well.

Ken and Laura were also now parents of one-year-old Maya, and Ken was raking it in, living in Society Hill, which was as wealthy and bourgeois as it sounds, in a 1790 three-story town house that had been completely renovated. He gave me my own keys, which lured me to visit every other weekend from Washington. I had my own bedroom and a ten-block walk to Tequilas.

THE OWNERS OF THE building on Locust Street didn't want to deal with David but were happy to negotiate if Ken was involved. Ken had cachet, a reputation. The young man from New Mexico who rose from poverty to prosperity, the epitome of the American dream.

Ken could have gone anywhere: California, or back to New Mexico, as he had once promised. But he'd chosen to stay in Philadelphia, expanding his law firm to Trujillo Rodríguez & Richards, now one of the highest-profile firms in the region. He loved his law firm life, a page out of the favorite book of his teen years, *The Partners*. Big-time litigation provided Ken with a lifestyle and level of prestige that would have been unimaginable to his father and inconceivable in Durango, Colorado. He traveled to Florida, New Orleans and the West Coast and spent nearly six months living weekdays at the Waldorf Astoria in New York. Bourgeois indeed.

He was the one whom Philadelphia's establishment now embraced. When Ken began to make some headway, David perked up. The more he thought about it, the more he liked it.

This could actually work, he told me. The two would own the twenty-thousand-square-foot building jointly, and Ken would purchase 5 to

10 percent of the restaurant. David actually asked for this because he wanted Ken invested in the restaurant. The liquor license was owned by Tequilas and the company holding it was named using the initials for their kids, DEDMA, Inc., for David, Elisa, Daniel and Ken's toddler, Maya.

The deal was fragile from the beginning. The bank was asking David for collateral that he didn't have—not the millions of dollars required for the size of the real estate investment. David put up his house, but Ken said he would not, insisting he would look for outside investors. That wrinkle sent Annette, David's wife, into a rampage.

Annette felt that if Ken was an investor, he needed to pony up his house as collateral. Ken felt that his interest in the restaurant was minimal and with a newborn he did not want to risk his house.

Ken brought in some outside money, in Annette's view, too little, too late. David was forced to look for outside brokers with huge interest rates. David closed on the deal in late 2000 and construction began almost immediately. The two never signed an agreement and kept it verbal, based on friendship. That was the beginning of the end.

David had grandiose ideas. He plotted every move with a goal: he would bring Mexico to Philadelphia in all forms and shapes. His furniture wouldn't come from just anywhere. He wanted authenticity. Guadalajara. Every item—bar stools, tables, chairs, glasses, plates, silverware . . . hell, even the bar itself—would come from his native hometown. He wouldn't call the place Tequilas anymore but Los Catrines Restaurant and Tequilas Bar, a name he toyed with for months. We would spend night after night at Tequilas trying to help him come up with the right name. It would give patrons, from all backgrounds and nationalities, a chance to feel they were back in Mexico on that magical weekend, sipping that margarita, or authentic tequila, in their Mexico.

If I'm not going back, I want to bring Mexico with me, he explained.

Nearly twelve months into the renovation project, David was growing impatient, restless. Often, whenever he visited to see how work was advancing, he found the union men on break. Once, a construction worker and his men were milling around the room when one of the workers broke a piece of the chandelier. He headed to Home Depot to buy a replacement crystal, but he was told that the piece was irreplaceable.

This is a chandelier from the 1800s. I doubt Home Depot carries that, David said sarcastically.

David stormed out of the building and plotted plan B. He wanted his own workers, which didn't sit well with a strong union town. The unions came in and shut down the work, objecting to the use of non-union craftsmen from Mexico. Ken intervened with the powerful union leader, convincing him that only Philadelphia workers would do the job.

Finally, in the spring of 2001, David called me as I curled up in my apartment near Capitol Hill, a two-story brownstone, with neighbors, Wayne and Everina, the most savvy wine lovers I'd come to know.

I lived just ten blocks from Union Station, which made for an easy escape route north to Philadelphia on Amtrak at any given time. This was one of those times. The place is ready, David said. Come see this beauty.

Tomorrow, I said. I'll be there.

It was a fresh spring day, the kind when you know that, at last, winter is definitely behind you: the trees were still bare but had a ripeness, an excitement to them. I came up on the train on a Saturday just ahead of the grand opening that Monday and found David huddled with his servers and kitchen staff. They seemed out of breath. His staff was led by Oscar, Manuel, Dino and Silvio from Ecuador.

The Poblanos outsized everyone. Their numbers had doubled, tripled, David corrected me. No one really knows anymore, he told me. Some say twenty thousand. Others put the number at thirty thousand. Still others, like the Mexican Consulate General office in Philadelphia, said as many as half of the three hundred thousand Mexicans in the tri-state region of eastern Pennsylvania, southern New Jersey and Delaware, originated in Puebla.

An earthquake in 1998 only seemed to push those numbers up. Claudio, one of David's cooks, and Mario, his assistant, pioneered a new batch of friends fleeing San Mateo after an earthquake literally broke the old place apart. They walked the equipment and furniture to the new spot. Inside, Mexico's spirit was already ingraining itself into the new building. David had hired Pascal Architects from Mexico City, whose avant-garde, modernist work was behind some of the most iconic buildings throughout the country. He hired a painter, also from Mexico City, who spent three months working on a floor-to-ceiling mural that seemed to depict, at first glance, an homage to Mexico's Day of the Dead: *calavera* skeletons jumping out to greet visitors.

But whenever anyone made that comparison, including me, David would lash out. No way, he said. That was beneath him. Mexico's Day of the Dead was one of those holidays increasingly embraced in the United States—tainted, David would say, by association with Halloween. He was more thoughtful, sophisticated, urging us to look closer. Yes, only a trained eye could understand the hidden political, anticapitalist messages behind the skeletal characters originated by José Guadalupe Posada—mentor to José Clemente Orozco, Diego Rivera and David Alfaro Siqueiros, the three most famous twentieth-century muralists of Mexico.

David's muralist was Orozco's grandson, José Clemente Orozco Farías.

I offered to help with the move. David looked at me and said no. You can't.

But I was a farmworker, I said.

Now you're just a dandy from Mexico City, a *fresa*.

Perhaps he felt sorry for me, seeing me there with nothing to do, so he sent me to the old place to make sure nothing had been left behind. David was so focused on reopening in less than twenty-four hours—so driven toward the future and occupied with the task at hand—that he didn't seem to be feeling the force of memories that swept over me like a tsunami when I stepped into the old Tequilas.

As his staff moved like an ant brigade up and down the block, dismantling the old Tequilas and setting up the new one, David fretted about where to put each item. I did my job heroically: I sat there and waxed nostalgic. This was where we had met and come of age; it became our own cathedral of confessions, angst, moments of renewal and defeat. The worn red carpeted stairs leading up a narrow passageway; an old wooden bar at the entrance and tables along the wall; a secluded romantic section beyond the bar with four or five tables, including Table 21. It was like the end of an era, the flickering of the off button on the past. So much had changed: America, Philadelphia, this block, us. All four of us, now in our forties and beyond, were but a memory of those insecure young men on the cusp of rejection or acceptance, hashing and rehashing every night in this very spot. I left and walked down the block.

I took a peek at the new place. Even in the disarray, you could see it was going to be spectacular. A day later David opened Los Catrines Restaurant and Tequilas Bar in the spring of 2001. The name Tequilas lingered.

I planned on returning that night to Washington. He would have none of that. He insisted that I stay overnight.

It's not every day that you can celebrate a Mexican from Guadalajara with real estate in Center City, he said.

He was excited about what lay ahead.

I was scared shitless for him, and worried about the friendship between David and Ken. Two different mind-sets. Both were convinced their venture would succeed, although signs pointed to disaster for our friendship.

I took the early train back to Washington and worried that David, who had already proven he could sell $20 plates of enchiladas, would now be able to fill a whole dining room three times the size of his old one. Would Philadelphia treat Tequilas like a novelty for a few months, then forget about it? More importantly, would the friendship survive?

That spring anything seemed possible.

SECTION V

Homeless

17.

The Blame Game

In Washington in early September 2001, the city was preparing for President George W. Bush's first state visit. An invitation was extended to Vicente Fox, Mexico's first opposition president in seventy-one years. That was the underlying purpose for my coming to Washington. Maybe these two men would finally shake up an otherwise predictable U.S.-Mexico relationship.

As much as the demographics of the United States were changing, Fox also wanted the nature of the relationship between the U.S. and its southern neighbor to transform, to become more equal, so that Americans and Mexicans would think of the neighborhood as a region and not two countries shrouded in political divisions. They were now one destiny. By this time more than nine million Mexicans lived in the United States, and one million Americans lived south of the border.

The U.S. government had historically dictated the relationship. For much of the past thirty years, the United States carried the big stick, pushing Mexico through Operation This and Operation That. This was particularly on the time-honored issue of drug trafficking, which was a festering issue, growing only more pressing from the U.S. perspective.

But the one-dimensional approach—fighting drug trafficking through the War on Drugs—ignored the other two facets of the problem. One U.S. administration after another failed to accept that Americans' insatiable demand for drugs was the source of the problem, along with its liberal gun laws the source of weapons for the cartels. The U.S. Treasury perennially added names to its kingpin list, freezing assets. But even that strategy didn't do enough to target the assets of criminal elements on either side of the border: Mexican drug trafficking organizations had amassed an army of "ants" who would bring back small amounts of cash—less than $3,000 to avoid detection—and weapons south of the border.

From Nixon to Clinton, the focus had been national security, and the agenda had not wavered much, except for an expansion into economic terrain with the passage of NAFTA. Nixon had talked about legalizing drugs but then ended up shutting down the border for seventeen days. In Mexico, foreign policy had been framed by a belief that governments should remain neutral toward other countries, withhold judgment and respect one another's sovereignty. It was a passive approach that didn't sit well with Fox and his advisers.

Fox knew the United States better than most. He had been a marketing guru and overseen Coca-Cola's division in Mexico. He felt comfortable with the American mind-set. He was making international news as the cowboy candidate cocky enough to think he could topple more than seventy years of single-party rule in Mexico. PAN had been steadily gaining ground in local and state elections since the mid-1980s.

However, the presidency, until that July 2, 2000, remained a pipe dream. Fox had an Irish grandfather who lived in Ohio. His grandfather stood over six feet tall and later immigrated to Mexico and owned a large cattle ranch in wealthy Guanajuato State. Fox didn't give two shits about political correctness.

Fox said what was on his mind. He had little to lose and everything to gain, and he quickly became a champion of *"el México de allá"*—of all Mexicans whether at home or working abroad. He began to fight for their right to vote using absentee ballots. His bet was that many of the émigrés exposed to true, functioning democracy in the U.S. would favor his opposition underdog party. It was a brazen message and scared Mexico's elites—by and large tied to the ruling PRI.

His time in politics had been limited to being a *diputado*, or federal congressman, followed by governor of Guanajuato. I first met Fox in the city of León, accompanied by my colleague Dianne Solis, over green chile enchiladas. He compared himself to Subcomandate Marcos, the rebel in Chiapas who had led an indigenous uprising turned agent of change and gradually became more irrelevant as the country opened up politically. During his term as governor Fox visited Texas so frequently that after a while his visits weren't making news. His public relations representatives were Texans, one born in San Miguel de Allende, the other an advertising expert from Dallas. They envisioned a Bush-Fox partnership.

In the early days of his presidency, Fox stumped from Los Angeles to Dallas and made his priorities clear to both the Mexican and American public: he wanted immigration reform and broke from Mexico's historic position of total sovereignty, neutrality and non-intervention. Fox insisted on changing priorities. He would treat the U.S. government *de tú a tú*, as equals: this time Mexico would set the agenda, or at least try to.

Now, in that fall of 2001, Washington eagerly awaited Fox. My fifteen years as a journalist came down to this moment, covering Fox's White House visit and address to both houses of Congress. I had covered Philadelphia, the border, the Southwest, Mexico and now Washington. This was my story. For days I couldn't focus on anything else and ignored calls from David, who persisted so much that I finally spoke to him, fearing the friendship between him and Ken had finally exploded and I had to play referee.

¿Que onda? (What's up?)

Guess who's been coming to the restaurant?

Santana?

I was wrong. His latest customers: the Chilean rock band La Ley. The lead singer was one of the most fascinating people he had ever met, he said. And guess what? Their new album, *La Ley: MTV Unplugged*, was sensational.

For a second I was intrigued and wanted to drop everything and jump on the Amtrak train north. Music, new tunes recommended by David, remained a weakness. I almost forgot about Fox.

I'll get to it as soon as Fox leaves, I said.

No, *güey*, David replied. I have a CD for you. Come over. Relax. Washington is making you too serious. I don't recognize you anymore. Think I preferred you in Mexico to this stale, oppressive world.

In the background I could hear Beto Cuevas moaning in one of his songs like an animal, a song appropriately called "Animal." Sounds interesting, I said.

Ken, too, kept calling me at night. David's wife, Annette, was driving him nuts, he said. I thought I was going into business with David. No, it turns out my partner is his wife.

Sorry, can we talk another night?

Fox was coming to visit Washington and I had tons of work. Angela would be visiting, too.

Fox arrived in Washington on a stunning fall day believing he had much ground to gain, especially since Bush had taken up residence in the

White House at the same time that Fox was settling into Los Pinos. The two presidents were expected to work closely, given all they had in common. As a Texan, Bush was more comfortable with Mexico than most presidents; he spoke a little Spanish and understood how immigration and U.S. policy played out in the real world. One couldn't live without the other, at least according to the rhetoric. He and Fox were rural bred with a cowboy culture in common, plus Bush's brother Jeb was married to Colomba, a native of Guanajuato. Both men boasted of straight talk.

Fox would be Bush's first state dinner guest, an honor that included a full military color guard ceremony. It was Bush's way of thanking Fox for hosting him at his ranch in San Cristóbal months before in Guanajuato.

I couldn't wait for Angela to arrive. She traveled to Washington to cover President Fox's visit for television viewers. We were giddy. I promised her dinner at Tequilas and a flight back from Philadelphia after Fox left. I had been commuting to Mexico City every month or so, determined to make the relationship work, even long distance. Angela visited as much as possible.

We prepared for that moment and planned to travel to Toledo. Fox and Bush had big plans. They organized the Amigo Tour, in America's heartland, sort of a homecoming for Fox, who recounted his Irish American roots. We had become so binational, so bilingual, that Fox and Bush embodied, for the moment, what seemed inevitable.

We were eager. We walked to the Smithsonian days before with an air of electricity. I told her I didn't miss Mexico City as much as I thought I would. The Northeast felt right. Maybe we should give the region a chance. I repeated a line from a State Department official back in Mexico City: Mexico was now a democratic country. What's more boring than that? The United States, on the other hand, was facing a demographic explosion. This could get interesting.

We'll see, Angela said. I'm just getting adjusted to Mexico City.

I ran into Carlos González Gutiérrez on the grounds of the White House. In the background I saw many of the traditional White House correspondents who normally didn't give these gatherings, a Mexican and American, that much importance. This wasn't a leader from Great Britain, Israel, or even Russia. Still, it wasn't every day that a U.S. president hosted a leader from a Latin American country, like Mexico, for a state visit. Plus Fox generated buzz. He spoke his mind in simple, plain language and one of his campaign promises had been pushing immigration reform. This could be the moment. A year before, immediately after his historic victory, he gave me his first interview as president-elect. I knew him and some of his closest advisers. I felt I belonged.

Fox didn't disappoint. He entered the U.S. Capitol with a throng of photographers and journalist literally shadowing him. Dressed in a dark gray suit and red polka-dot tie, he raised his voice to a fevered pitch in a speech to Congress, where he urged members to "give trust a chance" and help both nations re-create their relationship.

"No two nations are more important to the immediate prosperity and well-being of one another than Mexico and the United States," he said, to a big round of applause.

Like Reagan, Fox envisioned a borderless zone spanning from Canada to Mexico, much like the European Union where people cross borders as members of the same region. But not everyone applauded. Fox created an uproar within the country's media elites and reignited America's timeless and fickle obsession, immigration. Fox was bait for the twenty-four-hour TV cable news screamers.

The crux of Fox's mission for immigration reform in the U.S. came on September 5, 2001, in Washington, D.C., in the White House Rose Garden. Bush was dressed in a light-blue suit and greeted Fox in front of a gaggle of photographers.

I waited with the U.S. and Mexican press under a bright sun, with the Washington Monument shining in the background. I stood near Carlos, the diplomat from Mexico City, and wondered why he was so tight-lipped. I tried reading his mind, and kidded with him some, but he begged me to focus, warning me, *Pon atención, cabrón.* This can be real newsy for you.

Bush began by introducing his *"amigo"* Fox, declaring that the United States had "no more important relationship than the one we have with Mexico" and used a Mexican proverb, heavily accented but spoken in earnest, to make his point: *"Quien tiene un buen vecino tiene un buen amigo."* He who has a good neighbor has a good friend.

He then invited Fox to say a few words to the press corps in the garden. Fox's remarks followed: "The time has come to give migrants and their communities their proper place in the history of our bilateral relations; both our countries owe them a great deal . . . For this reason, we must, and we can, reach an agreement on migration before the end of this very year, which will allow us, before the end of our respective terms, to make sure that there are no Mexicans in the United States who have not entered this country legally, and that those Mexicans who have come into the country do so with the proper documents."

I looked at Carlos. He slightly raised one of his eyebrows. We correspondents expected Fox to come to Washington and talk about immigration reform. But for a Mexican leader, a state dinner guest no less, to stand in the Rose Garden of the White House and dictate its agenda, even setting a timetable, was unusual if not unheard-of. That portion of the speech caught policy makers and the press by surprise. He sounded uncannily like Ronald Reagan in West Berlin asking Mikhail Gorbachev to "tear down this wall."

This was David's long-awaited attempt at standing up to Goliath, to tell the powerful giant how to run its business.

Bush responded and tried to dampen the expectations a bit. He recalled his conversation with Fox the night before during the state dinner when he said he would consider ways "for a guest worker to earn a green card status. And yet I fully recognize there are a lot of people who have stood in line, who have said, 'I'll abide by the laws of the United States.' And we're trying to work through a formula that will not penalize the person who's chosen the legal route and, at the same time, recognizes the contribution that the undocumented has made."

There was a momentary hush in the crowd, bewilderment. Bush tried to downplay what had just happened. Not us, the correspondents. Veteran U.S. officials and lawmakers were aghast: Was Mexico telling the United States what to do? What about the border? No one went more ballistic than Lou Dobbs, the CNN host. The enemy finally had a face and it wasn't just those Mexicans jumping over fences or being escorted to Border Patrol vans. His name was Vicente Fox. His face was splashed almost nightly on Dobbs's show.

The shock, pleasantries all around—even the goodwill—was temporary, lasting no more than a long weekend.

On Saturday, Angela and I spent the weekend in Philadelphia, visiting David and Tequilas. We later walked with a bounce in our step along Broad Street, almost in celebration of our newfound relevance as reporters covering the binational relationship between our two countries. Maybe we could be pioneers, coin the phrase "binational correspondents"? she asked.

Why not? I said. The way we crisscrossed borders was the way of the future.

She left Sunday for Mexico City. That evening I took the last train to Washington with a copy of La Ley's *Unplugged* album in my hand. I promised David I'd listen to every word on the album, and we'd dissect the lyrics in an upcoming Cueva gathering.

Two days later, as I walked out of the Metro station, I was still glued to the CD, oblivious to the fact that the first of two planes had already struck the Twin Towers in New York City. Minutes later another hit the Pentagon. The hope for millions of immigrants and Fox's vision of a seamless North American community had effectively ended.

I remember walking toward our office building two blocks from the White House that morning—Beto Cuevas of La Ley and Ely Guerra blaring into my ears "*Sin dolor no te haces feliz*" ("Without pain you're not happy")—curious why people were staring at the clear blue skies above. I ran into a colleague with a haggard look in her eyes and asked, What's going on?

We're under attack, said Michelle Mittelstadt.

Stunned, I ran into the office, made a rapid-fire game plan with my editors. Some headed for New York City. I headed toward Capitol Hill, because another plane was supposedly headed that way. I never felt as American as I did that morning running on Pennsylvania Avenue, dodging people who were rushing the opposite way toward the Metro or to find their cars to hightail it out of the disaster that was surely headed our way.

One woman, a lawyer, said, The chickens have come home to roost, a line I dictated to my editor, Carl Leubsdorf, who simply said, Be careful out there.

On Pennsylvania Avenue? I thought.

I continued running and looked upward, horrified that the plane would zoom by me—or something worse. I was huffing and puffing after some fourteen blocks, when I spotted a man on his knees in front of the deserted U.S. Capitol. He was a native from Poland who had just moved to the United States. He had tears in his eyes when he said the United States would never be the same again. He knew, he said, because he had lived in parts of the world where suspicions, rancor and fear became part of the nation's DNA. The U.S. would become a frightened nation.

That plane never arrived, crashing instead in a remote field in western Pennsylvania.

At the end of that horrible day, I ran into another colleague who got the implications for the U.S.-Mexico relationship right away and somewhat mockingly told me: "Freddy, tell Vincente it's over. It's over, Freddy."

"Vincente" was the name Washington had bestowed on Vicente Fox, the name cable news had adopted, probably because it came out more naturally, like the English "Vincent."

The U.S.-Mexico agenda fell apart before anyone could even get his name right.

A month later Fox returned to Washington, hoping to make amends to a nation gearing up for war. Few cared to hear what he had to say. Visions of immigration reform and living in a borderless continent sounded ludicrous. The nineteen terrorists who had entered the United States with student visas, or through Canada—the very ones who had brought those towers down—also further disrupted Mexico's timeless rite of passage north, and the U.S. demand for its steady growing workforce. Security, the likes we had never seen before along the U.S.-Mexico border, was poised to dominate U.S. foreign policy with Mexico even more.

While much of the national security establishment regarded the attacks as an intelligence failure, others in the White House viewed them as a failure of border security. The post-9/11 decade was just getting started. Right on the U.S.-Mexico border, in my own backyard.

Senator Byron Dorgan, a Democrat from North Dakota, demonstrated the tenor of public discourse when he said at a congressional hearing, "America can't effectively combat terrorism if it doesn't control its borders." The U.S.-Mexico border became a national security priority in a time of widespread fear and anxiety. In fiscal year 2003 the budget for border enforcement spiked by more than $2 billion. The U.S. would soon begin building seven hundred miles of border fence under the Secure Fence Act of 2006, to the tune of $2.8 million per mile.

President Fox sought to be a good partner to the U.S. and failed. Following the attacks, the Mexican authorities detained and interrogated hundreds of people with Middle Eastern backgrounds, restricted entry of people from Middle Eastern and Central Asian countries and shared information with U.S. counterparts. Fox proposed various measures to support shifting U.S. policy priorities, but hopes for a new level of a U.S.-Mexico friendship were now dead.

The Mexican government missed a historic opportunity to help the U.S. in its healing process. The band U2, from Ireland, showed us how it's done. They played their hearts out, as the names of the 9/11 victims scrolled on a big screen during Super Bowl XXXVI in New Orleans in 2002, with the band singing "Where the Streets Have No Name" ("tear down the walls that hold me inside"), and fans waving U.S. and a few Irish flags. Once disparaged as unworthy, hated immigrants from Ireland, America couldn't see the difference anymore. At the end of his performance, Bono opened his jacket and showed off a U.S. flag sewn into the lining. There was yet hope for Mexican immigrants, I thought, as I watched from Philadelphia.

In the decade following the September 11 attacks, the U.S. would spend approximately $90 billion on border enforcement. Along the way, a number of government contractors were paid handsomely for their work on the southern border. Boeing was paid about $860 million to create SBInet, part of the technology-based Secure Border Initiative. The "virtual fence" was ultimately considered a failure and canceled. A Halliburton subsidiary by the name of Kellogg Brown & Root got $385 million to build temporary migrant detention centers.

Weeks after the attacks, I sat down with Carlos. He looked as deflated as the city does after the cherry blossoms fall off the trees. He would be transferred to Mexico City. He had taken a job no one else even thought was possible anymore, making inroads with top Latino organizations in search of a soft U.S. policy landing for Mexico. He helped set up the Ohtil Award, a recognition by the Secretariat of Foreign Affairs for contributing to the empowerment of Mexicans abroad. Ken would later win that recognition. Two years later, Carlos was back in Mexico City, putting the pieces together.

I saw Carlos's fate as my own. Binationality, the idea of having two homelands, had no place in the United States. You were either American or not. Soon, I was convinced, I, too, would head south.

I'm sure we'll see each other in Mexico City, I said. It's all about security now. All the talk about the two countries integrating sounds hollow, empty. The screamers on cable news were turning up the heat with rhetoric that sounded nastier, especially when Mexico issued ID cards, echoing that of congressional leaders like U.S. representative Tom Tancredo, who later lambasted my and my colleague Ricardo Sandoval's coverage as not "articles" but "opinion pieces."

I visited Primo in Mexico City. He had spent months trying to cozy up to the incoming Fox administration, hoping for a slot where he could return to his organizing roots, joining Mexican immigrants in the U.S. to make a final push for absentee voting in Mexico and organizing undocumented people to lobby for reform. The Fox euphoria was fading, and the president saw the vote abroad as cementing his only legacy with immigrants. He wouldn't get immigration reform, but the vote initiative would help him show he delivered. The vote abroad became a reality in 2005, near the end of Fox's presidency. But in the first presidential election that Mexicans abroad were eligible to vote, the turnout was measly.

Tequilas struggled as 9/11 transformed the mood of the country. The restaurant's clientele remained steady somehow, but David and Ken's friendship was suffering, fraying.

David was especially bothered when patrons would show up and demand a coveted seat here or there, dropping Ken's name.

I'm friends with the owner, Ken Trujillo.

Sorry, but you have to wait, *sir*.

The patron would then call Ken, who would apologize to David.

But the damage was done.

This is bullshit, David would tell me. I've worked all my life, and I will not be treated like someone's lackey. Ken never paid a penny in collateral. I'm assuming all the risk.

The arrangement was on shaky ground. Weeks after 9/11, with anthrax scares, hoaxes and terrorist fears, I tried to numb myself by watching comedian Jay Leno on television. I was really plotting my return to Mexico. Ken said he wanted to stay in the deal but felt that David had to run everything past Annette. He wanted out. I listened to him and tried to reason.

Would you like for me to talk to David or Annette?

No, that will make me look weak.

David was furious and stubborn, especially when he was mad. Ken was cooler, calculating.

Each of them would phone me, calls that would last late into the night, each one complaining about the other. I started shuttling back and forth to Philadelphia to see each of them—separately—to try to smooth things over. Amtrak diplomacy.

Finally I had had enough. I tried to convince Ken to back down.

Cabrón, this was never going to work. You two are very different people. Friends can't be business partners, at least not you two.

Yeah, yeah, I'm New Mexican and he's Mexican, mocking me.

But, Ken, it's not about being Mexican, or New Mexican. You two are just too similar. Perfectionists, more similar than different. Set in your ways. Looking for respect, more than you think. I was trying to find the right words without hurting their feelings. Both were driven by ambition and money, except David was lofty about it. Ken was not.

Please don't make me choose, I thought. Please.

Someone has to swallow their pride, I told Ken. This is about friendship—*our* friendship. You may not care, but I do.

That night Ken and I talked endlessly on the phone. I urged him to give in, throw in the towel. Be the big man.

Take the high ground. Think of your family. Their decency, their sense of forgiveness. Your family forgave those who took their lands. Let it go.

After much prodding, Ken eventually gave in, halfheartedly. I will back off, he said, but it will never be the same again, he told me. I'm doing this because you asked me to.

He sounded like the victim, yet we were all on the verge of being victims, especially David. His family home was tied up as collateral. His monthly interest rate was burying him.

No, I responded, you're doing this because you care about our friendship.

David paid Ken $30,000 to part ways.

It won't be the same again, Ken said.

And it wasn't. Something like a border had been drawn between us.

18.

Sister Guadalupe's Unusual Spirit

I said goodbye to my friends in Philadelphia in 2003 and headed for the next big story, again to Mexico City. The terrorist attacks ended my intrigue with Washington. The border was now ground zero for hatred, fear. I had little time to dwell on the differences between Ken and David.

Besides, David had other worries. He was on the brink of an emotional breakdown. Life with Annette was ending. His marriage, long in trouble because of distance and differences, was falling apart. She wanted him to become a more dedicated father, slow down, spend more time at home. David was a doting father with his kids, but too often he would arrive home late at night and the only one waiting for him was his dog, Cholo. He grew lonely, as did Annette. They lived separate lives. She spent her time at the restaurant in the morning. He spent all afternoon and evenings there. They rarely spent time together. They would eventually divorce.

It wasn't just the restaurant that kept David occupied, but tequila. David was all too consumed with his search for the magical tequila, which remained elusive. He was spending more time in Guadalajara, running into walls he had sworn for years didn't exist. Yes, America was the land of opportunity, but David always maintained that he could be successful anywhere. Mexico challenged that belief to the core. He had tried to shape himself in the style of his tequila master idols: Don Julio, Don Felipe. But Mexico's rigid, bureaucratic system of strongmen and wealthy families, where your name mattered infinitely more than your willingness to work, shut him down before he could even get started. He was drowning in red tape created by the *licenciados* and the culture of *"Lo que pasa es que . . ."* ("You see, what happened is that . . ." or a euphemistic way of saying "No way. Maybe *mañana*, not today . . .") All of these frustrations coupled with three- to four-hour lunches that went nowhere frustrated David's efforts. He couldn't even register his brand. And when he did, his childhood friend turned attorney stole the name and generated a decades-long legal dispute. David already felt he had been betrayed by Ken; now it was another old friend.

At times I was convinced David would give up on tequila and Mexico. I understood his disappointment, disillusion. But I still gave him grief.

So much for Mexico as a land of opportunity, I told David. Is this the Mexico where all is possible, or is it the Mexico where people don't even have a chance to dream? Unless a powerful senator falls in love with one of those beauty queens from Los Altos de Jalisco, where the women are striking and everyone boasts about tracing their lineage back to Spain and France. Then and only then will new roads be built in record time, as was the case of Senator Diego Fernández de Cevallos whose love saga with a much younger woman led to a brand-new highway and a front-page story in the *Dallas Morning News*.

México duele (Mexico hurts), he said. *Pinche México*. Fucking Mexico.

Now, with the highway, all he needed was the spot-on tequila.

David had been thorough in his research. He read about the Cristeros in the 1920s and how thousands of rebels loyal to the Catholic Church were hunted and killed. Many of them lived in the highlands of Jalisco where he wanted his agaves cultivated.

He learned that some of the nuns and priests fled to the United States. Had any of them come to Philadelphia? he asked, aware of the strong Catholic presence in the city. He was shocked to discover that one of the original nuns lived less than a mile from his house in Merion. Sister Guadalupe Teresa Rizo, 93, was originally from Arandas, Jalisco.

One evening David, still wrestling with the ongoing upheaval of his personal life, went to knock on the door of the convent. When a nun appeared, she sized David up and down, and said, You're here to see Sister Guadalupe?

Yes, he said. Suddenly a tiny woman appeared and asked in Spanish, *¿Habla español?*

Yes, we were clearly wrong. We hadn't been the only Mexicans living in Philadelphia all this time. Sister Guadalupe had spent more than sixty years behind convent walls in Philadelphia's main line, praying, painting, trying to forgive another country, people, place and time. The two hit it off immediately and met weekly, sometimes more often.

David needed a taster; Sister Guadalupe was from Jalisco. Turned out she loved tequila. It was a spiritual union. He began sneaking bottles into the convent to get her opinion.

David helped her build a network of friends, including me. One evening David called me and told me about her. As usual, I was skeptical about his invitation. Going to Tequilas had become awkward. I loved the new place, but I missed Ken. He'd still show up, but he clearly looked uncomfortable.

Come. You have to meet her. *Es de película.*

Was this his latest way to lure me to his bar? A tequila-drinking nun? I'll see you.

I took the train north to Philadelphia to meet the nun. I found a quick-witted, petite woman who possessed a sharp intellect, a vivid memory and an unwavering curiosity about anything Mexico today. She also had a huge, ready smile that would disappear whenever I asked about her past. I was drawn to her immediately. She became my spiritual guide, away from the Cueva, for deeper, painful confessions about a homeland tearing at the seams.

One afternoon I showed up at the convent to visit Sister Guadalupe and stayed for hours. I told her that I had once promised my parents, particularly my father, afraid for my safety, that I would never cover drug traffickers. But what choice did I have? No sooner did I get back to Mexico City than I was sent to the border, to Ciudad Juárez and Nuevo Laredo, to cover rising crime. The United States had gone to war against terrorists, but so had Mexico, only the country had never officially declared war or, worse, prepared for it.

Are they terrorists? she asked.

Call them what you want, I responded. They're destroying Mexico and the government can't do a thing about it because they're in bed with them.

I think I've seen this story before, she responded, hinting at her past.

Mexico's drug war widened as Mexico's safety valve to the United States closed. I told her Juárez was falling apart and a new era of border security had now taken center stage. The big binational story felt ancient. I was suddenly running for my life. At least I had my U.S. passport and thus a means of protection and escape at a moment's notice. My Mexican colleagues were being killed without consequences. I was trying to understand the underbelly of Mexico.

I see Mexico hasn't changed much, she told me, tears in her eyes.

But she held back, instead asking me about my family. I told her my mother planned to visit my sister Linda, a student at Swarthmore, a small liberal arts college outside of Philadelphia, originally established by Quaker Friends. I'd be honored if Sister Guadalupe and my mother could meet.

Like me, my sister had wanted a career in journalism but then set her sights even higher. She wanted to get off the sidelines and say things that I only dreamed of, scream to the world what I could only write into my notepads and publish in articles. As much as I boasted of being from the border, Linda was the only one out of all of us to have been born there. After receiving a full scholarship to Swarthmore, she was outraged that so many people on the East Coast were oblivious to what was going on in Juárez. So she organized a conference about the feminicides, the term commonly associated with the practice of the killing of women in Juárez.

She would channel that passion and create a tutoring program at Swarthmore for migrant children from Kennett Square after she experienced the same pangs of homesickness that I did. But this time from one of the wealthiest zip codes in the U.S., where Swarthmore was located. We all joined her for the conference, including my parents.

My mother and Sister Guadalupe met and talked about their devotion to God. They seemed like long-lost sisters. My mother invited her to join us for dinner at Tequilas, which she declined because of her cloister status. They laughed. In Philadelphia we walked the streets where I came of age as a reporter. At night I took my parents to Tequilas. My mother seemed uncomfortable, in awe of Tequilas, as she walked past a mahogany bar that stretched along the left wall.

This is a Mexican restaurant?

Yes, I said.

This is what I wanted to do with Freddy's. Make it elegant. But we never had the money. We never had a chance. Her eyes teared up.

I know, *mamá*, but we got by. Because of your sweat, your dreams, my father's hard work and belief in this country, I've been given a chance to succeed here. Linda is at school at Swarthmore. Monica was at the University of Texas at El Paso and now the University of Pittsburgh. Most of your sons have an education. Thank you.

She touched the chairs, napkins holders, plates.

Everything is from Guadalajara, I said, trying to ease her fears about the newness, the same fears I felt nearly two decades before. I wanted her to feel comfortable so far from home in what was once the home of one of Philadelphia's oldest families.

I recognize everything, she said. *Nuestro México.*

She returned to the convent to say goodbye to Sister Guadalupe. As I might have foretold, my mother's natural skills as a conversationalist helped to open the wounds Sister Guadalupe had carried for decades. I often see my mother as more the natural reporter, a storyteller who can weave a narrative from beginning to end, with no detail spared, and similarly make others open to tell their stories. Skillfully and without knowing it, my mother began by telling her story of emigrating from Durango. The regrets and the nostalgia.

My father stood alongside, unsure what to do in front of a nun.

Sister Guadalupe suddenly opened up and shared her own story. Slowly, with plenty of pauses in between.

She had been born to descendants of Italian immigrants in October 1910, a month before the Mexican Revolution erupted. She was one of eleven children. Back in 1917, tensions flared with the introduction of the new constitution that placed severe restrictions on the Church: the clergy were banned from criticizing the government, only Mexicans could be ordained as clergy and the Church was not allowed to own property or run private schools.

During Mexico's civil war and into the 1920s, more than ninety thousand rebels loyal to the Catholic Church, known as "Cristeros," were hunted and killed. Catholics had long been viewed by the Mexican government with a growing distrust, perceived as being more loyal to Rome than to Mexico City. The conflict escalated when the government began enforcing laws that prohibited religious expression. A bloody hunt ensued.

The conflict reached a village near Sister Guadalupe's hometown of Jesús María, tucked in the highlands of Jalisco, where a sea of blue agave plants, used for tequila, bloom year-round.

Her father, José Trinidad, was the mayor of the town and one of its religious leaders. On Christmas Day 1917, assassins arrived. The massacre soon got under way. The targets were men—anyone, really—who got in the way. The slayings took place on a cold, dreary day in the town square across from the church, which was packed with bewildered women and children. She watched the massacre in stunned silence. She ran to the window and saw what she later described as the most horrible, ugly side of humanity. The killers took the men one by one and hung them in the plaza. And to make sure they were dead, they'd stick a knife into them, tear their hearts out or slash their throats. Among those killed were her uncles, neighbors and eventually her father, who died later of injuries sustained at the hands of his captors.

Years later, at the height of the rebellion in 1929, her brother Roberto defiantly confronted the army when the government tried to prevent young Catholics from worshipping the country's patron saint, the Virgin of Guadalupe, outside the main square in Guadalajara. He was shot dead. He was twenty-one. She ended up in Philadelphia.

Another massacre in Mexico was unfolding, my mother said. And my son is in the middle of it. Please bless him.

Sister Guadalupe reached up to make the sign of the cross. I bowed to hold her frail hands, trembling.

19.

Middleman, Siembra's Rise

The farther we drove out of Center City Philadelphia, the more uncomfortable I felt.

I was cheating on David. On Tequilas. For *French* food.

I began worrying when I noticed that my cell phone service was increasingly spotty. Must have been all the trees surrounding so many mansions that was interrupting my service. I wanted to call David, let him know I was fine and wouldn't make it to Tequilas after all. Ken had made other plans. He wanted to take me to a new eatery, anything that wasn't Tequilas. We were headed to a French bistro, Paris, where the portions were sure to be small, so tiny I'd probably want a snack afterward, and we seemed to be in the middle of nowhere.

Ken kidded that I worried too much.

You're not cheating on David, he said.

He had read my mind.

This is crazy, I said. I'm straying.

Relax, he said.

Deep down, I really missed Ken's old town house in Philadelphia's Society Hill, my nightly walk to Tequilas. But here, in Chestnut Hill, I felt trapped.

We drove into Franklin Parkway, past the Philadelphia Museum of Art, where the iconic Rocky character ran up the steps to the booming tune "Eye of the Tiger." We drove slowly, meandering past Boat House Row and the winding, leafy Fairmount Park, with the Schuylkill River running alongside it.

Now Ken lived around people who weren't just neighbors but potentially big-money donors for his political run, something he talked about with more frequency. A run for the U.S. Senate? Attorney general? Heck, maybe mayor. We zoomed past the Philadelphia Cricket Club, founded in 1854, the oldest country club in the United States.

I'm a member now, he said, adding that on weekends he was taking his daughter, Maya, seven, to take practice swings at golf balls in between month-long vacations in Hawaii, where she surfed Pipeline.

Think you'll ever take me to this fancy cricket club? I asked.

No way and no offense, he said, laughing. You need a jacket for that, nice pair of slacks, and you have neither.

Next time, I said, relieved.

Nice, isn't it? he remarked, pointing to immaculate, manicured green lawns on the course and the stately mansion that was the clubhouse.

Stunning, I said. Impressive. You've really made it.

It was 2006 and I was living the post-David-Ken-feud era, learning to balance life without them together, which wasn't easy. Sure, we'd sometimes hang out, grab dinner, a tequila every now and then, make small talk. The two tried hard to keep a semblance of what we once represented: four lonely men meeting on a cold evening in Philadelphia, respectful of the fact that success of one played a role in the success of the others, although perhaps we didn't fully understand yet just how much. Ken and David seemed cool, courteous with one another, cordial. But our get-togethers usually happened only when I was around and I tried avoiding awkwardness, mindful of the tensions between them. I didn't push reunions on them, often preferring to see them separately.

The feuding was wasted time, I thought. We all needed to grow up, I'd tell them, because the day would come when we'd bow over each other's coffins to pay our last respects.

Don't be so dramatic, Ken would tell me. Stop watching those Mexican soap operas.

I was in his E-Class E 550 Mercedes-Benz, with its new smell still present, headed toward his recently purchased home somewhere in the farthest reaches of northwestern Philadelphia, the wealthy Chestnut Hill section of the city. Ken was boasting about his new neighbors, who included an array of CEOs, the heads of Comcast and Urban Outfitters, and high-priced lawyers who spent long weekends in Montauk, Long Island. In the 1800s this was the place industrialists gravitated to because summers in Center City were too muggy.

As he took on all the trappings of the Northeast elite, he didn't entirely give up on his roots. As he climbed the ladder, he also threw himself into the Hispanic community, joining the board of Congreso de Latinos

Unidos, a fledgling Latino nonprofit undergoing upheaval. Within months he had to fire the executive director amid allegations of improprieties. That began Ken's decades as its chairman. He also headed the local Hispanic Bar Association and was on the board of Community Legal Services of Philadelphia. Beyond the lure of private practice, he wanted to do public service. It seemed like he was constantly looking for balance.

At times, I felt I was part of Ken's balancing effort in keeping two worlds from drifting apart from one another. I mean, he was an attorney and I was a journalist, rich and poor, one looking to keep his clients' secrets hidden and the other on the prowl for information. But Ken wouldn't allow our professions, social status or wealth—or *lack* of wealth—to ever get in the way of our friendship. Even when I felt uncomfortable in his new surroundings, insecure around his new friends or just convinced our friendship had run its course, Ken would surprise me by reaching out to me.

I began to live in this high-end world vicariously through him. One December we crossed paths at Club 21 in New York City. Ken asked me to meet him later at the Waldorf Astoria, where Pennsylvania's business and political elite kept a tradition dating back one hundred years, hobnobbing with each other's families, drinking dry martinis and gin and tonics to the sound of Christmas carols. I did, but I froze up around his crowd, which looked gracious but smug. In retrospect, maybe it wasn't them but me: I was too insecure and unsure of myself.

Something, however, was gradually changing between us for the better. I had found my place, stepped into my own big shoes with my foreign correspondent's job, and was now moving away from Coyoacán to the neighborhood of La Condesa—a step up, I thought, to a cosmopolitan art deco neighborhood that attracted many of Mexico City's foreign diplomats, journalists, writers, actors and actresses who walked their dogs around forested parks.

Everything he went through in those years, I was there. Marriage, death, promotions. But more often than not, we had to get far away from everything, everyone, before Ken would relax. We traveled to Havana together and I saw a different Ken, the one not so driven by ambition but curious about how highly educated Cubans were living in poverty. Humanity mattered, and they were the most charming people, he'd say. But basic freedoms mattered, too, and Cubans had little to none. One couldn't work without the other. We rode in the backseat of a convertible along the Malecón, enjoying evening sunsets and the rants of Cubans. He'd smoke a cigar and we'd sip mojitos late into the night, debating with Cubans young and old about our capitalist model and how an island just ninety miles from Florida had survived so long, four decades in fact, in what seemed to us to be total isolation.

Maybe David had been right all along, I said to him, at least about how personal will, sheer determination, is key to survival.

I think Ken agreed with David, but the feud imposed itself on everything and he looked conflicted.

The best of times were in our hometowns. Wealthy life makes him humble for his roots. He's visited me in El Paso, met my family, ate at our restaurant and sent Christmas cards. One holiday he asked me to join him in New Mexico and southern Colorado, part of the necessary pilgrimage he made to reconnect with his ancestral roots. I was swept away by the beauty of the early winter sunsets over Española and Taos, reawakening a lifelong debate within me. Why did Mexico give up this land up for a meager financial return? The beauty around us seemed worth fighting for. Ken had no answer, nor did he care to weigh in. That fight was settled hundreds of years ago. He wanted to point out the beauty of it all instead. We drove north.

Laura kept him rooted in New Mexico.

It wasn't all laughs or celebrating success over the years. One morning Ken called me, devastated. He was on his way to Colorado. Pops, he said, had lost his long fight with diabetes. I waited for him to cry, but he was stoic. He wasn't the oldest in the family, yet he carried the responsibility bestowed on him by his father. He sounded so sad that we agreed to reunite in Havana or Costa Rica. I'd rather be anywhere in Mexico, but the rich had discovered Costa Rica, which became too trendy for Ken to avoid. Anywhere you want, I said, knowing how Ken would suppress his feelings, like he did everything else. But I tried to pressure him to talk, reminisce, not bottle up his emotions.

Just the fact that he was calling underscored the loneliness he felt.

We went to Costa Rica. We sat on a long stretch of beach, with seagulls flocking above us, turtles crawling on the sand, in silence. We lay in hammocks drinking beers, not saying much, staring out at blue skies before clouds moved in. I let him be.

Then morning broke along with the dam of emotions he carried inside. He buried his face in his hands. I couldn't tell whether he cried, but he began recounting everything his father meant to him: his inspiration, motivation, integrity—everything. I just listened, relieved that Ken was talking nonstop.

He didn't have much time to mourn.

Ken returned to Philadelphia and left his high-paying job, went back to public service and became Philadelphia's city solicitor. In that capacity he ran the 150-lawyer Philadelphia Law Department. His first year was spent negotiating Phillies ballpark and Eagles stadium transactions. He sued handgun manufacturers, helped plan the RNC convention and settled a decades-long prison overcrowding case. All the while, he had an urgent issue to take care of: to settle the case of MOVE, the radical movement whose Osage Avenue compound in West Philadelphia had been bombed by Philly cops in 1985. The saga exploded literally as Ken moved into his third year of law school, just over a year before I arrived in Philadelphia as a cub reporter for the *Journal*. The bomb destroyed sixty-one homes, which the city later rebuilt. But shoddy workmanship and a corrupt contractor meant that the homes had become a danger by 2000, with heating systems that released hazardous levels of carbon monoxide. The city had been in some form of litigation for fifteen years. Ken proposed an elegant if not practical solution: pay the home-owners $150,000, twice the value of their homes and moving costs. That would still amount to less than the never-ending litigation. The mayor agreed and so did most of the homeowners. The settlement was front-page news in the *Philadelphia Inquirer* and other news outlets and ulti-mately brought to end an ugly chapter in Philadelphia's history.

Serving as the city's top lawyer invigorated Ken. He would later tell me that those two years were the best "decade" of his career—that's how much he worked. Public service was his calling. The city was even more culturally diverse, vibrant. He wanted to be a player, to help navigate Philadelphia's future more closely. He could see it now: Senator Trujillo, Mayor Trujillo. I'd tease him and, like any good politician, he dodged it.

Maybe someday, he'd say. Right now I'm just too busy. But he was sure that if he ever ran for office he wouldn't do so as a "Hispanic" candidate. His last name touted his heritage. He needed white, African American voters.

Speaking a little Spanish wouldn't hurt, I'd said.

I think that's obvious, he'd responded.

Every move Ken made seemed calculated, as if part of a plan to achieve greatness, and he made emotional sacrifices in his pursuit of a goal that must have seemed unlikely to everyone but him. Every step was not just about living a life but fulfilling a destiny. He even had a German shep-herd named Tango. I really didn't see what I had to offer him. He kept up very high walls and rarely let anyone see the humble but hungry guy from New Mexico.

We sat at the restaurant Paris and drank red wine, which only made me feel guiltier.

This isn't Malbec, *chach*. This is better, he said, mocking me with a bottle of Bordeaux.

Just wished David was here.

Chach, you feel guilty about everything. That's why I'm not Catholic.

This has nothing to do with being Catholic, I thought. I just miss David being with us. But I didn't say any of that. I just raised my glass and toasted to his new life.

THOUSANDS OF MILES AWAY, David finally did what he set out to do, create the perfect tequila. After nearly twenty years, he had his own tequila. He also had a name: Siembra Azul, with a tagline: "The Future of Tradition." David wanted a name that honored the past but looked the future straight in the eye. He wanted a bottle that reflected his commitment to transparency in tequila production. His bottles' labels detailed every aspect of the production process. He even made his tequila kosher, meaning a rabbi from Guadalajara would visit the plant and offer a blessing in Hebrew. The tequila had another distinction: it was made only in winter, when a slower fermentation produces more complex flavors. I once visited the plant where Siembra Azul was being produced in traditional *hornos*, clay ovens, with workers carefully cleaning the ovens between each roasting to remove the waxy residue rather than once a week, which is the low-end standard.

I paid his factory a visit in Jalisco and marveled at what David had done. I stared at the ovens from a ledge up high, struck by the sound of classical music, a practice used by the French to make wine and champagne. Mozart and Vivaldi played continuously to reduce environmental stress via the musical waves and inspire the yeasts to work their magic on the open vats of bubbling juice.

Siembra Azul was finally being cooked.

In the spring of 2005, David had his first batch in a barrel of Siembra Azul tequila ready to debut to the world. I suggested he get away from the comforts of Sister Guadalupe and find new, eager tasters, journalists and *camineros*—a special group of journalists who gathered annually in the spirit of La Cueva to toast friendship. David rolled into the driveway of a hacienda in Mexico City's iconic Coyoacán neighborhood. Our mutual friend, foreign correspondent Ricardo Sandoval-Palos, lived in a sprawling home that featured a two-story all-glass greenhouse and three thousand square feet of lawn and garden. The greenhouse was used for receptions and was attached to the stucco house with thick wood columns inside. At the center of the garden was a terra-cotta patio under a massive elm tree.

We had decided to throw a party to midwife David's tequila into the world. We invited all the foreign correspondents, Mexican journalists and other friends. Unsurprisingly, everyone showed up and brought a friend. David and Ricardo figured some 130 guests came out for the event. It was a good thing David had come prepared. That first distillation—160 liters—was contained in a beautiful oak barrel that had been ferried by van from Guadalajara.

David brought with him a top "tequila-expert sommelier" to lecture the crowd on the intricacies of the distillation process: the cultivation of blue agave, the ancient methods used to cook and then crush the inner core of the agave's root, the *piña*. He moved on to the careful fermentation in steel vats, the aging in old Virgin American oak barrels that gave the *reposado* its golden hue.

It would have been enlightening had we not already been so drunk.

The correspondents, a rowdy amalgamation of free-drinking gringos, Brits, Irish and Mexican hacks, were pissing on the front lawn and sloshing David's precious tequila like it was Modelo beer. Primo danced the night away with his new paramour, Yolanda. Angela, in a hot-pink *rebozo* shawl and flowered dress, elegantly strolled the grounds with a tequila snifter in hand. I would keep a picture of her from that night, looking as lovely as ever, on my desk for years.

Even as the sun came up, a number of journalists were still wound up and insisted we all cram into a caravan of cars and drive to Jalisco state to spend more time with David's tequila—at the source. After all, Carlos Santana and Maná were hosting a private party for David back in Guadalajara. We passed.

Sister Guadalupe made us recount the story months later and we all laughed hysterically.

The only one missing that night was Ken, who said he was slammed with work. That was probably true. Nonetheless, we felt his absence.

20.

Hardening the Line

I'm still not sure when the loss of innocence set in—the moment I first questioned my lifelong quest about belonging to Mexico, and only to Mexico, and began to ache for the other side, feeling all the more rejected by both sides.

I was done with Mexico and eager to make amends with the United States. The violence in Mexico was exploding, first in Nuevo Laredo and now heading for Juárez, signs that the restructuring of cartels was leading to increasing violence that only seemed to underscore the reasons why more security on the border was needed. Make America safe. In the backdrop of the post-9/11 era was a country in ebbs and flows.

People still had phone books. "Social media" wasn't even a term. Facebook was starting to take hold of college students across the country, but it had yet to swallow up our free time. Smartphones didn't exist, and just a few years earlier George W. Bush had stood beneath a banner on an aircraft carrier that read "Mission Accomplished."

I was covering the growing number of people dying as the interplay of drug trafficking and demand for drugs in the U.S. began to change in both countries, for the worse. I was covering the strange saga of a U.S. informant caught in a messy situation. Mexican authorities had discovered the bodies of twelve drug traffickers in the backyard of a middle-class neighborhood in Ciudad Juárez. Documents obtained through U.S. authorities revealed that the killings were supervised or partly committed by a U.S.-paid informant who'd crossed the border on foot with a recording of the most recent killing and sat with ICE agents to transcribe the screams and agony of the latest victim before being buried six feet under the house.

Why would the U.S. government allow this to happen without raising Cain?

I flew to Washington to be interviewed by U.S. congressional investigators who followed my stories and were interested in holding hearings, but in the end none were held. Nothing was really done. No accountability, other than a few scapegoats losing their jobs. It felt hypocritical and my friends from Philadelphia came down hard on me.

I tried changing the subject, congratulating David on the *New York Times* naming Siembra Azul one of the best tequilas available. But that didn't seem to excite him. All he talked about was how bad things were getting in Mexico. Things we once overlooked—corruption and lawlessness—now permeated the country. Seemed like everyone was on the take. Residents were growing fearful of even coming out of their homes.

And you want me not to report on this? I asked. Secrets are killing Mexico. Look at me. I looked the other way, too, trying to hide the sun with one finger, to repeat a popular Spanish saying. Impossible.

¿Cuándo toca al fondo todo esto? he asked. Where is the bottom? *Está va de mal a peor.*

I cannot see it myself and I'm in the middle of it, I answered.

Why risk your life reporting these stories when nothing really changes? he said. U.S. society doesn't seem to care enough to curb their demand.

It's not just about the U.S., I countered. We can be a better country. We can set our own path and our own destiny. But, quoting Primo, Mexican immigrants need to be part of the answer.

I can understand that, but be careful. You have family, friends. Maybe you should consider moving back to Philadelphia.

And what, go into business with you? I asked, half joking.

Just take a step back, he urged.

He didn't have to tell me that. I found myself running away from Mexico every chance I got, searching for solace in my parents' backyard, where I looked for answers. We were hanging fruit for politicians.

One hot spring afternoon, David called. He sounded remorseful, not his usual cheery self. He was sad. I heard heartbreak in his voice.

I had been meaning to tell you, he began. But I know how busy you are and I didn't want to upset you more. She's left us.

Sister Guadalupe? She's dead? I asked.

She had been sick and I had been meaning to visit her.

Yes, she died last night. Went slowly, peacefully. Said to say goodbye to you and Angela. To take care. How happy she had been to meet you both. How she will miss talking to you. Hearing your stories, sharing your guarded optimism.

I didn't want to hear any more and simply cursed myself for not having made time. Always running. I got into my 4Toyota Runner and rested my face on the steering wheel, then popped a copy of a CD I had made for Sister Guadalupe with *boleros* that she enjoyed and raised the volume to Agustín Lara's 1937 song "Noche de Ronda." Then I drove away. Despite her long-term ailments and age, the news came as a blow. She had become more than a friend. She held some spiritual key for me that I hadn't found anywhere, even in the Catholic Church I was raised in. In her company, over hours of conversation and confession on my part, I felt I was in the presence of a godly person. She had prayed for me, and she had kept the violence unfolding in Juárez in perspective.

She would say, Alfredo, how's Mexico? And I would tell her, sadly, of the latest massacre.

Oh, so many more died in Los Altos, en La Cristiada, she would say—not to minimize the violence but to remind someone like me what Mexico had lived through before. What Mexicans were capable of. The real heart of the matter is that this violence is meaningless. My family fought and died for what we believed in, she said, our right to practice our religion in the face of violent government oppression. What do these young men and women fight for, die for?

To keep Americans happy and fed with enough drugs to ruin their own country, I'd say. And blame Mexico.

It's about lack of values, a lost society, she said, and sadly our values in Mexico are nothing to be proud of. Mexico needs prayer.

No, I'd tell her respectfully. We need more than prayer. We need to shame those in power, hold them accountable. We need a revolution, a bloodless one.

Prayer is powerful, she said. You should try that.

I wasn't in the mood for praying as tears welled up. I continued driving along Paisano Drive in El Paso and spotted even more shiny white-and-green Border Patrol vans crawling alongside a freshly built fourteen-to eighteen-foot fence. The agents inside seemed bored, guarding the world's most powerful country from possible terrorists, but mostly from Mexican men and women. The vans were parked next to the rusted fence that divides two neighbors, one bloodline, facing long historic tensions, protecting soaring trade headed to about a million dollars per minute, or $1.4 billion per day. The marriage between the U.S. and Mexico, the one that Primo once talked about, felt so trite, reduced to finger-pointing. Something was amiss.

I opened the sunroof to see a helicopter thump-thumping above, over the concrete ditch where what's left of the Rio Grande flows, dividing El Paso from Ciudad Juárez. If not for the ditch, you'd assume the two cities were one, a single urban sprawl blanketing a valley between two desolate mountain ranges. Only when I headed west did the border become distinctly visible, a straight brown line jutting into the scrub desert. I could see a metal fence that divided my two countries.

The vans helped block the view of the Chamizal National Memorial, once the symbol of friendship, established by a treaty envisioned by President John F. Kennedy and his Mexican counterpart, Adolfo López Mateos. Back then, when JFK went to Mexico in 1962, he noted that three million U.S. residents had origins in Mexico. By now that number was on mark to surpass 35 million in the next ten years.

How did America get this way? Seeking an answer, I looked toward the sky, a sea of blue dotted by military helicopters. Below me, toward the horizon, I saw white vans. I was surrounded by more agents, Border Patrol and National Guardsmen trying to seal the once so-called open door and giving the appearance of a new order on the border, something the country ached to see in the post-9/11 era. Ironically, the tightening of the border led to unintended consequences. Yes, fewer undocumented immigrants were crossing the border, but once across they stayed longer in their new homes, forcing many to set roots down and grudgingly wave goodbye to their Mexican dream. The Kennett Squares of Pennsylvania kept growing.

The drug trade revenue was calculated at between $10 billion and $40 billion and rising annually. New, deadlier kingpins took aim at Mexico with its weak civil society, a rule of law rarely enforced, constitutional laws that exist solely in textbooks, and greedy lawmakers who give in to temptation too easily and hide behind legal immunity. Mexicans are quick to say that the U.S. creates demand, supplies the guns and launders the money. Mexicans suffer the consequences, laying down bodies, suffering the deaths. But there is no shortage of blame coming from either direction.

Searching for answers on both sides of the border, my heart tore at its seams. The so-called tortilla curtain was now made of steel.

SECTION VI

Homelands

21.

Walls

W e left the refugee camp as the sun was setting in a pink glow over Vienna, and by the time we roared onto the highway the night was as black as shadows. I rubbed my hands together as the heat from the car thawed my fingers.

Our driver and guide, Ignác Nagy, sped us along the four-lane highway while he jammed to a mix created by his sister back in New York City. Gladys Knight's rich voice filled the car. "Midnight Train to Georgia" was the perfect song for this moment, a man leaving on a midnight train, searching for a simpler place and time.

We were on a two-and-a-half-hour drive between Austria and Hungary, composing a part of the so-called Schengen Area of free visa travel across the European Union. I strained to see some invisible line between both countries. Crossing international borders was as easy as traveling from Pennsylvania into New Jersey. The "border" was only an electronic checkpoint, no wall, no fences, no guards, nothing resembling the militarized Texas-Mexico borderline that was tormenting me.

On the Hungary-Austria border there was no one to ask me for my nationality—no gun-toting guards as along the Serbian border or on the El Paso–Ciudad Juárez frontier. No ICE helicopters or airplanes buzzing above the valley near my home in the Shadow Mountains of El Paso's Westside. No Border Patrol agents in vans circling their prey, kicking out the third world masses when the first world was done exploiting them.

Since the creation of the European Union, leaders had done what many of us had only dreamed of: created a pragmatic world of coexistence. I rode up front beside Ignác (pronounced "Ignas") with three students from the Walter Cronkite School of Journalism at Arizona State University riding in the backseat.

It was spring break.

I had walked away from journalism and was giving teaching a chance, mentoring students through Hungary, along the Serbian border and through Austria, talking to refugees in free-travel zones near double rows of razor-wire fences. High-tech watchtowers equipped with search-lights, motion sensors, cameras and loudspeakers. The scenes resonated with me. I was also here to understand my slice of the world back at the U.S.-Mexico border.

After more than twenty-five years as a journalist I was testing whether leaving my entire way of existence was as difficult as I had feared.

Was I ready for a new adventure?

Two of the students, Celeste and Sarah, were falling asleep, tired and drained from a long day of reporting on the refugee crisis. The darkness of the night made an oil refinery appear like a magical city in the dark as its industrial lights glimmered against the sky. Ahead, wind farms with blinking lights looked more like flashing red stars, spaceships preparing for takeoff, similar to the windmills straddling the California-Arizona border.

These windmills generated energy for the European Union, a conglomeration of twenty-eight nations now crumbling under the weight of migration. The tidal wave of refugees arriving on its borders and shores threatened to unravel decades of open-border policy and threaten a region with a declining birth rate.

Ignác puffed on a cigarette.

He had a small build and was handsome and rugged-looking with three or four days' stubble. He was an intellectual, with a ready opinion on just about everything and everyone. Ignác was an aspiring lawyer—a driver only as a favor to a mutual friend, Dora Beszterczey—and took pride in his near-perfect American English, the product of a few years of schooling as a young boy in New York City and many years of immersing himself in American TV, film, music and a job at a Starbucks in Washington Heights.

He seemed fascinated by the United States, asking me questions about the current political climate and what it meant to be Mexican American, something I had little interest in rehashing at the moment.

I deflected.

Wasn't this the reason I came here? To get away from the violence, the death threats, which led to a growing depression over my life, an inner fistfight over things I once believed in and now doubted.

Traffic slowed as we neared Hungary, a country that tore down its border fences when it joined the Union in 2004 to show it was shaking off its isolationist, communist history—a sign of its openness to the world. Hungary was the first among the former Soviet satellite states to take down its barbed-wire fence with Austria, creating an opening in the months leading up to the fall of the Berlin Wall for East Germans to escape to West Germany via Hungary and Austria.

The current crisis was sparked by a mass exodus of people escaping violent conflicts, or economic crisis, who were now making their way across Europe, some of them voyagers navigating with the help of stars and cell phones. The scenes were already familiar: hordes of desperate migrants from war-torn Syria, Afghanistan, Iraq and Africa, growing in population at twice the rate of European countries, as well as home-grown terrorists launching deadly attacks on European capitals. The Hungarian state became the first to re-fence its border with Serbia and Croatia in an attempt to keep out the biggest wave of refugees since World War II and preserve its way of life.

Prime Minister Viktor Orbán was the architect of the new policy. He called himself the only European leader willing to defend the continent's Christians, saying that Muslims were threatening Europe's Christian identity, framing the issue as a clash of civilizations.

Despite initial condemnation, Hungary had now set in motion a chain reaction across Europe as countries sought individual solutions, trumping the Union's common agenda, to cope with an endless stream of migrants.

The Schengen Area for the moment seemed ideal, though reality was fast closing in. The days of borderless travel seemed numbered, here and everywhere.

Border fences were going up in Austria, Serbia, Slovenia and Croatia. The very concept of borderless travel on which the union was founded was being tested as other countries followed suit. The United Kingdom, Norway, Sweden, Slovenia, Austria, Germany, Belgium, France and Denmark were all now questioning the EU open-borders policy.

At times, desperate migrants and asylum seekers flooded Europe by the tens of thousands. The parallels to Mexico and the United States were everywhere. Trains packed with migrants, many apparently seeking refuge in Germany, were stalled at the Hungary-Austria frontier for hours. Confusion ran high about how far west the trains would go and whether all their passengers would be permitted to continue traveling.

These refugees reminded me of the asylum seekers I met on a route from Tenosique, on the Guatemalan-Mexican border, to Mexico City. They clung to the top of a train known as the Beast as they crossed the Boca del Cerro bridge. Many of them were youngsters making the journey on their own, like those pouring into Texas from Central America, a region devastated by drug violence, poverty and U.S.-backed conflicts. The very same immigrants who were also testing Mexico's tolerance for outsiders. I rode alongside the train route of the Beast to interview men, women and some of the children abandoned at migrant shelters. They talked of shakedowns, rape, losing a limb and their friends who never made it, victims of coldhearted coyotes. I interviewed several more at the Annunciation House shelter in El Paso. All were looking for any sign of hope.

They risked their lives atop the Beast and faced the dangers of rape in every unknown corner of the world that led them to America. In one stop, bordering Veracruz and Morelos, I witnessed a group who stood alongside the train tracks handing out burritos, *gorditas* and water to the weary headed to the America of opportunity. They headed for the U.S., where people groaned at the very sight of them.

Hungary, like many of its neighbors, was an aging country with a declining birth rate that could use new blood, evident by a series of campaigns that included promoting dance parties for young people to meet, fall in love and start families. But although refugees had little interest in staying in a country whose economy offered so little, the Hungarian government, justifying its hard line and new fences, churned out propaganda to instill fear in residents about the strangers among them, inspiring them to regain control, revel in nostalgia and become a strong nation again, something many found attractive enough to keep Orbán in power.

Ignác's mix was now playing Michael Bublé's "Feeling Good." He wanted to impress his guests with his knowledge of American music. While her fellow Arizona State students slept, Courtney Pedroza grew animated, transformed, having for the first time envisioned her future as a foreign correspondent.

Her enthusiasm made me also realize how much, at the moment, I missed reporting after an adrenaline-fueled day in which nothing worked as planned but we, guerrilla journalists (a term I coined that day when we had to innovate on the spot), managed anyway, finding ways to meet with weary refugees who shared their stories with an unsympathetic world.

Courtney shared the story of the secret love affair of her great-grandfather, a photographer in the United States, with two families, one on each side of the U.S.-Mexico border. She had relatives she had never met, a country and a language foreign to her, a culture she ached for, a curiosity awakened by the newness around her and the growing hatred against Mexicans back home.

I listened to her, yet I was fixated on the wind turbines, silently counting them. The scene unfolding before me reminded me of Don Quixote's epic battle with a field of windmills, a battle that was all a figment of his imagination. In the darkness, the landscape looked just as surreal as Quixote's dream.

I stared at the windmills and couldn't escape our own internal battles with the so-called *others*. Ignác called this very time and place, the Hungary-Austria border, the end of the West. Globalization petering out, he reasoned, replaced by fear and anxiety.

Yet, as we left the "border" behind and barreled toward Budapest, Ignác quietly confessed he felt as if he'd been "exorcised" of his cynicism. I asked him what he meant.

Maybe it was during interviews earlier that afternoon, he said. We had talked to refugees, people with nothing but their blind faith in a better life ahead. If they could believe so deeply in hope and human brotherhood, how could he not? How could *we* not?

Here were people plowing ahead, looking for any sign of humanity and clinging to any show of kindness—people who still believed in a better world. Their goal was Germany. Some also talked of eventually ending up in Michigan, Minnesota, Nebraska or Arizona.

Their unabated hope inspired him, Ignác said, shaking his head, puffing long on his cigarette, fiddling with the music.

I felt the same way, I said, and smiled.

We all needed to believe.

These are different borders, continents apart, but sewn through with the same heartbreak.

Migrants are universal—not so unlike the men, women and children from Hungary who fled for Cleveland, Chicago, New York City and Philadelphia after the revolutions of 1848 and 1956 or who fled hunger in the late nineteenth century. Or those like my parents who over the past century had fled Mexico for reasons of poverty, family reunification, violence, seeking a better life in a country they hoped would welcome them.

Despite the heaviness of our trip, we were suddenly filled with childish hope, laughing ourselves silly as Ignác rolled down the window and blew more smoke from his latest cigarette.

By now I'd lost count of the windmills. For the first time in ages, Ignác confessed, he knew that even if the world wasn't the place he had imagined as a little boy sitting in his grandmother's living room, it would somehow get there. He turned to look at me a long time and, in a low, serious tone, asked the question I had been dreading this whole time.

What's going to happen in the U.S. with the presidential election?

As a Mexican, does this billionaire worry you? he continued.

I wasn't ready to imagine the answer or discuss it too deeply, afraid to ruin the moment. Instead, I watched the flickering yellow lights of Budapest up ahead, our journey almost at an end.

I changed the subject by firing rapid questions about his music selection. Bublé? Country music? I equivocated, wishing I had no past, just a new beginning. I was part of that Schengen Area that for the moment seemed ideal even as reality was quickly closing in, reminders of fences going up.

Ignác simply stared back, growing impatient for an answer.

OK, I finally blurted out, breaking an awkward silence. Yeah, I thought he was a cruel joke. Amusing. And once I said that, the flashbacks engulfed me, punching me in the gut. Those hurtful words made me curl in the front seat of the car as I recounted to Ignác in bits and pieces the moment when I got off the plane at Phoenix's Sky Harbor International Airport.

I was looking for Angela. We were there to interview for jobs at the school of journalism at ASU. Dean Chris Callahan wanted me to accept an endowed chair of the Borderlands Initiative. Angela would serve as a Borderlands Director for Cronkite News, teaching broadcast students to cover border issues. Instead I found Trump. Announcing his candidacy for presidency.

No way, I thought. Mexican rapists? Murderers? Drug kingpins? And maybe some of them are good people?

What the *fuck*?

I wanted to get back on the plane and return to Mexico City. I wouldn't have even considered Arizona if it hadn't been for Angela. Arizona still had SB 1070 on the books. Passed in 2010, the law allowed police to use traffic stops to check the immigration status of drivers, and advocates said racial profiling was rampant. Another section of the law, struck down by the U.S. Supreme Court, made it illegal for day laborers to stand on city streets and sign up for work on construction crews. Other states with historically racist reputations—Alabama, Georgia, South Carolina—passed similar laws.

Angela and I had managed a long-distance relationship for more than twenty years. We were looking for a fresh start, much like Mexico was looking for a new narrative, away from the violence that had marked us.

ASU offered us the opportunity to live under the same roof for the first time in a decade and prepare a new generation of journalists to cover the border, to do what we loved. We weren't sure we could walk away from our current jobs, mine as bureau chief of the *Dallas Morning News* in Mexico City, and Angela's as bureau chief for a group of television stations. She had been relocated from Mexico City to the border and was based in El Paso, a city she loved because she didn't have to explain herself to anyone in a binational, bicultural, bilingual region.

Saying no to Cronkite also meant saying no to each other.

Besides, journalism felt like a sinkhole.

Angela was facing budget cuts and shrinking interest for border stories from her employer, which had recently sold its television division to Gannett, the nation's largest owner of newspapers and a major broadcast powerhouse with television stations nationwide. The company was notoriously ruthless about its bottom line. Whether Angela's bureau job would last was just one concern. She also worried about having the flexibility to report on the stories that mattered to her, and whether she could tell every story in a less than one-minute-and-fifteen-second package, which had become the norm industry-wide.

At the *Dallas Morning News*, stories were increasingly localized and the company faced increasing financial pressure, so it was constantly looking for ways to cut costs. The Mexico City bureau was once the largest of any media company in North America, but the business had changed on us. A buyout seemed like the right thing to do.

All those months ago I had looked around the airport at the faces glued to the flat screens, watching the latest presidential candidate vilify Mexicans. He appeared to be calling for a lynching.

Trump had been fooling around with running for president since the 1980s, when I worked at the *Journal* in Philadelphia—all trial balloons that popped in the air as soon as he let them go.

It had to be a ploy to boost his TV show's ratings. The usual scapegoating, fanning the flames of fear, and Mexico, again, fit the narrative.

But blatantly sacrificing Mexico and its people, those living with and without documents in the United States, made no sense.

The candidate's words reverberated throughout the airport like a foreboding nightmare.

I continued walking, looking for Angela, assuming I was one of the good Mexicans.

I DUMPED ALL OF this on Ignác.

At first wanting to leave the past behind, but with so many contradicting emotions, all I could do was share and not offer much else: no explanations, no illuminating thoughts. Everything was just raw.

Budapest loomed before us and we all became quieter.

I rolled down the window a crack and put my hand out to feel the frigid wind. The moment took me to another time, another place: that night in Philadelphia in 1987 when I first discovered Tequilas with Primo, Ken and David.

The Danube, the longest river in the European Union, came into view. The river's meandering waters reached the Chain Bridge, which was blown up during the siege of Budapest in 1945 by the retreating Germans. On the horizon, my eyes lit upon Buda Castle and Hungarian Parliament Building.

Sometimes, I told Ignác, I feel like a tired, broken bridge, but a bridge nonetheless. I can see clearly from this corner of the world that the United States had once opened its arms to millions of us, immigrants from all over the world. A nation of immigrants. Well, now that country seemed distant, foreign and out of reach.

As the journey came to a close, I wearily made my way back home, bridging a country engulfed in fog.

22.

The Pope in a Nativist Land

I often felt nostalgic for that kid I used to be in California. The one who listened to George while loading tomato bins. As a Vietnam veteran, he felt like his own country had abandoned him. He was just another guy sent off to fight our wars, but no one cared about George after that, where he would work, what his new identity would be, a broken man in violent times. By the early 1970s George had already given up on America as he plowed his hands into her earth, just as I was getting acquainted with her. As a new immigrant, I hoped that the best was still to come. I wasn't desperate, just eager for the next tomorrow. Even as a reporter covering horrors in Mexico and injustice in the U.S., I tried to retain some sense of optimism.

And yet I couldn't shake off George, couldn't escape him. This new voice of America that felt angry and abandoned was an old voice. It sounded like George, except George wasn't racist. Or, more accurately, he didn't fear the unknown.

I put on my most earnest face at a Republican rally in Phoenix. Ignác was visiting Phoenix for a reunion and he was beside himself with excitement because his visit coincided with that of candidate Trump, the phenomenon in the flesh. I invited him to join a group of Cronkite reporters, including Courtney, to Veterans Hall to see the man himself. He grinned and jumped out of his chair to light up a cigar.

As usual, Courtney was obsessed with capturing the scene. She was in no mood for intellectual, ideological rants but offered that her Mexican grandmother was curious about whether her favorite granddaughter, born in California and raised in the red state of Arizona, supported Trump.

Was she as brainwashed as the rest of this country? her grandmother wondered.

She asked, *Mija*, what do you think of him? Courtney recalled. And I responded, I think he's awful, Grandma, and she's, like, Oh, thank God. If he wins he's going to deport me. Where will I go? Mexico has already deported me. I'll have no country.

Her grandmother had been deported by her own government when, after moving to Mexico with her family, she discovered her father's other family there. The family had overstayed their visa, prompting the government to deport them. And they did.

But I told her that she would always have me, Courtney said.

Courtney looked warily at the angry crowd and stayed close to Ignác. Oddly, she wasn't shooting photos. Instead, she looked around and took in the crowd as their chants fluctuated between a burning desire for a wall and a seething hatred for the media. Fuck you. Fuck You. Not you, Fox News. You're okay. And then proceeded to point to the rest of us and the chorus continued: Fuck you.

This is fucking horrifying, said Courtney, who I learned usually curses when she's uncomfortable. Who are these fucking people?

Your neighbors, I answered.

No, your generation, she complained. Not mine. My generation is more tolerant.

Just shoot, I told her.

I watched her disappear, her face hidden behind her Canon, lips pursed.

I picked two men in the crowd as they eagerly awaited Trump's entrance. At least they didn't appear to want to bite my head off. I turned my recorder on.

They were actually quite polite when I introduced myself as a reporter.

I said I was just interested in the fascination with Trump. In my mind, I was painfully aware that I'd never had to give these qualifiers to others, I simply asked for an interview. Now I felt I had to make them comfortable just to be around me. I felt like they had to know my intentions. I wasn't there to crucify them or humiliate them. I was only there to understand.

I told them I taught journalism just a few blocks away and also wrote occasional stories for the *Dallas Morning News*, hoping the name Dallas would suggest a bastion of conservatism, albeit fading.

It seemed to work.

What do you like about Trump?

He's got the balls to tell it like it is, said one.

He's rich, so he knows what it takes to be rich. He doesn't need to be doing this, but he believes in this country and has a plan to make it great.

Yeah? What's the plan?

We're not really sure, but he'll deliver. That I'm sure of. He's a man of his word. He's a billionaire, not a politician. He doesn't need the money. He just wants to serve his country.

I pressed him for specifics, but another man lurking in the background stepped in and asked to see my press credentials, then dismissed me.

Where were you born?

Mexico, I said.

So why would you even pretend to understand any of what Mr. Trump has to say? You probably don't like the man or what he stands for, like building a wall and making your country pay for it.

Sir, I'm a U.S. citizen and I'm just a reporter trying to understand your views. I want to understand the phenomenon.

You're looking at the phenomenon. We're not talking to you anymore.

Thank you for your time. I looked at the two other men, father and son, a minute ago amicable and open, now seemingly distant, mouthing something about building a wall. "Build the wall! Build the wall!"— so went the chilling, vicious chorus, the voice of a lynch mob, with supporters standing up in unison. *They* were the wall. Divisions formed. So rabid were the Trump supporters that he could have called for a wall with Canada and they would probably have yelled their lungs out in support.

One of the men, the father, smiled, almost apologizing for the rude behavior. I reached out to both of them and shook their hands and stood for a few seconds, maybe a minute; but clearly everyone seemed uncomfortable, so I walked back to the stage with the other downtrodden reporters and took my place, questioning my lifelong role: an objective reporter on the sidelines. As if I had no feelings. I was pissed, and scared shitless.

A succession of local politicians had given short speeches denouncing open borders. We can't be a country without borders! they screamed. The illegals, the terrorists, are pouring in.

Wrong, I thought.

I had gone on wild-goose chases already.

Once I crossed to the Mexican border town of Ojinaga to look for chemical weapons after a source and a U.S. document said terrorists were planning to smuggle the weapons through Big Bend National Park. Even though the information was based on raw, unvetted intelligence, the *Dallas Morning News* assigned me and a colleague to spend weeks investigating everything about the claim.

Other than a sheriff with outlandish claims of having found a Koran inside a motel, I found nothing. Pressed for evidence, he couldn't even find the Koran, just a photograph.

Another time Angela and I spent an entire day looking for ISIS operatives across the Rio Grande in Anapra, a poor neighborhood on the outskirts of Ciudad Juárez, following a report in the conservative website Judicial Watch that alleged the terrorist group had set up a training camp there. We spoke to dozens of U.S. and Mexican intelligence sources and locals, including a man from Chihuahua who swore he could tell whether visitors are from Zacatecas, Durango or Coahuila just based on their accents. Arabic and foreigners stand no chance here.

We got your back, he said, after calling his family in El Paso across the river that day.

Again nothing.

So many illegal aliens are taking your jobs, another said.

Wrong, I wanted to scream. Labor shortages are real. Crossings of undocumented migrants are falling dramatically.

And they're not even paying taxes.

Wrong, I thought again.

I walked around and saw another strange sight.

Diversity.

Yes, the majority of people were white, but there was also some people of color. African Americans. Hispanics and Italian immigrants peppered the crowd. One Iraqi and many white women. They were women of all ages, shapes and economic backgrounds. Two held signs that read: "Make America Great Again."

As I scanned the crowd of Trump supporters, my discomfort deepened.

Maybe we were all racist. Were we all, all of us, afraid of and angry at the unknown?

Weeks later, a black Uber driver in Cleveland left a lasting impression when he gave me his rundown of race in America.

Trump is like the white Obama, he said. It took Obama to run to get us all excited, dancing our asses to the polls. Trump is inspiring all racists to vote and speak out. He's making them comfortable enough to be themselves. Man, this isn't about jobs. None of us can find good jobs. Automation is killing mankind. It's about race, immigration. Fear of us. You get me?

I remembered that night so well: the Uber's GPS was down but he didn't want to stop by a gas station to ask another person for directions. He just wanted his signal back. However quick we are to identify problems in our society, we are much slower to actually create solutions.

Maybe this America is nothing like George's, I thought. He welcomed me with open arms, shared his heart with me, treated me just like any other brother toiling in America's fields.

But this wasn't that and didn't feel like that. This was one stuck in the past.

George's heartbreak in the 1970s had turned into anger and fear in 2016.

What are we supposed to do with so much emotion?

The digital revolution, automation in factories, self-checkout and smartphones are practically phasing us out. The jobs of the 1980s economy, even the 1990s economy, had evaporated. I thought about the travel agency in Philly where I booked my tickets to El Paso.

Gone.

But you can't rage against a machine. A computer. A smartphone.

So people started to rage against others. Preferably someone who didn't look like them. Mexican. Muslim. Asian. African American.

I was engulfed by that same rainbow of humanity during Pope Francis's visit to Philadelphia, when the faithful walked, celebrated and cheered the first pope from Latin America. He had introduced himself to America as the "son of an immigrant family" and as a "guest of this country, which was largely built by such families."

The faithful came from all over the world, particularly Latin America, Mexico. They brought along their children, who on behalf of their parents asked for a miracle: immigration reform to keep them together as families in uncertain times. I remember walking down the Benjamin Franklin Parkway, looking for people to interview.

Fear of sharing names was palpable. I noticed workers from the restaurant industry. They greeted me but waved me off when I asked for comments.

La cosa esté caliente, said a waiter who worked at a fish restaurant and who, like most, was also from Puebla.

I saw a couple I had met earlier, Reyna Trinidad Morales and her husband, Camilo Hernandez, both from Puebla. They worked at the Italian market on Ninth Street; their clients included David, who liked their homegrown squash blossoms. The couple also sold peaches, tomatillos, and jalapeño peppers, all planted in their backyard in Camden, New Jersey, just as they had done back in Puebla.

They hadn't been in Mexico in more than twenty years. They weren't legal. They spoke with a sense of urgency. Some in the family were U.S. born. They feared separation.

On that day, the couple marched for about an hour with some sixty other Mexicans from Camden, across the Benjamin Franklin Bridge and later near Independence Hall. They came to pray for protection from President Obama's deportation machine.

Reyna cried as the pope stood outside Independence Hall next to a statue of George Washington and called for tolerance toward America's immigrants.

"You should never be ashamed of your traditions," he told the crowd.

I watched, taking notes for a story for the *Dallas Morning News*, mesmerized by the Latin American pope speaking Spanish in front of the building where the Founding Fathers signed the U.S. Constitution.

"Do not forget the lessons you learned from your elders, which are something you can bring to enrich the life of this American land," he said. "I repeat, do not be ashamed of what is part of you, your lifeblood."

Francis exhorted newcomers to be "responsible citizens and to contribute fruitfully to the life of the communities in which you live . . . By contributing your gifts, you will not only find your place here, you will help to renew society from within . . ."

Americans, he added, had forgotten that the most famous refugees in all of humanity were Moses and Jesus. They had forgotten the foundations of their own country.

"Do not forget what happened here over two centuries ago," he said. "Do not forget that declaration which said all men and women were created equal."

The next morning David and I took a peek from his window and observed throngs of the faithful, children walking with parents with signs calling for amnesty, family reunification, and an end to deportations.

I rushed down and met a Mexican family traveling from North Carolina. They said they believed in miracles and not necessarily in voting. They didn't have the "legal documents" to vote.

I looked them up and down and thought of the untapped potential in front of me.

How fragile and defenseless they were.

You shouldn't have made the trip, I thought. Instead, you should be saving for the trip back to Mexico. Because you'll be deported.

Our home is back in Mexico, the father said. We're just here working, raising our family, but we're going home one of these years.

There were so many Catholics, so many Mexicans, I figured—so many who believe in miracles—but few who actually do the small things, like vote, to improve their lives. I took down their names, and promised I would look for them someday back in their towns in Guanajuato.

Behind me were rows of nuns walking one by one, their hands in the shape of a cross. I stopped and looked at them closely, hoping that Sister Guadalupe somehow got a free pass from heaven that day in order to return to earth. I missed her so much and wished she were still here with us, at least for this one day.

23.

Thirtieth Aniversario, the Celebration

The yellow cab pulled to the rain-drenched curb at Rittenhouse Square in Philadelphia. I leaned in close to the window, looked at the bare trees, still haunted by memories of my old stomping grounds.

I was so lost in thought that I forgot the cabbie, who now turned his head to make sure I knew what I was doing. I had already changed my destination and asked him to drop me off at the corner of the square. He told me this was the first cold day of the year and my destination, Tequilas, was still two blocks away.

A chill rain poured and I didn't have an umbrella. He seemed more worried than annoyed that I insisted. I opened the door and immediately felt both the cold and rain, faint reminders of the weather when I first came here so many years ago.

Let me drop you at the door, man, he offered.

No, thanks, I said, paying the fare. I'll walk from here.

The truth was I needed to be where I was, in this square, at this moment.

I had a romantic attachment to the park with its towering trees, curving pathways and bright restaurants and condos lining the streets around it. I missed those Quaker-gray, quiet, low-key evening walks.

I didn't mind pulling my black carry-on a few blocks in the rain for another reason: I felt nostalgic and wanted to savor the walk there alone, remembering the first time I found the spot, Philadelphia, my shelter from *whatever* the storm. This square was also where over the years I'd come to think and marvel at the city's old-fashioned beauty and its history.

I pulled my blazer up over my head and walked against the rain.

If ever I needed friendship, Tequilas, some Quaker love, it was now.

I rolled my carry-on bag past old and new landmarks via Walnut and made my way across to Locust, revived by memories of Le Bec-Fin, which was no longer here, victim of the aging demographics that doomed the original as a relic in the first place. I was now headed to Los Catrines Restaurant and Tequilas Bar, still Tequilas to me, now one of the oldest restaurants in Center City and part of the Mexican food dynasty that had doubled in size from the late 1990s.

It was September 29, 2016, the thirtieth anniversary of the opening of Tequilas.

I wanted to remind myself of what it felt like to be a reporter back in Philadelphia, especially when I no longer felt like one, and that absence created a deep emptiness within me. I was still mourning the loss of Juan Gabriel. A few weeks earlier I drove up and down Locust and Walnut Streets, just minutes after the announcement of his death, listening to his remake of Creedence Clearwater Revival's song "Have You Ever Seen the Rain," blasting it as I drove aimlessly.

Creedence Clearwater Revival? asked a musician on the corner of Walnut and Twelfth.

I shook my head.

Fogerty? he asked, increasingly perplexed at the sound.

No, Juan Gabriel, I said.

Who?

Juan Gabriel. He was just a Mexican whose music knew no borders. He died today.

I waved at him and smiled. It was the only American song Juan Gabriel ever sang, at least that I could remember. Of course, he did it in Spanish. I kept on driving and searched for "Para Qué Me Haces Llorar" on my smartphone.

On my way, I ran into Mexicans from Puebla: waiters, dishwashers I had met over the years in Philadelphia. I knew them only by their nicknames. One of them was Gordo, a veteran server from Puebla. So many Poblanos lived in Philadelphia that he and his buddies organized the annual "Puebladelphia," a parade to mark Cinco de Mayo in an old Italian market and to promote Mexican traditions to a younger generation.

Will you join us this year? Gordo asked.

Count on it, I said, and kept walking.

Another waiter was El Rojo. He still carried the emotional scars of a traumatic journey north: days spent in the Arizona desert and then locked for nearly four hours in the trunk of a car along with five or six other men between Nogales and Phoenix in the summer heat. Once in Phoenix, he spent the next three days in a *coyote*'s holding cell, waiting for documents—fake, or borrowed, he didn't know—and a plane ticket to Philadelphia to reunite with his friends from San Mateo. They had fronted him the $3,500, money he'd pay back.

His story was the norm. These were Mexico's wayward sons and daughters—waiters, dishwashers, cooks, throughout Philadelphia and New Jersey—who would become adults overnight and could only dream of ever seeing their parents again, of walking their hometown streets once more.

I asked him: What do you remember?

I was just a boy, El Rojo said. I didn't know any better. I didn't think I'd make it through the desert, much less in the trunk of the car.

He looked away and gazed out in the distance. I'd known El Rojo for nearly a decade, back when he was wide-eyed, with an easy smile. Small in build, with curly hair, El Rojo was now a bit pudgy, the shine in his eyes wiped away, his face seemed drained, with a pallor to it.

He came originally for adventure, to make some money and return home. So much enthusiasm, hard work; he wasn't so sure anymore.

Sometimes I don't know where home is, he said quietly. Sometimes when I walk in Philadelphia I close my eyes and imagine I'm back in San Mateo, and it's easy because so many of my friends are here. That's how I get through the day.

He has no plans to return to Mexico. Maybe tomorrow. Not now.

I'm nostalgic, he said. I miss my family, my town. But I can't imagine making three or four dollars a day, depending on the peso-to-dollar exchange rate. That was the daily average salary in Mexico. More than thirty years after NAFTA, Mexico's salaries remained virtually the same.

I approached Tequilas. Outside the brownstone, four waiters on ladders were putting the final touches on an anniversary sign that read: "We are humbled for the opportunity to have served you for 30 years. Join us in celebrating the past, present and continuing into the future."

Thirty years. Tequilas had survived, thrived, outlasted three generations, from the Boomers to Gen X, millennials and now aiming for the Gen Z. Above the building an American and a Mexican flag flapped in the rainy breeze. A sign hung below the flags: Tequilas, Alta Cocina, Est. 1986.

Appropriate, I thought.

In these times of uncertainty, a nativist era, Tequilas was a reminder of Billy Penn's spirit of inclusiveness.

David's achievement did not come without bittersweet moments for everyone on both sides of the border. Efren, the first Poblano in Philly, died. Nostalgia overtook him and he hit the bottle too hard. After a few years of living in the U.S., his liver gave out on him. He was buried in San Mateo.

I thought about Efren as I pushed the door open into Tequilas, where the dimmed lights spoke of warmth and I could almost taste the *pastel de mousse de chocolate* and smell the *chile habanero* and feel the burn of tequila *blanco* in my throat as I lugged my carry-on through the door, headfirst.

I looked for David, spotted him rushing past the bar and chairs, busy seating customers, telling each one how happy he was to serve them. I smiled as I observed the latest exchange and recalled Ken. Tequilas, he once told me, was the place to hold on to the Latino pieces of us that were slowly being chipped away.

Outside, people walked by with their heads down against the weather, fighting renewed rain. Among them I spotted Ken. He was glued to his cell phone, looking for a place to park. I felt relieved he was joining us. The rift between him and David seemed permanent but he made sure to be here this night. Nothing felt truly the same again between them. As long as we didn't talk about the deal gone wrong, we were fine.

I heard David's voice, his heavy Mexican accent still firmly in place, interrupting my inspection of the murals. Good evening, sir. Table for one, or would you like to sit at the bar?

No mames, güey, I shot back—the Mexican equivalent of "Don't BS me, dude." *¿Qué pedo, güey?* (What's up, dude?) It's me, *cabrón*.

David laughed. He knew all along and was just giving me shit.

Güey, he said, mocking the years and shades of gray in my hair. He quickly took my bag. I didn't recognize you. I see you're aging well, and even becoming wiser. But you're still two hours late.

He was even grayer, his hair practically gone; even his salt-and-pepper mustache was thinner. But he still wore the mustache with distinction. We wanted to believe we had more charm to compensate for our fading looks. He could still lure me into confessions of the heart with just a sly smile.

David handed me an unsolicited glass of Siembra Azul Blanco, now available throughout the eastern seaboard and from Texas to Illinois to California and even Australia. For Tequilas' thirtieth anniversary he was launching his latest tequila, Siembra Valles Ancestral. Siembra Spirits was no longer limited to the highlands of Jalisco but also the lowlands, known as the valley of tequila. He was also producing mezcal, Metl, reuniting the agave spirits family. Long lost in tequila's shadow, mezcal had for centuries been the socially frowned-on drink of Mexican peasants, even more than tequila.

David had formed the Tequila Interchange Project with a group of bartenders and academics nationwide to lobby the industry to promote sustainability and best practices and increase consumer awareness of the process of making tequila and mezcal. The goal was to do the impossible: rewrite its narrative and get the story right. With mezcal they had a chance. He brought TIP members on trips to Jalisco, Oaxaca, Michoacán, and taught them the history. Until recently mezcal's contact with the outside world was best described as nefarious. Visitors to Mexico had long seen it as a kitschy souvenir: a drink with a worm inside, the kind you hid in the kitchen cabinet following that beach vacation. Yet mezcal was an even more sophisticated drink than tequila, he said.

I disagreed, but what did I know?

David's newest business partners, the family of Don Emilio Vieyra, a former *bracero*, and his son Emilio Jr., born in Houston and now living in Michoacán. For years the family had peddled mezcal as underground bootleggers. Now that American appetite had soared, the family had joined with David. Mezcal exports more than tripled to two million liters in 2016, with 63 percent of those exports headed for the United States.

You should try mezcal, he insisted.

I like my tequila. It's smoother.

Alfredo, how many fucking times do I have to repeat myself?

Shit, I thought. I did it again. David, like Primo, rarely if ever uses such language.

I don't like you using that stupid word, "smoother." There is no such thing as a smooth tequila. You are only degrading the integrity of a spirit that is loaded with complex flavors and aromas extracted from the soil, from the heart of Mexico's divine land. The agaves could spend up to a decade exposed to the elements absorbing the nutrients, the flavors, receiving the sun's energy.

Damn, here it comes: the bat story.

The agave plants are evolving for millions of years in coexistence with one of the most effective pollinators in the world: bats, he said. Yes, bats, you heard me right.

Over the past twenty years David had been working on a bat project with Rodrigo Medellín, who is considered the world's leading expert in bat conservation.

This is authentic tequila, the real stuff. Not smooth, he said, taking a long sip. Fuck that.

At times like tonight, I still pined for the old place, back when he wasn't so preachy and I could still say dumb things. The original Tequilas was now an Irish pub. I missed being greeted by the altar to the Virgin of Guadalupe and the photos of leftist revolutionary leaders.

The new place still captured the spirit of the old, in murals depicting a left-leaning, anti-capitalist, anti-globalization message. But it was too sophisticated for me, so grandiose and elegant, you still had to study the paintings to capture their meaning. Orozco's grandson's masterpiece captivated guests nightly, although, like me years before, few understood the larger political subtleties.

The *calaveras* on the walls of Tequilas were dancing, ranting, raving, fighting caricatures of the Mexican Revolution—wicked political and cultural satire. The style revealed David's disdain for Mexico's political elite, the corruption within an insidious government and the struggles of the working class.

The mural projected those traditional images and others: Mexicans marching north to seek a better life, a new beginning; limousine neo-liberals signing away the country's future and what was left of its sovereignty by signing NAFTA; two former presidents, Mexico's Carlos Salinas de Gortari and George H. W. Bush, tossing Mexico's poor to the vultures of capitalism. Another wall depicts a church, with Saint Michael stepping on the throat of a feathered snake, the pre-Columbian god known as Quetzalcoatl. In other words, taking Catholicism to task for destroying pre-Columbian religions.

I sat at the bar, staring at the murals and waiting for Ken. I then spotted Luis Tuz, one of my favorite waiters, and waited in anticipation. Luis is a Mayan performer and a former circus trapeze artist from Yucatán. He usually quiets the place with flare. He walked by casually with four margaritas on a tray atop his head. By twisting his head ever so slightly, he made the margaritas turn round and round. Customers clapped. Luis would twirl again. Again. And again. He loved the attention, acknowledging the applause with a smile.

By Mexican standards, Luis was born into a wealthy hacienda in Yucatán, with maids and workers on the premises. His father was a landowner who made a living from selling pumpkin seeds and raising chickens, turkeys and rabbits. Daily, workers would dry chilies, corn, bean and squash to take the seeds out. In the evenings, as the sun set, vendors, all women, would arrive to purchase bags and sell them in the open market the next day. Despite the profitable business, Luis was curious about the world. He joined a circus owned by a family friend and traveled throughout Latin America. Between seasons he worked as a waiter in Cancún alongside his pal Oscar Serrano, a native of Chiapas, learning the habits of Americans and enough English to get by. A consummate talent scout, David was tipped off by his former boss in Cancún, who raved about Oscar's work ethic. Oscar was married to a woman from Philadelphia, making David's recruitment easier. Once at Tequilas, David admired his leadership and saw similarities in their old-fashioned schooling, their belief that customers came first. He liked him so much he later promoted him to general manager, his right-hand man, as David dedicated more time to Siembra Spirits.

Oscar called me one day and said, You want to work in Philadelphia? Luis remembered. We can use your talent here.

Yeah, said Luis, but I don't want to go there illegally. At the age of seven he was bitten by a snake on his left ear, forming a welt that required a plastic surgeon to remove it. His nose had already been surgically repaired after his brother sliced it by accident with a machete. He still has scars. Now he feared an agonizing death, trapped inside the trunk of a car or an overheated eighteen-wheeler. No way.

Luis had a job in Cancún. He could afford to wait.

He waited three years for a work visa that Tequilas paid and sponsored. He arrived in Philadelphia three months before 9/11.

Homesick, he then spent thousands of dollars to move his own family, which included his wife, sister-in-law, brother and nephew, to join him in Philly.

Like most immigrants, he didn't wait for America to assimilate his family. Lucky to be living in Philadelphia, he took them to the national monuments, bought them a Spanish-to-English translation book and played tourist guide on rare days off.

On weekends he worked in the early morning at a food cart that specialized in *tacos de barbacoa* alongside his sister-in-law, a specialist in *barbacoa* who owned the business along with her husband, Benjamin Miller. The food stand generated a cult-like following, with customers flocking from as far away as Connecticut, New Jersey, Delaware and around Philadelphia. Even in the dead of winter, clients, wearing Eagles jerseys, hats and scarves, stood in line for a taco. The humble operation was so successful, the family soon opened a restaurant and got even more attention. The magazine *Bon Appétit* named South Philly Barbacoa the sixth best restaurant in the United States in 2016.

We're all very proud of the recognition, he said. It wasn't easy. But this place—he pointed to the murals I was looking at earlier—has set the example. It's set the bar high.

Philadelphia has been so good for him that he's now saving to buy properties in South Philly, near the five-block Italian Market, long the magnet for fresh produce and restaurants with an Italian flavor, now dominated by Asians and Mexicans. On Ninth Street, the newest entrepreneurs sell pizza stuffed with mole sauce and picadillo. The place is not far from Geno's Steaks, whose owner once threatened to withhold service to anyone not speaking English. The sign "This Is America. When Ordering 'Speak English'" is about the only thing that survived his death.

Ken finally walked into the bar, and David and I flagged him over. The bartender, Vincent Martinez, or Vinny, greeted him with a glass of wine. Ken put on a valiant face. His lifetime political ambition had ended prematurely and the stress of running a mayoral campaign had taken a toll, an unforgiving experience but understandable. He pulled out in order to care for his ailing mother. As the *Philadelphia Inquirer* reported, Ken spent two years planning his campaign for mayor. His candidacy was an anomaly. A Latino who hired New York mayor Bill de Blasio's campaign manager and a former federal prosecutor who called for mandatory body cameras on police, Ken could not be easily pigeon-holed.

On the other hand, at times he looked like an insider who didn't quite connect, political strategists told me. Had he come too far from his poor working-class roots? The *Philadelphia Business Journal* touted him as the business candidate and simultaneously weekly newspapers hailed his progressive platform.

Ken saw no irony.

His view was that you could do well and do good. In fact, if you did well you better do good. A first-time candidate, Ken raised eyebrows with supporters like Governor Ed Rendell helping him raise more money for the race than any other candidate and building a formidable campaign war chest.

Five months before the primary it looked like his campaign might take off. Ultimately, a lifetime of political ambition ended prematurely.

He needed to spend much of the next few months at his ailing mother's house back in Colorado. Eileen Trujillo was diagnosed with kidney cancer and would eventually die. She ended up spending nearly a year living with Ken, Laura and Maya while undergoing chemo and surgeries at the University of Pennsylvania.

Ken had also long been fighting diabetes and was careful about everything he ate and drank. Diabetes had taken his father prematurely and he vowed to beat the disease that is so prevalent among Hispanics.

As I saw him make his way through the crowd at Tequilas, I gave him a hug.

Glad you made it, I said.

I wouldn't have missed this, he replied.

David ordered us a round to get the night going.

I, David, Ken, Hilary, Dick, John Carlano, the people from *Esta Es La Noche* back in Guadalajara—everyone had arrived. Raul Garcia, one of the early Mexican pioneers in 1972, Steve Larson, a physician who founded Puentes de Salud, an organization that for three decades provided affordable health services for immigrants. Everyone except Primo.

It had been months since anyone had heard from Primo, not since he told us he had been barred from setting foot in the United States again. Primo had placed all his faith on change in Mexico—change that had come painfully, slowly, and been woefully incomplete. He was so confident in Mexico's future that one day he walked into the U.S. embassy to give back his green card. The U.S. officials were shocked: they could not understand why he would take such a drastic measure.

Wasn't he there to *renew* his green card?

Primo insisted he had no use for it anymore. In his late sixties, he said his most productive years were behind him.

One of the agents looked at him and said, Mr. Rodríguez, do you know, people die to get this green card, and you're giving it back.

I know. I used to be a human rights activist in Chicago and Philadelphia.

Then they added, Sir, you can also apply for a U.S. visa. You know that, right?

They thought he was a crazy old fool.

Primo finally told them he was there to send a message: he wanted to be a minority within a minority—those who gave back their green cards. He left feeling happy he had gotten some attention.

The agents hardly noticed and took the card.

Weeks later Primo had second thoughts. He returned to the embassy and this time in a more humble tone asked for a special visa to travel. He realized that the Mexico he really longed for was up north, not just south of the border.

There was another problem that complicated Primo's life. He had succumbed to his theory of foreign interference and had penned a column for the influential leftist Mexico City newspaper *La Jornada* crying foul on many of his compatriots fighting for democracy, claiming that the U.S. government was bankrolling one of the more influential NGOs, *Alianza Cívica*. And he pointed a finger directly at the head of the organization, his college buddy Sergio Aguayo, who made his name as a democracy promoter. Aguayo didn't take the criticism lying down. He sued for defamation in a Mexican court, and he won. Primo was ordered to pay 400,000 pesos, a fortune he didn't have. In the end, Aguayo suspected Primo of being a bitter man who never succeeded in Mexico as he thought he would one day. Primo shrugged off Aguayo's criticism and claimed the suit was based on a lie. Nonetheless, he ended up paying 32,000 pesos, a loan from his brother. The legal dispute still shadowed him.

This was a sore topic, one we rarely talked about, particularly on this celebratory night.

Salud, he said over the telephone. *Adelante jóvenes y galanes.* To another thirty years.

We raised our glasses.

We walked into a back room of Tequilas, big enough to accommodate the large crowd that had shown up and seemed in no hurry to leave. It was an eclectic crowd, with the wealthy—lawyers, accountants, doctors—standing next to immigrants, some without papers. All were happy to witness a milestone. David stood up and thanked the crowd. One by one the clients told stories of their first time at Tequilas and why they continued to come to celebrate anniversaries or birthdays or just to say hello to David. David thanked his family and introduced the next generations, Dave and Luca, his grandson. He saved special words of praise for Ken: without him, we wouldn't be enjoying that evening at the building on Sixteenth and Locust. Ken didn't expect the words of appreciation.

That was nice of David, he said afterward. Very classy.

David later came over and gave each of us a long hug. For a moment old wounds were healed, although Primo's absence made the night feel incomplete, a blank page in a friendship that now spanned nearly thirty years.

24.

Arcadio's Legacy

We tried to beat the sunset, driving through the desert, shadows falling over green mountainsides, signs of a good rainy season. The rivers looked full. Trees, ocotillos, green. Standing tall. I drove with my parents and brother to San Luis de Cordero. Juan's Mexican wife, Yedsmin, accompanied us. He hadn't been back in years. In fact, he couldn't remember the last time he was here. My mother thought bringing him here for *Dia de Muertos*—Day of the Dead—would be good for Juan, revive old memories, help him understand where he came from and how far he'd come.

Juan, an accountant, liked the drive, although he had his hand over his head because the sun was now setting, blazing into our faces. He, too, worried about the sun going down amid an expansive, lonely landscape that made us feel even more vulnerable with darkness just hours away. With Chapo in jail, and the order he once presided over in disarray, the *Chapitos* were running amok, extorting people, asking for protection money without repercussions from higher-ups. In a country with weak judicial institutions, sometimes the best lawman is the criminal himself, but Chapo was behind bars back in a federal prison near Ciudad Juárez. We had zoomed by hours earlier.

For the moment, my parents had bigger things to worry about. This was the perfect time to get my parents away from the toxic political environment that kept them awake at night and glued to the television. As we got closer to our birthplace, I noticed my parents' mood change: they wondered whether leaving Mexico had been the right thing to do.

¿Valio la pena? my mother asked.

So many years later, they now questioned their own sacrifice. I downplayed their worries, and turned the volume higher on Juan Gabriel's

"Siempre En Mi Mente," or "Always on My Mind." Juan Gabriel's music had always been a sure pick-me-up.

Not this afternoon.

The scandals that followed Juan Gabriel's death, particularly fathering children that he allegedly refused to recognize and abandoned without any protection after his death, irked her. He fell out of my mother's good graces. I turned off Juan Gabriel and switched to boleros by Javier Solis. But my mother spoke above the music.

I had no choice but to face her insecurities and questions.

See, this wasn't my mother's first choice. Or second, or third. Becoming immigrants and moving to America was more than just leaving all that she knew behind, because leaving Mexico also meant that my mother would betray her father, Arcadio.

My mother was only eleven when the prolonged drought in San Luis de Cordero, Durango, derailed all. The drought had been going on for so long that locals still couldn't remember when it actually started: in 1950, 1951 or sometime after. But they remembered the clouds—dark, low-hanging clouds that swirled in magically and made promises they didn't keep. The clouds threatened rain, teasing farm and ranch families into a frenzy of hope and prayer, then disappeared, leaving them disappointed, kicking dust and pondering the future.

The farmland turned to desert that seemed to stretch forever. Rivers turned to dust. Cattle strained to feed. Arcadio Jiménez worried about one hundred or so head of cattle that foraged between San Luis de Cordero and Piedras. They were starving, no pasture to graze. He grew so desperate to feed them that he took to tying a tank of gasoline around his waist and spraying the *nopal* cactus with flames to burn off the thorns the way a chef might crisp a crème brûlée and make them edible for his cattle. One late morning the hose broke and doused him in gasoline so fast that he caught fire and was engulfed. His son, Chey, thirteen, watched his father scream in anguish. The frightened teen threw dirt on him to tamp out the flames before getting him to a clinic in Gomez Palacio more than one hundred miles away. But Arcadio was so badly burned that the doctors told him to go home and die with his family. Arcadio put on a brave face and ordered his children to stop crying as he drank *sotol* and *tequila* to ease the pain. He died a day later. A band showed up for his funeral and played his favorite waltz, "Recuerdo," as he was buried next to his mother. His eldest daughter, Herlinda, led the funeral processsion. Here comes Arcadio Jiménez, she screamed, tears streaming down her face.

I was born on my grandfather's birthday. I should have carried his name, Alfredo Arcadio, but the family preferred just Alfredo—more modern, and less of a reminder of those dark days that helped define our destiny. My grandfather was a stocky man with light-blond hair, light skin, green eyes, a dimpled chin and a bushy mustache. He beamed confidence, with a deep nationalistic pride and an unwavering belief in the Mexican Revolution. Two of his brothers—Manuel and José—had fought alongside Pancho Villa, who was said to have buried treasures in the area. To this day, locals keep digging.

His death changed everything and everyone's destiny. Arcadio's life-long lesson to his three sons and three daughters was tested.

Don't ever leave for the United States, he'd tell them. No guest-worker program was good enough for them. No promised job north of the Río Bravo would ever fulfill them. The U.S. works you to death and then deports you when they're finished with you, he'd say. No mighty dollar was worth breaking up the family. We might be poor, he'd tell his children, but we'll always have plenty of food. If you try hard enough, Mexico will provide. Mexico had boundless possibilities. The United States was beneath their dignity. Mexico was home.

With his death came cruel reality.

He was everything, Mama said, and we were everything to him. Once he died, we were on our own, facing drought and poverty.

My mother, Herlinda, took a job as a maid for the rich in Gomez Palacio and sold *marranitos*, homemade sweetened bread shaped like pigs, on weekends. My uncles took over the cattle business but the drought defeated them, too. Eventually the push north began.

Esperanza and Hermila, Arcadio's daughters and my *tías*, were the pioneers. Esperanza was "abducted" by her then boyfriend, Antonio, a *bracero*, who lured her to Ciudad Juárez, where they married. They headed for the fields of California. She was sixteen, so homesick that she urged her youngest sister, Hermila, to join her. Hermila left her job cleaning houses in El Paso and with the help of a tourist visa headed to Dos Palos, California, to join Esperanza. She planned to comfort her older sister and return home. But once in California she met her future husband, Jesse, the Vietnam veteran turned labor contractor, and the first Mexican American to marry into the family. She joined her husband in the business, recruiting workers from Mexico—especially her hometown. Esperanza and Antonio did, too. Together, the sisters followed the fields and did their part in emptying out San Luis de Cordero.

My mother's resistance ended when her first daughter, two-year-old Lupita, drowned a day before Easter in 1964. Mama was inconsolable. She was still mourning her father and now she had lost her only daughter. Herlinda had a voice that the whole village remembered; with the tragedies, she stopped singing. Now she longed for a new beginning, a chance to reunite with her absent husband, Juan Pablo, also a *bracero*. He was the kind of man my grandfather railed against: those traitors who didn't give Mexico a chance. But the dollars my father earned and sent home paid for a good life in our town—a small store my mother ran stocked with dry goods and toys–and we always had enough to eat.

Did we do the right thing? my mother asked as she looked at the road ahead of us. To sacrifice everything that we knew—was it really worth it?

She echoed the same question we—David, Ken, Primo and I—had been asking for years. The question that consumed me from the moment I left El Paso all those years ago: Was the sacrifice worth the price?

We were nearing our hometown, now just over the hills. San Luis was an old silver mining town that was originally influenced by Spaniards, French and even a few Swedes during the mining boom of the late 1800s and early 1900s. Locals who remained there survived by ranching and raising corn and cattle.

I could see glimpses of a line of tiny homes with fresh coats of paint, pastel colors, some signs of life but still ghost towns. Kids ran on paved streets, darting here and there. Donkeys strayed and left their turds just ahead as neighbors sneered, holding their noses with their fingers. Some giggled. New houses under construction, homes ordered built by immigrants who left years ago and now, as age crept up on them, wanted to return. This time they seemed serious.

Things up north didn't look so promising anymore. They loved you when you were young, healthy, with a strong back to pick the crops, wash dishes, make beds, take care of the elderly, their children. Now they were aging, some more than others, growing restless and scared of this so-called nation of immigrants. More homes were under construction. In the distance, roosters crowed.

My mother had had enough of roosters, she said. She had had enough of Trump, whom she likened to an orange rooster. We all laughed except for my father.

We crossed a creek that at one time had been a lush river. That was before the drought took it all away, all they had, before all the lofty talk about rule of law, back when Mexico seemed to have a plan for economic development, to create jobs and not depend so much on the mercurial neighbor up north. We passed cattle, cornfields. Just across the creek, my mother said, was a ranch my father owned. He raised cattle there. Fig trees lined the area. Corn from our fields roasted in the afternoon glow, mines surrounding us. Occasional raindrops fell. We still have a picture of my uncle Delfino holding on to his tiny nephews—I'm in the picture by that creek—while my father picked cotton in Texas and sent money every two weeks like clockwork.

In hindsight, everything was great, I told my mother.

Oh it was, she said. Really was. Without a doubt.

I gave her the benefit of the doubt.

My mother turned to my father and again asked a question that perhaps had no real answer, having much deeper implications than we could understand at the time. Was it worth it? she asked again. Was it worth selling our home? Giving up everything?

My father didn't want to face the hard-hitting questions. He just wanted something to eat.

In order to give her some kind of solace, Juan admitted that it was too early in the trip to respond to such questions. He wanted to walk the streets of his hometown, take in the moment, before he could really wrap his mind around everything. My mother wasn't satisfied. She turned to me.

Yes, Mama, thank you and Father for making that decision. I again listed the accomplishments of my siblings, her children, grandchildren, great-grandchildren. None of this could have happened without you.

Then I asked her: Was it worth it for you?

The silence between us spread like the growing distance, the gaping gulf between the United States and Mexico, the sliver of river that was meant to unite us, not separate with such vastness between us. She didn't respond immediately, her eyes locked in the past, with San Luis de Cordero closing in on us.

We left only with our memories of the past and hope for a better future, she said.

She asked me to put on a Juan Gabriel song, one that sang to her pain, to her nostalgia, and no one—no matter what Juan Gabriel did or didn't do—could do that better than "Juanga." I went for the jugular, "Amor Eterno," the live version. We grew silent as San Luis suddenly appeared in front of us. Two little boys in shorts chased a ball.

That's you and Juan, she said, back when you were boys, before our lives were disrupted.

I turned to my mother, who was now teary-eyed.

Was it worth it, Mama? Your sacrifice?

She didn't reply. Instead, my father spoke for her.

I don't like that you make her cry. Turn that song off. Put on something happy. A *norteño* song.

No, my mother said. I want to hear the song. Freddy always knows what to play for me.

When you're young you leave everything behind, my mother said. You think something is better up there. You forget everything you believed in, everything you grew up with, and you don't ask questions. You work from sunup to sundown, wiping that sweat off your forehead. And for what? And now I'm back and I ask myself: What if we had stayed here? Put all that sweat, all that effort, here in my San Luis and done everything to make this a better place. Not one that looks forgotten, lost, abandoned.

I wanted to tell her that we probably wouldn't have amounted to much. Maybe I could have become a merchant and eventually would have been forced to pay a bribe to some criminal group, become part of the informal economy that now represented more than half of Mexico's overall $1.046 trillion economy. Or the best scenario, I could have saved enough money to go up north and maybe found myself a job as a waiter or busboy in Philadelphia, where the tips are generous, I thought.

But why break her heart even more?

Instead, I, too, grew teary, wishing I could assure her.

I drove slowly, careful not to run into a burro or a kid chasing a ball. I reached back and searched for her hand and played with her fingers as I did when I was a child and I tried every trick to wean myself back from California to these lonely streets where the boys nonchalantly kicked a ball, running down the streets like Juan and I did all those years ago. Back then my mother would take the remittances sent by my father and head for Gomez Palacio to shop for linen so that my paternal grandmother, Mama Rosa, could sew us new shirts, shorts with our initials stitched on them. We had a pretty good life as kids in Mexico. We walked the dirt streets of San Luis de Cordero, Durango, as though the streets belonged to us.

We're here, I said.

We passed by my grandmother's house, where I was born, in the shadow of the steeple of a church that my mother once cleaned.

We never forgot, I reminded her.

Yes, but at what price?

As the sun set, we arrived at Uncle Toño's house, not far from the cemetery where my grandfather Arcadio, along with Nina, Mama Rosa, my sister Lupita and others were buried.

A DAY AFTER ARRIVING, we drove in separate cars to visit cousin Toño's restaurant in the town of Nazas some twenty miles out. My mother and Yedsmin rode with Lucy and Alfredo, my mother's niece and her husband. They once worked in California and Chicago. My cousins were in another car. I drove with Juan and my father, passing San Juan de La Boquilla, a tiny village with no sewer system, just a few miles from San Luis de Cordero.

That's where I was born, he said.

Some fifty years after he had left this land, my father was in a rare mood to reflect, to break his silence. His past had caught up to him. He was spirited, talkative. He said he dreamed of becoming a drummer, until California and the easy dollars got in the way. He played in just about every *quinceñera* and wedding he could, even during his periodic visits to Durango. Los Pajaritos was the name of the group, a five-member band made up of every brother: Alfonso, Edmundo, Ardolio, Delfino, Eutemio and him, Juan Pablo. He was the best drummer anywhere, though he liked the dance beat more. Sometimes my uncle Mundo played the saxophone with so much passion that my father would leave the drums behind and grab the prettiest girl and break out and dance, annoying his brothers, who needed the drumbeat. He didn't care. Couldn't give a damn. He loved women, booze and music. He saved enough money to buy a boom box he carried in the back of a pickup truck while riding with his friends and fellow *braceros*, Chuy Banda and Isidro Borrego, the volume blaring, playing *norteño* music—Los Alegres de Terán, Los Cadetes de Linares, Los Relámpagos del Norte—till dawn.

The band broke up because they all headed north. With the exception of two, all his brothers ended up working and dying in the United States.

Those were probably the happiest days of my life, he said.

I put a song on for him, "Un Puño de Tierra" by Antonio Aguilar, a song about a wanderer who wishes for his remains to be returned home someday.

His eyes seemed to dance. He broke into a story. Got animated.

You and your mother think calling *ese cabrón* a rooster is funny, he said.

He was referring to Trump.

No, I corrected him. Not just any rooster, but a mango rooster with the face of a monster. Those are Mama's words.

Sometimes old roosters are the most dangerous, unpredictable animals you'll ever run across, my father explained. He pointed to his scar on his forehead. His hand movement commanded attention.

Every evening, as the sun set over the mining hills of La Boquilla, my father, then twelve years old, oversaw the rounding up of the family goats, donkey, roosters and chickens. He then had to make sure all the critters were inside a wire cage to protect them against prowling coyotes.

In the morning he'd check for eggs, carefully treading around the rooster, who once poked him with his beak when my father wasn't looking. The rooster was old and stubborn. Nightly the rooster would run away from his grasp, flapping his wings as if taunting him. My father would usually let the rooster go and wait for him to return to his chickens. One afternoon the rooster didn't come back. My father, tired of waiting, left to hang out with his friends and did what kids did then: throw rocks, whistle at the girls walking by, try not to get in trouble. When it came to spanking, his mother, Mama Rosa, was known to have a firm hand, even if she rarely used it on her spoiled child, the youngest one. A kid showed up and told him he heard a rooster crowing, alone on a ledge, sitting atop a rock.

That's your rooster, Juanito.

Juanito left to retrieve the rooster, afraid that losing him wouldn't sit well with Mama Rosa.

The rooster was on the edge of a ledge.

Juanito noticed that the only way to reach him was by jumping over a rock. He didn't want to disappoint his mother or raise the ire of his brothers, who would surely never let him forget that the beloved golden rooster died on his watch. Juanito jumped as far as he could and fell just short from the rooster. He landed on his forehead and bled heavily. But he got up and picked up the rooster. The boys laughed as Juanito walked home cradling the rooster.

The old rooster almost killed me, he said now. I thought I had him cornered and he outfoxed me. That's why roosters make me nervous. They're self-absorbed.

On our return to San Luis, I drove with my cousin Alfredo, the undersecretary for the state's agricultural department. There are so many Alfredos that we call him "Alfredin." He was eager to show me that this was a different Mexico, a place of opportunity. His wife, Monica, joked that the town was collecting donations and putting the money into a piggy bank to break later and help the United States pay for Trump's wall for both sides to piss on.

Let them build the wall, Alfredin chimed in. Just don't take away trade, the economic, cultural integration. Breaking us up; is that even possible?

Esta cabrón, I replied.

More than one million head of Mexican cattle were being exported to the United States, he explained as we passed by a new cattle processing plant.

No, the jobs didn't pay high wages, he said. Nonetheless, the impact would be felt for generations to come.

Compared to your generation, *primo*, kids don't grow up thinking the U.S. is their only option, he said. People just want opportunities, something good enough to stay home for.

Put plainly, more Mexicans preferred walking across a street or driving a mile to a job than set out on an unpredictable journey. Criminal groups shaking them down. Americans looking down on them and constantly threatening deportation. Plus, following the U.S. recession, jobs weren't as plentiful. And now the leading U.S. presidential candidate hurled hatred toward them.

Dozens, if not hundreds of Mexicans are returning to San Luis de Cordero to reclaim a tired, thirsty land. Some want to retire here. Others just had enough of the U.S. Signs pointed to homes under construction all around us. Two of them belonged to cousins in California and Colorado, both descendants of Arcadio and Nina. Ruben's house was halfway built. He thought so many more Mexicans would follow him south that he even thought of opening a business to sell concrete blocks, convinced the exodus from the U.S. was about to explode.

What's changed, Alfredin pointed out, is that teens aren't planning their future around the wants and needs of the United States.

Alfredin was one of four, the youngest, with political aspirations. His parents, Lucy and Alfredo, operated a meat market and raised cattle. Like many Mexicans, their family was divided between two countries. Their daughters all lived in Colorado. Noemi taught at an elementary school in Longmont.

Noemi contradicted her own brother about a Mexico rising. She was born in Chicago, although she lived in Mexico longer than anywhere else, certainly more than in Colorado. She saw Mexico as a place to visit family and celebrate holidays but not much else.

Anytime I thought of why we ever left Mexico, her words resonated with me.

Mexico, she once told me over dinner in Longmont, is a beautiful, precious rosebud. It just never opened up for us.

Now her youngest brother talked of a new nation. He sounded as determined and committed to his country as his great-grandfather and Toño, his grandfather.

We can't give up on Mexico, he said. A nation of more than 120 million people, Mexico represented the fourteenth-largest economy in the world, and second in Latin America after Brazil. But corruption remained endemic. Crimes unpunished still hovered over 95 percent. More than half of the population lived in poverty, and more than two hundred thousand had been killed in a drug war that showed no end in sight. Given Mexico's higher inflation rates, wages in Mexico were lower now in real terms than when NAFTA took effect. From 2001 to 2015, Mexican hourly wages in U.S. dollars grew by only 9 percent, less than in the United States and far below the 120 percent increase in Brazil, according to a Moody's report. The minimum wage was still roughly $3 a day. To make ends meet, the majority of Mexicans held a second job, many of them in the underground economy.

Alfredin knew all that. He had heard the numbers. He didn't need me to repeat it.

I've never liked the United States, Alfredin said. For me it's a place to visit, not to live. This is home and we're the answer, he told me one night as his proud grandfather looked on, complaining of weak legs, natural for a man of eighty-five.

Tío Toño wasn't doing well.

His daughter Mary arrived two days earlier, having left her job cleaning the homes of the elderly back in Longmont. She took two buses to get here, one in Denver and another from Juárez. It took her nearly twenty hours straight to be with her father.

Both countries are aging, she told me over *semitas* and the sound of a burro across the street. The sky was brightly lit with an array of stars that seemed to fall low from the sky. A chill wind swirled in a town filled with immigrants honoring their departed friends and family members during Day of the Dead festivities. Mary's customers back in Colorado, all of them elderly, called nonstop. They missed her so much, they were collecting extra money to entice her back and make sure she stayed through Christmas. No one wanted to be alone during the holidays. Not them. Not her father. She was torn.

That evening her daughter, Gris, called to tell her that her cancer had returned. Mary broke down in front of her father and said she had to go back.

Perdón, but I have a life on both sides of the border, she told him.

My uncle Toño looked at me and said what he feared the most was now true. The women had picked up and left, leaving the old like him alone.

Everyone flocks around their mother, he said. You did. Once the mothers leave, the community dies.

I listened to him as I was glued to game seven of the Cubs-Indians World Series with a weak antenna signal. He watched with me before falling asleep. His snores interrupted the game, which went into extra innings. When the game ended, a cheer from the town disrupted the silence of the starry night, a reminder of ties to the United States and, especially on this night, to Chicago.

25.

Lessons from Israel

The Mediterranean Sea rose in the early dawn, glistening from an encasement of land almost completely covered by waters that stretched from the Atlantic Ocean, separating Europe from Asia, seas once used by travelers and merchants during ancient times.

On an early-morning flight from New York City, Tel Aviv was a sight that incited a gasp of excitement.

I was there to search for my ancestral roots—if any.

David and I had long obsessed over what, if any, ties we had to the Middle East. Ken was, too, but for different reasons.

He had long suggested I go to Israel to understand political lobbying via expatriates abroad. Roberta Jacobson and John Feeley, two top State Department officials and close observers of the Mexican American experience and diaspora, had also suggested I study the model. Roberta didn't appreciate her own roots until she lived in Argentina, where she learned not just her family history but the key to political empowerment. No, Mexican Americans weren't as homogenous as American Jews, Roberta cautioned, nor were they Cuban Americans, fierce and united in their opposition of Fidel Castro. Nor were they assimilating as fast and with as much ease as John's Irish and Italian ancestors. However, Mexican Americans represented an untapped voting potential with a remarkable political empowerment and Israel, the Jewish model, provided valuable lessons.

It was while working in Argentina that Roberta came to understand her Jewish roots, meeting survivors of the Holocaust.

To me Jewishness is not a nationality. It's a religion, she said. We may be Zionist, but we're not Israelis and that's the core we share anywhere in the world. That sense of core, I tell her, is missing from the Mexican American community.

Americans with roots in Mexico is such a vast group—their numbers surpassed 35 million—that it's harder for them to form a sense of community, be part of a core group.

For years I was obsessed with my family origins. Corchado. Jiménez, my grandfather Arcadio's last name. Where did the names originate? I once traveled throughout Spain seeking information about the family, chasing leads from Madrid to Seville, where I first learned that Sephardic Jews, many with the name Jiménez, fled the Spanish Inquisition. The people I met kindly claimed me, but answers were incomplete. Eventually I forgot about the search and let the journey take over.

I thought Israel could provide some direction or answers to my Sephardic Jewish roots. But I was also really there to understand the growing hatred of "others" and make sense of the bloodshed over religion. I didn't adhere to any religion.

My late evenings with Sister Guadalupe taught me about my own mysterious spirituality, questions that lay deep inside. I couldn't really identify with any man-made institution, ruled by tradition and habit. But I felt spiritual in my own way. Why else would I spend so many nights inside the convent when all the nuns had gone to sleep?

Beyond those moments with her, I couldn't really find myself in the spiritual realm. There was no answer, no arrival in some illuminated state. It has always just been a private dialogue with someone out there, somewhere.

So I guess I was really here hoping to reconnect with some infinite spring of hope to resuscitate my depleted reserves. Find answers.

We traveled through the tiny strip of land of about eight million people, journeying through the stunning Mediterranean and Dead Sea, a region that was no stranger to the world stage or ancient conflict. But the visit to Israel only underscored the complexities of the conflict and raised questions.

An outing to Palestine was forbidden. Several of us asked to visit, but the organizers refused, saying they couldn't guarantee our safety. Besides, the purpose of the trip was to give us a more comprehensive, deeper understanding of Israel, not its conflict with Palestine. For some of us, the tour felt incomplete. Israel's 1948 takeover of Palestine territory reminded us of lands our own ancestors lost following the 1848 U.S.-Mexico War under different circumstances. The eighty thousand Mexicans who lived under the Mexican flag in territories that stretched from Texas to California weren't displaced from their land like Palestinians were. But a parallel remained constant. Mexicans lived alongside a powerful neighbor walling itself off to keep Mexicans out and keep America safe. Trump promised a bigger wall and, if elected, would take a page from Israel, a country that in addition to a wall has armed guards to keep terrorists out.

We walked through the Holocaust Museum in Jerusalem, with Aharon Erich as our tour guide. He was a short, balding man with wisps of white hair. He stood in front of a video screen with black-and-white images projected on it. It was 1938 and Hitler was parading through streets flanked by cheering crowds. Aharon told us how Jews were banned from working in public services and prohibited from studying at universities. He told us about the 184 calories rationed per day during 1940 to starve people to death.

He talked about how the museum was made up of official documents from the Nazis. They documented everything, he said, reminding me of the importance of journalism, storytelling. So many stories of horror and hope, so well preserved. For generations the young and old have experienced or heard them told firsthand, he said. The museum served as a warning for the growing hatred across the world, Aharon said.

Before we left the museum, Aharon asked for one favor.

He asked all his visitors to remember one of the victims. She was less than one year old.

The night grew darker. And the reason we were really there in Israel became clear. The 2016 presidential election and the nefarious role of Russia.

As we boarded the bus, we were greeted by Avi, our guide, whom I immediately suspected of being a spy. He cuddled a web of conspiracies that usually involved Hillary Clinton. Hillary was an alcoholic. The Russians had proof. Hillary this, Hillary that—and making the case about why Trump was America's savior. At the moment, our patience was low. The anger rose inside me and as it did with others like Macarena Hernandez, a former editorial writer with the *Dallas Morning News*. We started challenging him; voices were raised.

Avi, we just walked out of the Holocaust Museum, Macarena said. Do you know what Trump has called Mexicans, us, the very people you want to create an alliance with? Rapists, murderers, drug dealers and maybe a few good people?

I looked to Avi, turning my recorder on, and added: This is the man you want to lead the United States? The man who offends the people you want to align with? How about taking a stand, showing solidarity for common humanity? You invite Mexican Americans to tour Israel, and you don't even know what Trump has said. You don't know who we are. You get a Spanish translator for us, who by the way we love, but the point is half of us don't even speak or understand Spanish well.

Avi looked surprised, a bit sheepish.

Israel clearly understood statistics, as in the demographic growth of Latinos. But Avi made it clear that at least this group from the Israeli government understood very little about us. The bus fell silent. We were all emotionally drained. As evening descended on Jerusalem, we had dinner with a woman named Hanna, who was Avi's boss.

I told Hanna about how the museum made me question things differently, raising alarms and fears about Mexicans. She stressed the importance of learning history, the Holocaust.

Hatred can wipe out societies, she said. I lost most of my family and sixty years later the pain eats away. You'll be fine if you learn the lessons from the Holocaust.

I stayed up that night, into the wee hours of the morning, watching CNN, and I couldn't help but imagine an apocalyptic outcome. Mass deportations. Chants of "Build the wall!" With those vivid, graphic images of the Holocaust Museum still fresh in my mind, I thought of the words I had just read, words from Martin Niemöller, a prominent Protestant pastor who emerged as a public critic of Hitler displayed on the museum's wall.

Over the years the words have stirred controversy as they have been printed in varying forms, referring to diverse groups such as Catholics, Jehovah's Witnesses, Jews, trade unionists or Communists depending upon the version. Nonetheless his point was that Germans—in particular, he believed, the leaders of the Protestant churches—had been complicit through their silence in the Nazi imprisonment, persecution and murder of millions of people.

I, too, had heard the words before, but never in such a powerful fashion, in a place where the past seemed all too present. I turned off the TV, rolled into bed and looked up the words and mouthed them slowly, hoping to make them part of my vocabulary:

First they came for the Socialists, and I did not speak out—
Because I was not a Socialist.

Then they came for the Trade Unionists, and I did not speak out—
Because I was not a Trade Unionist.
Then they came for the Jews, and I did not speak out—
Because I was not a Jew.
Then they came for me—and there was no one left to speak for me.

Were we making the same mistakes?

THE REALITY SHOW HOST loomed like a threatening menace with echoes of the past we thought had been buried.

Now I sought more than roots. I needed a deeper understanding of political empowerment.

Over generations, Israel has nurtured bonds to overseas Jews. Over the past twenty years Birthright Israel and countless other programs have brought half a million young American Jews on free summer trips to Israel for an intensive course of indoctrination. They've also brought in athletes, musicians, actors and writers—even Hispanic writers like us, thanks to hundreds of millions of dollars provided by the Israeli government and charities from around the world, particularly the United States.

All are expected to return as ambassadors for Israel—or better still, in the case of Israeli Americans, devotees who will immigrate to help in a demographic war against the Palestinians, a strategy that younger generations of Jews increasingly question.

They're expected to be Israelis like Bracha Katsof, our young American tour guide whose father's organization back in New York City and Philadelphia helped fund the trip.

I spent long hours listening to her story and her quest to merge her two worlds. As long as she could remember, she said, she lived a life between oceans and couldn't imagine being just American or just Israeli.

She had to be both, especially in a world that seemed to be shrinking against mounting forces.

Her journey, she said, was a way to keep her two countries close to each another. She hoped to find love, a Jewish husband, hopefully in the Holy Land, to keep her culture, language and religion intact.

I could imagine tens of thousands of young Mexican Americans returning to Mexico. Yet Mexico's outreach efforts were laughable, pitiful, limited to the Institute of Mexicans Abroad with only some four hundred visits by community leaders and academics, a number that was on the decline.

THROUGHOUT MY JOURNEY IN Israel, I remember thinking once, twice, three times on whether or not to make good on a promise I had made to my mother. She wanted me to be baptized in Israel.

There before me was the Jordan River and an African woman singing in her native tongue as a priest beckoned me to the middle of the water.

I put on a white gown and left behind a bag with my shoes, socks pants and shirt inside.

I didn't know how to swim, but I took a leap of faith and followed the priest from Africa, as the woman sang by the edge of the river on a hot afternoon.

The priest pushed my head backward and I pushed back. He tried again and again. I pushed back.

Have faith, he said. Let yourself go.

I don't know how to swim and I'm not a man of faith, I said.

As the sun shone above my head, the African priest laid his hands down on me.

You are here, he said. You must already believe. Otherwise you wouldn't be here.

No, if I didn't want to believe, I wouldn't have found myself along the Jordan River wearing a white gown, searching for any opportunity for rebirth and a prayer against growing nativism.

I looked at him, smiled and nodded my head. I rolled my head and waited for him to push me back. He did and I felt light as the water carried me.

I didn't feel a zap of enlightenment. My head didn't feel numb by some crown of infinite light falling upon me. No, it was none of that. I walked away with a sway in my step, feeling no difference other than the fact that I had allowed myself to believe, even as my fear of the unknown was growing.

26.

The Wisdom of Doña Lidia

M y mother said we're all birds who one day return to their nests, David told me as he walked me to what he said would be my room, on the third floor of his new apartment in Guadalajara, complete with a private bathroom and a spectacular view.

The United States just doesn't feel like home anymore, he added. He was coming home. He really was. All those talks back in Philadelphia, pure fantasy, really, and he was finally here, easing back to his old life in Guadalajara.

David didn't invite the entire neighborhood to his housewarming party, but he did have a lot of friends there, including some bartenders from the United States. All gathered to toast David and Marité, just weeks after their marriage, with barbecue and fresh guacamole and quesadillas. The three-story apartment also served as Siembra Spirits' international office.

I remember David quoting her years ago when his mother, Doña Lidia Piñera, lay dying of pancreatic cancer in the living room of his home back in Merion. She said that we were nothing more than migrating birds and that David's journey to America was one that would eventually bring him back home.

He believed it now more than ever. His father had died, though he didn't know details, not even when, or how.

Is it really that easy to come home again? I asked.

How many tequilas have you had?

Haven't had a damn thing to drink other than Topo Chico mineral water.

I'm coming home, little by little. And that's that, he said. At this moment it just feels right. You should, too. The U.S., the one we knew back when we were young in Philadelphia, had been a farce.

Primo, too, thought Guadalajara was ideal.

His mother had died and he traveled regularly to look over her home in La Perla Tapatia. He looked fit, a bit sad, but still danced the salsa twice a week, Fridays and Saturdays. He was still addicted to photography and mostly, even if they were no longer a couple, maintained an unusual friendship with Yolanda, his last and longtime girlfriend.

Every Sunday, he said, they share a meal and a watch a movie with her son, Leo, and his girlfriend, Jessica. It's a good life, a simple one.

Ken was there, too. He was still reeling from the fact that Pennsylvania had turned red during the presidential election, but he was on the mend. He sounded hopeful again. It was time to turn a new leaf, plant a new seed—literally, he joked. Ken told me he was looking into applying for a medical marijuana license in Pennsylvania.

I wasn't sure what to say, other than to point out that nearby was a bar where I used to meet up with a U.S. investigator, a veteran FBI agent named Arturo Fontes.

One night we drank an entire bottle of tequila there, I told Ken, as Fontes dryly predicted that the bloodshed from the drug war in Mexico would be eternal.

I now looked back and also thought of the falseness and the duplicity of it all. U.S. agents so coolly blamed Mexico for the drugs and violence and rarely, if ever, acknowledged the role of U.S. demand and enforcement and the web of deceit. I thought of Marco Antonio Delgado, my classmate at UTEP. An El Paso lawyer, he turned confidential U.S. informant and was later convicted of conspiracy to launder as much as $600 million for a Mexican drug cartel through a myriad of ways, like setting up a scholarship at Carnegie Mellon University, where he served as a trustee. Marco once invited me to meet his friend, now Mexican president Enrique Peña Nieto. I was late for the meeting and missed my chance. Once he was captured by U.S. authorities, Peña Nieto's office vehemently denied any connection to Delgado. Marco was now rotting in jail, facing up to twenty years in prison for wire fraud and money laundering.

I told Ken about a series of stories I had worked on with a colleague of mine, Kevin Krause, for nearly a year about how U.S. agents were entangled with criminals and had triggered massive violence in an entire region by splintering Los Zetas and the Gulf Cartel.

This, thanks to a plea bargain that the U.S. government made with the top leader of the Gulf Cartel, Osiel Cárdenas Guillén. He agreed to plead guilty in federal court to drug dealing, money laundering and the attempted murder of U.S. agents. He promised to turn over more than

$50 million. He received a relatively light prison sentence of twenty-five years. Once Los Zetas smelled the rat, as in U.S. informants, all hell broke loose. Hundreds of people died. Cárdenas's personal attorney had been gunned down at a shopping center in Southlake, Texas. With his death, secrets were soon known.

All this information, I said, was thanks to a source, Gary "Rusty" Fleming, who once worked undercover for the FBI and infiltrated a wedding hosted by Los Zetas' top leadership. He posed as a photographer and took pictures of the Treviño Morales family, brothers Miguel and José posing.

For weeks Rusty called me, telling me he had some "goodies" to share. We met at a downtown bar in Dallas and he wouldn't let go of a box he carried. Finally, after catching up and plenty of small talk, he said, "Fredo"—a term he used because he could never say "Alfredo"—"you might want to have this."

As long as there is no human head inside, I said, taking the box.

Might make for some interesting reading, Fredo, he said. Make you see why people are dying or fleeing Mexico in mass numbers.

The box was heavy, filled with documents he had obtained that showed that the U.S. government knew full well what the consequences of their decisions would be. Yes, they got information that would lead to a major takedown, but their actions would result in massive bloodshed in Mexico. Could the DEA have done more to protect their informants and their families? The U.S. government had blood on its hands. But of all the stories I had written on violence in Mexico, of all the times Mexican sources implored that I reveal the U.S. hand in Mexico's drug war, this was the first time I had it all on paper: barely redacted U.S. government documents proving exactly what U.S. agents did.

After the stories ran, a federal court-trial ensued. All pleaded guilty. No secrets were spilled, other than the ones we wrote about. Thereafter, Rusty tried reaching me several times.

I was thinking of that meeting that never took place with Rusty. He had called me weeks before, saying he needed to talk. It was urgent. On the day of our scheduled meeting, as I prepared to leave for the airport, his wife called to tell me Rusty had died, days after his car ran off the road and crashed, right in the middle of the highway, headed for El Paso.

Foul play?

No, she said, I don't think so.

He had been overly stressed, he told me once. Wasn't sleeping well. Sometimes he was a bit paranoid. He had lived in the fast lane, too. He knew sleepless nights, hard drinking and he was now paying for it, he feared.

As Ken and I sipped tequila, I told him that poverty was no longer the dominant force pushing people north. It was increasingly security fears pushing the middle class from cities like Guadalajara. They were the new immigrants.

And now—hundreds, thousands, tens of thousands of deaths later—Americans wanted their marijuana to be legalized.

I'm sorry, I told him. I'm not blaming you, or pot, cocaine, meth, heroin. There was and will always be something else, something new, for criminal organizations to control so long as Mexico remains a pathetically weak-rule-of-law country and the U.S. maintains this level of demand.

Marijuana is bread and butter for Mexican cartels, but a low-margin product. Legalization in the U.S. cut into their profits, as they increasingly turned to heroin and meth. Demand for heroin had soared in the U.S., thanks to widespread abuse of prescription opioids, while methamphetamine was cheap to produce and easier to smuggle through legal ports of entry. As Ken talked about new opportunities with legal marijuana, I listened and cringed.

I'm just thinking of the dead, the faceless victims, I told him. I saw the human consequences of the drug trade in Mexico up close. I had been watching in horror for too many years.

I felt so wrong for believing the U.S. served as the best example for Mexico. The horror kept spreading across Mexico. As the Mexicans saw their market up north tighten because of legalization, they turned inwardly, domestically, and carved a new, growing and bloody market. The drug violence in Mexico soared. And no one gave a shit. Just Mexicans killing one another, I told Ken.

After our talk, I went in search of David, hoping for a less disturbing conversation about homecomings. I ached for Mexico and my old job. Despite its problems, Mexico felt more hopeful than the U.S. It was a strange irony that in Mexico, with its infinite problems and daily difficulties, Mexicans seemed less fearful of the future than Americans did in the United States.

THERE WAS NO WAY to talk about coming home to Mexico without addressing the election, the fuel that had fired us all up about leaving the U.S. I told David how I had awakened on November 9 in Arizona with the television still on. Angela and I were in Nogales to cover the elections with a group of ASU students eager to learn about the border, the Latino vote and the political process. The news of Trump's win blared, a shrill reminder that the great "sleeping giant" of Hispanic voters still didn't have the ability to stop someone like him. Angela and I missed being on the front lines, reporting. Instead we were behind the scenes, helping new journalists find their step. But the news was so big, we looked at each other that morning and asked what the hell we were doing. Why did we walk away from journalism? I looked at us now. We had grown distant, easily irritated with one another, short-tempered. We were miserable. We longed to return to our old lives as journalists, our old partnership that found so much romance in the work we did together.

As she prepared to leave, I startled Angela by urging her: Pack your bags, *güerita*—blondie, my term of endearment for her.

She looked at me, perplexed. What are you doing? I thought we were staying another day.

Let's just run across the border and return to our jobs, I told her.

I wish I could but I'm on deadline, she said, explaining one of her students had a meltdown. Gotta go. But I like the way you're thinking now.

Cable newscasters, the enablers, blabbed in their shock-and-awe voices. The usually robotic anchors suddenly turned human, showing emotion: surprise and elation on Fox, shock and dismay on MSNBC and CNN. I regretted leaving the TV on and turned the sound off as I began to pace the floor, exploring my options, thinking of my family. I called my parents. My mother said she and my father were sitting in the kitchen back in El Paso, waiting for my call, for a few consoling words.

How are you doing? I asked.

My mother paused and in her saddest voice asked when I was coming home.

She continued: We're in a state of loss, not sure what to do, just staring at each other, pondering selling everything and moving back to Mexico. We're thinking of friends and relatives who face deportation to a land they know little about.

How's Dad?

He's angry at the low Hispanic turnout. He feels betrayed. What happened?

I have no idea, I said.

I couldn't even console myself. How could I console my mother? Why even try? Why lie? Tell her the overall culprit was a low voter turnout?

That politics was so divisive we could face another Civil War, hope-fully bloodless, because remnants of black and white issues still lingered and things had turned even more complicated with so many Muslims, Asians and especially Latinos? That would just scare them more. Instead, I kept my thoughts to myself.

I wanted to tell her I just wanted to go home, curl myself with them and watch telenovelas and *Home for the Holidays*, listen to Nat King Cole. But that would show weakness. She needed me to be strong.

No se que decir, mamá. (I don't know what to say.)

I guess I have to watch Jorge Ramos to see what happened, she said.

I took this as a dig. She usually used Jorge Ramos, Univision's top anchor, whenever she wanted to annoy me, and especially now because Jorge Ramos was dancing the line between journalism and activism. She knew it would get to me, especially now that I was no longer a journalist. Why couldn't I express my anger now? What was holding me back? My mother and sister would ask. I respect the profession too much, I'd say, though at times this sounded like a lame excuse.

Plus, I'm really curious now about why "they"—meaning Trump's base—hate us. How did we go from the shadows to the spotlight shining on us?

When exactly did we stop being a novelty and become a threat?

Let me know what Jorge says, I said, in a snarky tone. He might be at a loss, too. Univision spent millions to get out the Hispanic vote. In 2015, 67 percent of lawful permanent residents who were eligible to become U.S. citizens had done so, the highest level in two decades and a 20-percentage-point increase since 1995. The population of natural-ized U.S. citizens reached 19.8 million in 2015, a historic high that reflected both an increase in the population of eligible immigrants and an increased likelihood that those who were eligible to apply for citizen-ship would actually do so. But when it came to voting, they remained bears in hibernation. No sign of life.

I scrolled through social media and suddenly detested everything about it, the "likes," the addictive popularity contest, the outlandish, poisonous lies that spread without any accountability. Social media had changed our lives, and not always for the better. Our smartphones had become human trackers, emitting secrets of what we read, ate, loved and hated. We had been turned into like-minded warriors with a false impression of broader company or validation of who we really are. We were more connected online and more disconnected in reality than ever before. Our language was growing coarser, blunter and limited to

140-character outbursts. Trump was a master of the forum. And reporters, well, we sometimes had thirty seconds to react, a reflection of American conversation today. We were inundated by hashtags, people screeching louder over one another, pointing fingers and meltdowns caught live on breaking news. Everything was breaking news. And if everything was news, if everything was important, then nothing was important. Maybe it was the intensity of the news cycle that wore everyone out and made too many people give up and stay home from the polls. Our democracy had been poisoned.

We defend democracy every day, our publisher Jim Moroney would later say. But did truth even matter anymore? I wondered.

Journalism had been weaponized via talking robots to further divide red and blue states. Details would soon emerge about how Russia used fake news, drummed up by hacks in Macedonia, to spread lies and influence the outcome of the election. It appeared that the result the Russians wanted was a Trump administration.

Media companies were struggling to keep the powerful accountable, leaving communities without needed checks and balances. Once the stellar example of border and Mexico coverage, the *Dallas Morning News*, like others, was in the process of reinventing itself, trying to stay afloat economically and make the transition to online as Facebook, Yahoo and others swallowed up advertising dollars. This forced perpetual layoffs, cuts and buyouts, shrinking our newsrooms. Maybe it was too late for me.

But with Trump's face plastered on television, I heard the calling louder than usual that morning. I ached for journalism and wondered if my profession would forgive me for doubting it, for thinking that I could walk away. Wasn't it me who believed journalism was an incurable disease?

Now, inside the hotel in Nogales, I missed my pen and pad. Mexico.

I took out my BlackBerry and looked for an email I had sent Angela back when I was in Hungary and reread it.

Teaching is not for me, I wrote. I was out in the field today and I so much missed being a reporter. I'm glad I can help these young colleagues, but their curiosity, enthusiasm has only inspired me in ways I couldn't have imagined. All this job has done for me is underscore who I really am, how at heart I'm just a storyteller . . . how much I love being a reporter. How much I miss working on stories. We have to return to our old lives as journalists . . .

I rolled back into bed, hoping to fall asleep again. It wasn't working. All seemed clearer, as though clouds had lifted. I felt brave again, tired of the charade. I had an apartment in Mexico that I barely paid for. It had always served as my backup plan. A friend and colleague, Kathy Corcoran, shared the rent. She and I had talked about letting the apartment go at the end of the year. I didn't see the value anymore, as I wasn't visiting as regularly as I had intended to. Suddenly, I thought twice about that decision and called Kathy up.

Still interested in keeping the apartment in Mexico City? I asked her. I want to go back.

Maybe, she said. That sounds tempting. Let's talk.

I reached for the phone again and called my old editor, Keith Campbell, a tall, lanky no-no nonsense New York City native with an easy smile and a giant soft spot for Bruce Springsteen. I got to the point.

I'm ready to stop dancing, I told him. Are you?

Sara says I'm not much of a dancer, he said, referring to his wife. What do you have in mind?

I want to go back. I'm ready to be a reporter again, Keith.

There would be plenty of details to still work out but his response heartened me.

Welcome back, Freddy, he said.

I felt humble and grateful for a second chance.

27.

Tío Alejo's Funeral

We drove into the California rain, rain that at last gave respite from five years of drought. The weather matched my mother's sadness as she cried for her brother who never returned to his beloved town of Piedras, where as a boy he roamed with his father, Arcadio, to help keep the cattle together.

Alejo had died in California. So had my father's cousin, Chalio, that same week. Alejo and Chalio were contemporaries of my father's, destined to become *braceros*, until Americans grew politically fearful of too many Mexicans. So my uncles ended up working illegally, welcomed by growers with much *gusto*. The fields of California needed to be pampered, the state needed to continue being great, and it couldn't do it alone. Like me, their kids were part of the U.S. baby boomer generation—those born after World War II and before 1965—drivers of the nation's workforce.

I peeked at my father from the rearview window and saw only a shell of the man he once was, a proud man. He was eighty, hadn't had a drink in twenty years. An immigrant through and through: still young at heart with an unshakable spirit of renewal. I also saw a striking physical similarity between us. Many people say I look like my mother, but as I watched him, I thought: I'm looking more like my father as I get older, complete with the receding hairline. We were also just as imperfect, I wanted to tell him. Relax, *papá*. We came of age here.

He became a *bracero* in 1957. He was a cocky man, and for good reason: he could do it all, all the jobs the Americans wouldn't do—work the cotton fields, drive the tractors, run the big Caterpillars. American employers couldn't say no to him, either. He began by working the cotton fields of Texas. When he threatened to return to his native Durango to marry and not come back, his employer arranged for him to gain so-called special status, which permitted him open-ended, legal re-entry. To show how nice he was, the rancher helped him become a permanent guest worker. But the rancher made it even more enticing. Legalize the entire family, bring them over and don't return to Mexico, he said. Whenever Juan Pablo left, his boss confessed, he was constantly nervous my father wouldn't return. A green card for each family member guaranteed stability, a permanent presence.

My father agreed and spent more than a year working nonstop for the man he called Joe as we waited for our own green cards. Once legal, my uncles Eutemio and Edmundo urged their brother to move to California. The pay was better. My father reluctantly left and never came back, though he vowed to one day live in El Paso, just across from Mexico. Joe didn't lose him to Mexico, but he couldn't compete with California.

My mother and father left their sweat in these fields we passed by. Memories raced of early mornings when, dew still clinging to the sugar beets, I'd wait for an old man to sharpen my hoe. I'd look for Mama, who stood quietly alongside dozens of other men and women, all from Mexico. Some leaned on their hoes, yawning, hoping to get a last wink of sleep. Others lifted their hoes and carefully inspected them to make sure they were sharp enough to do the job ahead. They'd prepare for the long, arduous, hot day by covering their faces with handkerchiefs to protect them from the dirt and pesticides. They adjusted their straw hats, baseball caps and worn-out gloves. Their shirts were untucked, their jeans torn, their tennis shoes dirty from the day before. Nearby, my father's tractor roared, kicking up dust as he held on to his white cowboy hat. Suddenly, with the first glimpse of sunrise, the silence of these men and women broke. The rhythmic sound of *shhhh, shhhh, shhhh* could be heard across the fields as the long hoes weeded rows and rows of sugar beets that seemed to go on forever. We were shadows at dawn.

We headed for the San Luis Reservoir, surrounded by stunning golden hills along Pacheco Pass. My mother had never wanted us to get used to the beauty here. We never went to Disneyland, no matter how much we begged, because we couldn't afford it and were too busy studying, learning English, reading and math.

Assimilation, nonetheless, was under way, amid ebbs and flows. In general, the second generation—me and my siblings, my uncles' kids— did well, sort of. A study by UCLA that had longed measured the integration of Mexican Americans found that second, third and fourth generations spoke English fluently, preferred American music, increasingly leaned toward Protestantism and even voted Republican. They were assimilating linguistically, like previous waves of immigrants had, but unlike the Germans or Irish, Mexican Americans' overall political assimilation wasn't so easy. Second-generation Mexican Americans were three times more likely to earn a bachelor's degree than their parents. But the third and fourth generations failed to surpass, and to some extent fell behind, the educational level of the second generation. Moreover, the educational levels of all Mexican Americans still fell behind the national average, and poverty levels were almost twice the national average. Holding them back were historic institutional barriers, discrimination and repressive immigration policies, and too much competition from Mexican labor made integration that much harder.

Like every family, ours too had exceptions. Some became educators, medical technicians, social workers, police officers, business administrators and artists.

As I drove, I gazed at the rain now forming puddles in those fields facing us. They served as inspiration if not reminders of where we came from. As my cousin Geno, who taught sixth graders in Merced, once told me: our parents built the roads. We paved them.

My cousin Gisel Ruiz surpassed all expectations. She too grew up with us in the fields, hoeing cotton, working atop tomato machines for her father Pilar and mother Martha. Both had limited or no education and were labor contractors, who leased the land where my family along with Gisel and her sister worked. A cheerleader and tennis player at Dos Palos High School, Gisel's parents demanded she seek higher education. There was no other way, they told her. She ended up at Santa Clara University where she studied marketing and completed the university's real estate management program. One of her classes involved taking apart Walmart's philosophy. She was later recruited as a store management trainee. She had been there for more than twenty-five years, rising up to executive vice president of Walmart's International people division. She was now executive vice president of operations at the Sam's Club division. Gisel had also made Fortune's top list of the country's most powerful women.

My determination, tenacity represent my very humble roots, my community of Dos Palos, which always kept me grounded, she told me. But more than anything this is a reflection of my parents and their belief in us, she said, referring to her sister Elda. For them the only obstacle in front of us was whatever we imagined.

I looked back at my father, who stared at the rain falling harder. I also didn't remember my father complaining of the historic obstacles before us. He dutifully drove my brother Juan and me and dropped us off to wait for the buses to take us to elementary school. In the afternoons, the bus dropped us off near a long field. We'd kick dust and rocks and sometimes cry until Papa drove up and picked us up, seating us next to him as we drove home. We didn't say much. Whenever we'd protest for the long waits next to those melon or sugar beet fields, where we feared an attack from rats or mice, he'd lecture us about the need to get an education and not end up like him in the fields.

Many years later I understood why frustration led him to throw ice at me when I dropped out of high school. I tried making excuses, legitimate, I thought, like how I suddenly felt inferior in front of my classmates. I used to join the top students every year on a trip to San Francisco, a reflection of our good grades. One day, unexpectedly, I was pulled out of my class for separate instructions, all in Spanish simply because I was an immigrant. School wasn't the same again. I was something other than an American. I was once comfortable being both, and now I was none. My father couldn't care less. Study and work hard, he'd tell us. You speak English, right? You're getting an education, right? You have no excuse but to do better. He saw the extraordinary possibility in us. He wanted us, his children, to integrate and become a part of the social fabric of a country he admired. He liked living in a tolerant country filled with opportunity. He didn't know Muslims or Jews, but he boasted to friends back home that he lived in a country where he drove past synagogues, mosques, Catholic churches—all signs of tolerance. Now he was envisioning internment camps and massive deportations. Many of his *bracero* generation were now in their late seventies, eighties and nineties. A few even older. They are forgotten men and women who built America's dams, railways, roadways, mines and assembly plants, joined the U.S. forces and fought alongside Americans, lifted neighborhoods from the rubble, picked America's agricultural produce from fields now filling with rainwater.

We zoomed by, headed for the heart of California's San Joaquin Valley, in Dos Palos, for funerals. We left Highway 101 to connect to State Route 152, which links Gilroy to Los Baños, and headed right on 33 to Dos Palos.

Although California is a famously blue state, its agricultural heartland beats red. This is slowly changing as the valley diversifies and urbanizes and Hispanic workers earn the vote. But like so many other struggling areas in rural America, the region voted decisively Republican. Dos Palos and nearby Los Baños were bastions of conservatism. So it didn't surprise me to see Trump campaign flyers and posters as we drove in for Uncle Alejo's funeral. The region had weathered a long drought, and their fears eased shortly after the presidential candidate had visited the area and promised to cut regulations to ease the flow of water into their fields.

¿Quien va a levantar la fruta, las naranjas, la uva? Still perturbed by Trump's win, my father asked out loud, Who will pick the fruit, the oranges, the grapes? There will be fields without workers. Fruits unpicked. What will they eat?

By "they" he meant Americans, which is what he had become without knowing it. The ones who wouldn't do the work he did.

My father was full of questions and anxiety in these uncertain times. He'd lived sixty-three of his eighty years in the United States, never learned English and never given Mexico much of a thought. He sat in the backseat of the rental, lost in thought as rain soaked every pothole. We had been looking at preowned U.S. pickup trucks. Now he questioned whether we should even think of making a new investment.

Papa, you worked your ass off all your life in this country. Treat yourself. Go to Mexico in a brand-new truck, just like you did when you were a young, brash man. Return like the flocks of birds and take back your nest, I said. Ride La Paloma with you.

Instead, my father asked whether the government would also take away his and my mother's Social Security retirement money? What about Medicare? They had nothing left.

I looked back at my father, his eyes now watery.

Cito, my mother said quietly, using my father's nickname coined by my brother Juan. Don't you give up on me now. *No nos rajamos. Ni madre.* Are you crying?

I'm not crying, he said stubbornly. I'm just old. It's these cataracts.

Both my parents have been U.S. citizens since 1998. My father likes to go to the gym daily. Recently, my mother told me, he had asked her to make sure his documents were all in order inside his glove compartment in case he was stopped by ICE.

What documents? I asked.

His U.S. passport. I think this is why he's so depressed.

Yeah, that and watching so much TV, I responded.

What are you worried about? I asked my father. You're a *U.S. citizen*.

I don't think that matters anymore, he said, his face contorted. We're Mexican. Look at what's happening to the Muslims. I look Mexican. I will always look Mexican.

He's watching too much TV, I told my mother. We all are. Stories of fathers, mothers, without legal documents, who don't sleep anymore and drive nervously, fearful of the local police. Worried that any infraction, a traffic ticket, will do them in. Children stay away from school. Mothers prohibit them from leaving home, fearful of separation.

Recently, a man who does occasional work in the house showed up to see if we had any yard work for him to do.

Not today, I said. How are you?

Not well, he said.

Adrian had been living in the United States for nearly ten years. Four years ago he paid a smuggler $3,000 to bring his fiancée. They married and now had two children, ages two and four, born on U.S. soil. He feared deportation and separation. Yes, he'd take them to Mexico, but he was from the state of Mexico, where corruption runs deep, children are kidnapped and jobs are slim pickings. He wasn't exactly sure what kind of future faced him. He had a question, a proposition, for me.

If I'm deported along with my wife, would you consider taking in my children?

I looked stunned.

I don't need an answer now, Adrian said. Just want you to think about that as a possibility.

I felt at a loss for words but blurted out that, yes, I would think about it. I waved goodbye, feeling the depth of his worry.

MY UNCLE'S FUNERAL WAS filled with friends and family. My cousin Ruben, Uncle Alejo's son, and his family—Ruben Jr., Brenda and Jessica—sat across from our pew. My mother and her sister Esperanza sobbed. My uncle Chey could barely move his legs now, as if he had left them behind in some field he irrigated. He wore the Surgos company baseball cap, and during the simple service he insisted to my mother they'd talk at least once a week. My mother said she'd like that and reached out to touch his shoulder.

It seemed like everyone was dying. But we were also stubborn about taking ahold of time in order to celebrate my aunt Chala's one hundredth birthday. Her daughters, grandchildren and great-grandchildren were eager to celebrate a life that had absolutely changed not only our family but the fate of our hometown, San Luis de Cordero. Although many of the pioneers were aging, our memory remained intact, as did our appreciation of the "pioneers" before us, the *braceros* and my *tía* Chala.

In California, amid the excitement of the rain and the promise of work ahead, a tall man stood up and walked to the front of the church. Jesus Santillano was an old *bracero* who took over the mike and said kind words about Tío Alejo. He was one of the hardest workers he had ever encountered. He remembered several *braceros* who had also died that past year. He looked at the sparse crowd and dampened the already solemn mood with one question:

Will California have enough workers now to plow the fields and pick its crops? The question hung in the air as men and women bowed their heads to remember the departed.

We walked away from the casket and headed for the exit. Tío Alejo had gathered us, reconnected us once again away from the fields. Old *braceros* walked slowly to their cars, many using canes. My father lingered with them. Younger immigrants plotted and talked excitedly about the upcoming agricultural season, hoping the rainy season would create so many new crops that it would in turn open up opportunities for relatives and friends back home through a temporary-worker program to help keep up with demand. Wages would surely rise. Many had worked for generations at Del Bosque Farms, whose owner, Joe, said a worker shortage could force farmers to raise wages to drum up enough pickers that spring and summer after the rains.

My cousins Carmen, Lisa and Rene; new generations Allison, Sophie and Derek; and a dozen more greeted each other in mournful long embraces. We planned a toast for Tío Alejo that evening over pizza that cousin Patty left to fetch. Mama, Tía Esperanza and Tío Chey were the last to move away from their brother's coffin and only did so when I gently walked with them and insisted that we honor our fallen uncle with a few more moments of togetherness.

We walked outside and took in the fresh air.

For a moment the clouds held back their rain.

28.

Uncle Bill

I decided to return to Middle America, where, in some cities, Mexicans, once a novelty, had set down roots. I wanted to travel the roads of Colorado, Nebraska, Iowa, Minnesota, Illinois and Wisconsin, regions I had traveled two decades ago. I was curious to see how far Mexicans and Americans had come in learning to coexist.

The demographics were changing, at least according to statistics by the Pew Hispanic Center. The Mexicans' share of the total undocumented immigrant population had declined to 5.8 million in 2014, from a peak of 6.9 million seven years before. Mexicans simply weren't crossing like they had before. In fact, in terms of Border Patrol apprehensions at the border, agents arrested more Central Americans and other non-Mexicans in 2014 than Mexicans—a first. There were several reasons for the decline. The birth rate in Mexico did go into a tailspin starting in the 1980s as Mexican women began having an average of two children apiece, down from an average of seven. Over time, that meant fewer frustrated workers in younger generations. Although Mexico's economy was still struggling, and wages were depressed, more and more young Mexicans were finding ways to make ends meet at home. After all, border security had made crossing the border illegally an increasingly deadly prospect that, for many young people, just wasn't worth it anymore. The U.S. recession in 2008 and 2009 took its toll, as did the massive deportations during the first years of the Obama administration.

I cruised through Colorado—taking busy I-25 north, cutting east on I-80 through flat farmland and pastureland and a series of distribution warehouses and meatpacking factories—where I stopped to see family members in Boulder, Greeley and Longmont, cousins that I had grown up with in California. It wasn't a neat narrative but a tapestry of stories that emerged. Some had one foot in the United States and another back in Mexico. Others were firmly rooted in Colorado.

Cousin Noemi was six months pregnant and her latest child would be born in the United States. This should have been seen as good news for a country where the overall fertility rate was the lowest it had ever been. In the first quarter of 2017, the overall U.S. fertility rate fell to 61.5, putting the U.S. population below replacement levels. The influx of immigrants was compensating for the aging population in the United States that seemed to be living increasingly in isolation, like other countries including Japan and Hungary.

Noemi told me she planned to name her son Matthew, a biblical name. American, too, I thought.

Her parents, Lucy and Alfredo, crisscrossed the border two or three times a year for family visits.

Colorado offers us four seasons and it's beautiful, she said, as she sat next to her husband, Eraclio Rubio, and six-year-old Yaxkin. I was never really enticed by California and all those fields. Here there are more opportunities for us, especially educational ones for Yaxkin without the toxic politics, and fewer obstacles to success.

Others, like Ruben, worked in Greeley, but his heart was back in Mexico. He worked as a mechanic at a maintenance plant; he showed me pictures of the home I had just visited down the road from San Luis de Cordero. He was running out of money and joked that he might sell *menudo* and *gorditas* to finish the project. His home will include a new Jacuzzi, a master bedroom and even, he insisted, a guest/writing room for me. When we were boys, I looked up to Ruben as an older brother. I still do.

It'll have a great view of the mountains, he said. Do you remember them?

Of course I remember, I said, trying to hide my road weariness.

Slow down, he said.

Slow down? You're working sixty, eighty hours per week, I responded.

Eighty-four, he corrected me. But I get paid twice what I made in California and I'm saving it all to live in Mexico. He even signed up for a 401(k) savings program, unheard-of back in California. Not bad for a boy with limited education. He'd gone from running a movie house in San Luis de Cordero to working alongside me in the fields of the San Joaquin Valley for more than a decade and now was one of the top mechanics.

These days, he lamented, new workers are always coming in, a reminder that his best days are coming to an end.

But did you vote? I asked.

I was too busy working, he said.

Living in nostalgia for Mexico as you get screwed in the U.S., I said, sarcastically. Nice, *primo*.

His son, Ruben Jr., twenty-eight, looked on in amusement. He was still a green card holder, but after the presidential election he, like millions of other Hispanics, was saving money to become a citizen. Too much at stake. The application could cost $700 to file. He told me he hoped Bernie Sanders would run again.

Mary told me she made chicken tamales for me; she wanted to give me a taste of home, she said, reminding me of my mother. Her green tamales were especially delicious. Mary was in a bind. Both her sons lived in Mexico. One was deported and the other had his temporary worker permit status rescinded. He had no immediate plans to return to his old job as a maintenance worker in Colorado. Her daughter, still battling cancer, and grandchildren live in Colorado. She told me she had decided to spend her springs in Colorado with her daughter and granddaughter cleaning the homes of the elderly to finance winters in San Luis de Cordero, where she's building an extra room in the home of her father. Tío Antonio's health kept declining and she wanted to be closer to him and her sons.

Sometimes I wish we had never set foot in the United States, because you end up always comparing the two countries and you can't choose one over the other, she said. Both have their pluses and minuses.

Beyond Colorado and into the Great Plains, meatpacking plants welcomed arrivals from other countries to fill the slots that Mexicans were beginning to abandon—workers from Africa, the Middle East and Central America. Nebraska, the Midwest and Great Lakes region quietly defied the vitriolic debate over immigration nationwide. They didn't want labor shortages. In St. Paul, Minnesota, rooted in Scandinavian culture and the beauty of the Mississippi River, a network of workers from Axochiapan in the southern Mexican state of Morelos thrived in restaurants, bakeries and *tortillerías* alongside Asian and Muslim eateries and businesses. The state is home to the largest Somali community in the United States and some 185,000 Mexican workers.

I arrived in Lincoln, Nebraska, minus a few tamales.

I was used to engaging the cleaning lady at hotels, part of a reporter technique. I would usually stop to greet her and make small talk. It was a way to get a lay of the land in the area. Where are people from? I'd ask. What regions of Mexico are represented here? But I looked outside that morning and didn't find the usual Mexican cleaning lady.

Instead, I ran into Hussein, twenty-five, a refugee from Baghdad. I wondered whether he was one of the refugees I met while traveling through Eastern Europe back when I was visiting Austria. At first I thought he might be a maintenance worker too afraid to talk to me. To ease the awkwardness, I offered Hussein a tamale. He looked at it and seemed to have no clue what to do with it. I ran to look for a micro-wave and heated it for one minute, returned upstairs and offered it to him. He was about to eat it, cornhusk and all, until I grabbed it from his hand.

Wait—no, I said.

A Mexican cleaning lady who, I later learned, was from San Luis Potosi laughed from across the corridor. Her name was Eva and she came over. She unrolled the steaming *masa*, green sauce and chicken from the husk and handed the tamale back to Hussein, smiling. He took a taste.

Good, he said. Very good.

The exchange offered a peek into an evolving workforce in the United States, a mishmash of Mexican and Central Americans now toiling along-side a rising number of African and Middle Eastern refugees.

The last chapter of Mexican migration is over, for now. Maybe forever. A major upheaval in Mexico, or economic or natural disaster on either side of the border, however, can change that. No one discounts that.

Here in the Silicon Prairie of the Midwest, many hold jobs in the service industry and poultry and meatpacking plants. The Mexicans are leaving, or least they're not coming from Mexico in the numbers they once did. Refugees are replacing Mexicans, in the way Mexicans once replaced Japanese, Puerto Ricans and Filipinos. It was a new workforce that was vulnerable and increasingly threatened by the Trump adminis-tration's draconian immigration policies, aimed, in part, at slowing down the diversity under way across the country. The U.S. population was now 324.4 million. By mid-century, the United States was poised to grow to 438 million and become a majority-minority nation, a place where whites would make up less than half the population, while Hispanics and Asian groups were gaining new demographic prominence. Hispanics are on track to grow to 29 percent of the U.S. population;

Asians to about 9 percent. The African American population had stayed generally constant, about 13 percent. Anglos would fall to an estimated 47 percent of the population.

Nebraska and the state I long claimed as home, Texas, were both red. They cast lopsided votes for Trump, but as Texas lawmakers cracked down on illegal immigration and tried to limit the number of refugees resettling in the state, Nebraska and other parts of the Midwest seemed to be rolling out the welcome mat. Drive down to Lincoln and you'd see endless fields interrupted by just as many rows of monster wind turbines—some with blades manufactured in Ciudad Juárez *maquiladoras*. Cruise past meatpacking plants near Iowa, and across Nebraska. A messy mix of the latest weary refuge.

Not long ago, jobs, particularly in the labor-intensive meatpacking industry, went almost exclusively to Mexicans and Central Americans. Employers fearing a looming labor shortage didn't have many options at the moment. They were becoming more dependent on immigrants to keep America's labor force growing. Immigrants made up about 17 percent of the U.S. labor force in 2017, with about one-quarter of those immigrants undocumented. Political refugees were by and large legal and therefore not singled out by immigration authorities. Company managers told me over and over that they had tried recruiting American workers in Minneapolis, Chicago and Kansas City and few, if any, lasted longer than a week.

Community leaders and employers were finding ways to be more accommodating, demonstrating tolerance for newcomers. Muslim prayer rooms, outfitted with rugs, were installed for Middle Eastern workers, all the while employers pushed for a more robust guest-worker program to fill jobs once held by Mexican laborers. A period of transition was under way.

Roberto Rodríguez wore an L.A. Dodgers baseball cap. He's in his late fifties and had spent much of his youth in the poultry plants of Nebraska. A native of Zacatecas, he didn't like the work, and he hadn't received a pay increase in years. He always planned on returning home, but now his family had moved, thanks to amnesty. Nebraska was home. Rodríguez was working at a poultry-packing plant in Lincoln alongside mostly other Mexicans, many of them legal, some Central Americans without documents and increasingly Middle Easterners. Americans rarely lasted more than a day, or two, he said. Who can blame them? This is hard work. He found it challenging speaking with the newest arrivals from the Middle East and Africa, but was convinced they represented the future.

So, he tried communicating through hand signals, he said, referring to his new coworkers. Working with Arabs is something I never imagined doing. I thought the pipeline of Mexicans was forever. We just ran out of Mexicans, he said, laughing. No one wants to come anymore.

Several times a day his fellow Muslim employees paused to pray, he told me. At times he found the breaks a bit odd, even annoying, but added, I think we Mexicans pray all the time, too, especially in the meat and poultry plants, he laughed, making the sign of the cross. I try to be as hospitable as possible, because I think Mexicans understand rejection.

The latest drama in Lincoln unfolded at Klein's Corner, which embodies America's immigrant tale. It was built in 1928 to pay homage to immigrants from Germany, Sweden and other Scandinavian countries. Across the street is an Italian eatery for pasta and pizza. Rodríguez bought freshly made bread baked by a Salvadoran owner who expanded the business; the new workers from Africa and the Middle East also like the bread. They exchanged smiles and warm greetings in lieu of words.

Above the storefront was a sign that read "Esquina de los Hispanos." Klaus York pointed at it. He arrived from Germany at the age of five. We walked to the corner. A retiree, he pointed to the changing demographics and remarked, I can't feel anything but pride because I, too, was an immigrant and we weren't treated very well, either. People spit on us so I understand when people are not nice to immigrants. I try to be welcoming.

A block from there, worlds and cultures melted at the Lincoln Literacy Council, a brightly lit room with rows of long desks and walls of books. Service workers turned students, most of them from Africa, Laos, Mexico, Central America and the Middle East, sat with pens and notepads. Sandra Rojo, the English-language-learner coordinator, also saw newly arrived Mexicans. They were not so much coming directly from Mexico but fleeing states like California, which had become too expensive, and Texas, which was downright anti-immigrant. Just as thousands of undocumented workers fled Arizona years before, away from laws that discriminated against them, these newcomers were looking for a welcome sign.

Little things like a neighbor's smile make all the difference, she said. Makes you feel you are part of the neighborhood. We're all human and sometimes we're afraid of the unknown, she added.

IN WISCONSIN, I DROVE with Angela down Highway 50 and we got a glimpse of dairy farms where Mexicans milked cows and mowed miles of lawns and golf courses near Lake Como, Williams Bay and Lake Geneva and as far away as Kenosha and Janesville. I paid a visit to Santos, a *paisano* whom I had known for years.

I had been coming to the resort town of Lake Geneva in southeastern Wisconsin for years now with Angela. Both her grandmother and grandfather, native Chicagoans, had relatives who have lived there for generations, including her great aunt Lorraine, who loved the charming lakeside town so much she later moved here and taught art in local schools. They lived within glimpse of golden-age mansions, many of them owned by wealthy Chicagoans, including the gum magnates the Wrigleys—places where Santos pruned brushes, mowed lawns and tended to gardens.

Since I've known him, Santos's hair has turned salt-and-pepper and the circles under his eyes have deepened. He and his wife have lived in Wisconsin for more than twenty years after emigrating illegally from Oaxaca, Mexico. They raised four children, including three born in the U.S. Together, they ran a family-owned landscaping business complete with a recorded phone greeting by a polite man in perfect accent-free English asking callers to leave a detailed message. They raised their children to be of two countries, although they rarely set foot in Mexico. They'd walk their kids to wait for school buses, convinced their new lives would be worth their sacrifice. They attended PTA school meetings, met with counselors, watched their kids play baseball and sing in school plays. Now they talked about college, careers and the most pressing priority.

These days the family was in constant communication, making sure no one had been deported. They had a secret game plan to keep the home and business running.

It's all detailed, although I have no idea what I would do in Mexico, Santos explained. Everything is here now. For now, the key is to keep a low profile.

Even so, there was life to live. They celebrated baptisms, *quinceñeras* and weddings in a big way, hiring *norteño* bands to play live and loud.

Once Santos invited me to a wedding in nearby Burlington. I got lost on the way and ended up next to Fred's Burgers, known for the best burgers in the area, the place where a young Tony Romo grew up and ate before going on to fame playing quarterback for the Dallas Cowboys. Romo's father's roots were in Mexico. His mother had roots in Germany. I rolled down the window of the rental and asked two young women if they knew of a wedding. They laughed. Follow the music, one said. They were right: around the corner, *banda* and *taconazo* music was blaring. I peeked inside and saw Santos with his friends, natives included, dancing the night away.

Celebrations, parties, are the best way to bring everyone together, Santos explained.

My visit with Angela coincided with Cinco de Mayo festivities. Restaurants all over town offered drink specials on tequila and margaritas. The holiday, so beloved in the U.S., was really minor and mostly forgotten in Mexico. Cinco de Mayo isn't Mexico's Independence Day, as some Americans believe; it commemorates the Mexican army's unlikely, albeit brief, victory over French troops led by Napoleon III during the Battle of the Puebla on May 5, 1862. The French attacked Mexico, in part, in hopes of collecting on the country's unpaid debt. It was the middle of the American Civil War, and the French were aiding the Confederacy. The French loss left Confederate troops without the resources they expected— long enough to give Union troops time to recover and prevail in the ensuing battles. The battle at Puebla also represented a truly American concept: the triumph of the underdog over a richer, better-armed foe. Today, the holiday is more of a beer fest, easier to say Cinco de Mayo instead of *Dieciseis de Septiembre*, Mexico's Independence Day.

Angela wanted to visit her ailing uncle Bill at an assisted-living home in nearby Williams Bay. Her trips had become more frequent since 2012, when her uncle suffered a stroke, leaving him partly paralyzed. Angela was the daughter Bill never had, and Bill represented a father figure of sorts for Angela. I tried to accompany her whenever she went to see him, because I knew how emotionally draining it was for her since the trips made her miss her mother, who died in 2007.

I waited for Angela and her uncle in the dining hall. Most of the employees were native Wisconsin residents. But a few were from Mexico and the Philippines. The patients were usually locals of German, Polish or Irish descent. In one room there was a sea of wheelchairs. A woman called, "Help, help, help." Others roared with laughter holding virgin margaritas. A nurse's assistant walked in with one of those oversize Mexican party hats, the type you see during spring break in Cancún. Some ladies were wheeling around, saying, "*Viva, viva Cinco de Mayo,*" and acting tipsy, although the nurse assured me there was no alcohol in their drinks.

Tom, a patient with a foul mouth, spotted me and wheeled over.

Are you really Mexican? he asked.

I'd known him for about a year. He was from Milwaukee, a welder, a union man all his life. A Democrat who voted for Clinton. He had a full head of hair and wore a torn blue T-shirt. He was constantly plotting ways to escape from what he called a prison cell. He had a spirit that reminded me of the Randle Patrick McMurphy rebel character in Ken Kesey's *One Flew Over the Cuckoo's Nest.* The nursing home had only recently taken away his motorized wheelchair, which he used to cruise the halls at full speed. He would zip outside and harass the smokers.

He looked dejected this afternoon. Cinco de Mayo had awoken an old yearning.

You're a real Mexican, right? he asked again.

As real as it gets, I said, I am so Mexican, I have a cactus stamped on my forehead.

I don't see it, he said, not understanding the popular Mexican saying *con nopal en la frente.*

'Cause it's invisible, I said.

Cut the bull. How far is O'Hare from here?

Roughly ninety minutes or so, depending on traffic.

I need you to smuggle me out of here and take me there. Take me to Mexico.

I know nothing about smuggling, I told him.

BILL WASN'T FEELING IN high spirits, either. Angela promised him pizza and wine for dinner.

Chicago-style, he said.

Whatever you want, Bill.

None of that franchise stuff.

Don't you worry Bill. We'll find the best.

The best is in Chicago, he insisted.

He broke into a story of his better days in Chicago, where he ate at the finest restaurants and closed down bars. No other city—well, maybe San Francisco, where he lived for years—came close, he said. What he really wanted was to go to Chicago for pizza himself, but he knew that was impossible. The idea of his niece leaving his side was even harder.

There's some good ones here, too, he said.

We'll find you the best, Bill. We'll be right back.

We returned with pizza and a bottle of wine. Bill savored his first sip of cabernet sauvignon in years, a bottle of Perez Cruz from Sonoma Valley that we bought at the Green Grocer just a few blocks away. We listened to "My Way" by Frank Sinatra. Bill, too, had a few regrets that on this night he didn't want to share.

Salud, amor y tiempo para gozarlo, he said, raising a glass in a toast, remembering his visits to Cuernavaca, where his mother and sister once lived, where Angela was almost born during a car ride to the American British Cowdray hospital in Mexico City. He lifted his glass and Angela and I toasted with him: Health, love and time to enjoy life.

Later that night, after Bill headed for bed, Angela and I made a beeline for Anthony's, a favorite place. The kitchen workers were from Mexico. They battered, broiled and baked platter after platter for Fish Fry Friday, a tradition I'd grown to enjoy, except for the fact that Anthony's had a poor selection of tequila. Why would they invest in a good selection, after all? Their clientele was mostly older Italian immigrants and younger American families. But over the years I would see more Mexican families on those Friday nights. I offered to help the bartender with a list of tequila selections, with Siembra Azul spirits at the top of the list. The bartender, a stern woman who in the past rarely smiled, actually exchanged a few nice remarks with me. Her younger sister joined in the friendly banter.

Angela watched the scene in amusement.

Looks like you have finally charmed them, she observed.

I think we're all a bit more comfortable with one another, I said, grimacing at the poor-quality tequila I was forced to drink. David had really ruined me.

As in the Southwest, and the Southeast, and now the Midwest, Mexicans had left elements of their food and culture embedded in communities. Tamales in Mississippi, tacos in Nebraska and music in Milwaukee, home to Kinto Sol, whose music attracted younger Mexican Americans, known as *malinchista millennials*, and increasingly mainstream crowds.

They left their sweat in the landscaping fields of North Carolina, the oyster-shucking industry of the Outer Banks, the apple orchards of the Yakima Valley; the dairy farms of Vermont and Wisconsin; the cotton fields of California; the grape vineyards of Paso Robles, Napa to Willamette Valley; in the agricultural fields of Arkansas, Texas, Pennsylvania, Ohio, Michigan, Minnesota; the service industry of Arizona, Colorado, New Mexico, Idaho; and the poultry and meat packing industries of the Midwest. And in just about every kitchen across the country, assisted living and daycare centers. Even on Trump's construction sites. Everywhere a job required a hardworking human, a Mexican was there.

29.

Four Friends, Philadelphia Reunion

TEQUILA

Friends sit
at a low table

Siembra Azul
clear as anything

in short crystal
glasses—

expense & conversation
danger of saying too little

or too much
at midnight

we'll walk along
the tracks of Union Pacific

& sing
to the low, loud-mouth moon

IRISH POET JONATHAN C. CREASY, MARFA, TEXAS, 2016

I couldn't remember the last time we were together, the four of us, at Tequilas, and in the same city. We were just in Chicago together for a program I helped organize for the University of Chicago's Institute for Politics, moderated by Angela. After all those years of our own personal conversation, David, Ken, Primo and I gathered together to talk publicly about the current climate of immigration, offering our own glimpse into a divided nation. It was May, the anniversary month of David's moving Tequilas into the new building.

A photo shows us around a table of Mexican water glasses with the cobalt rims, waiting for the server to bring tequila. David looks like a Mexican Sean Connery, with a trim white beard and a winning grin to hide his growing worries. Primo doesn't smile beneath a black mustache. He has the intense stare of a poet. Ken, a bit uncomfortable and rounder in the face, thinner overall, smiles happily, and I look like a deer in head-lights. I'm wearing my trademark jeans and a blue sports coat—like the one from JCPenney but nicer.

It was a Friday night. A bartender poured Siembra Azul, and again I shook with delight. Savor it, David said. You never know. Like Siembra Azul, other privately owned smaller brands were fighting to survive in a cannibalistic market ruled by giant corporations.

We all looked at each other and commented that we hadn't been here all together in years. After the elections in November, we really thought we would never be in Philadelphia together again. It felt like a big deal.

Primo looked at me and said, Alfredo, I know you miss Mexico and consider Mexico home, but you would have never become as Mexican as you are now, here, in this country, in this city.

I knew what he meant. He stayed quiet and took in the moment.

If we didn't have to decide anymore about *who* we were—both Mexican and American—we did have the right—the responsibility, even—to decide to stay and make a difference. I could see that David and Ken had turned a corner. They seemed comfortable alone.

It was clear as I looked at David and Primo that we now had two souls, or maybe we had always had two souls, souls that belonged to either side of the border. We were constantly searching for a part of ourselves, only to realize that as we found ourselves on one side of the line, we would inevitably remember the other. Perhaps this whole geographical thing was just a figment of our own imagination; perhaps throughout our journey to understand ourselves as immigrants, we were really just searching for a way to coexist with one another.

I marveled at how a group of four American students, which included a Korean American and one with roots in Bolivia, at the Chicago event, had renewed my belief in a country that felt as if it was imploding. It inspired me to rethink America and its polarized mood. Michelle, Nicole,

Olivia and Elle talked about taking back their country and really, truly making America great again.

Chingón, no?

Agreed, they said. We were so inspired that Guadalajara didn't seem so imminent anymore.

Perhaps we were morphing into something else, something better, Ken said.

Ken remained optimistic about better days ahead, calling the latest low turnout among Hispanic voters a momentary blip. He'd been helping his daughter Maya apply to universities across the country and studying Hispanic educational gains. Over the past decade, he said, overall Hispanic educational attainment remained the biggest challenge, but the Hispanic high school dropout rate had declined and college enrollment had increased, even though Hispanics still trailed other groups in earning a bachelor's degree.

Ken's rosy outlook may have been colored by the latest data showing Hispanic dropout rates kept falling and his daughter Maya's own college search. A top student, Maya was looking at the Ivies and other elite universities.

It's really amazing, Ken told me. The percentages of Latinos getting into top schools is growing. You have thousands of top Latino students getting in to Harvard, Stanford, Yale and Penn. I never thought I'd see this many Latinos at Penn. I love the fact that Maya is competing head-to-head with top students around the country. Who knows where she'll go, but I'm confident it will be a great school. Not quite my experience.

More than a third of Hispanics were enrolled in a two- or four-year college, up from 22 percent in 1993, a 13-percentage-point increase. Sure, they had a lot of catching up to do. Just 15 percent had a bachelor's degree. That compared with 41 percent for whites, 22 percent for African Americans and more than 60 percent for Asian Americans.

Look, I agree, Ken said. When it comes to political empowerment, there's a lot of work ahead. But numbers are on our side. Demography is destiny, citing stats that more than one million Hispanics would become new citizens by the midterm elections.

David's son, Dave, thirty-one, wasn't buying any of the lofty talk at the moment. He was David's heir apparent, working the floor at Tequilas. He took a moment and sat down with us. He was reflective, confessing a sense of betrayal. Dave was the eldest of three; Marcos and Elisa were his brother and sister. Like his siblings, Dave conceded he was more Italian than Mexican, but the latest mood in the country had pushed him to protect his Mexican side. He'd grown up in Tequilas. I remember holding him as an infant and watching him grow in the shadow of his father. David even sent his son to stay with Angela and me in Mexico City and we later accompanied him to San Miguel de Allende in his quest to learn Spanish. The experience, plus countless trips with his father to the agave fields and plants in Jalisco, helped him take stock of his Mexican heritage. Because of the Trump effect, Dave now passionately defended his food, music and spirits in ways his father hadn't been able to teach him about all these years.

Dave reposted his father's message on Facebook to show solidarity with Mexican workers, joining a nationwide movement to honor immigrants by closing businesses for a day that depended on them. The message read:

"In the birth city of our nation, in the great City of Brotherly Love, we respectfully closed our business today to honor the humble spirit of immigrants, their past and present, especially those who founded the United States of America, and those who keep the promise alive . . ."

He looked at the institution his father had built from the ground up, with the sweat of Mexicans from Guadalajara, Mexico City, Puebla, Chiapas, Yucatán, Quintana Roo, Guerrero; Colombians; Ecuadorans; and even the children of some of Tequilas' original workers. Edith, a DACA recipient, was twenty-two. A native of Mexico State, she came to Philadelphia when she was thirteen. Like many "Dreamers," she had become politically active, inspired to engage in the U.S. democratic process. We need to be part of the solution, not the problem, she said. One way or another.

The only way to make a difference is to get involved, she told me. Politicians play with our lives, our future. Political activism is the answer, she declared, explaining that she spent evenings and weekends organizing immigrants with and without documents.

Another was Nicky, a cheerleader for the Philadelphia 76ers and a Tequilas hostess during the off-season. She was the daughter of Oscar, from Chiapas, David's top lieutenant. He had raised her to be American first, at the expense of speaking Spanish. For her own good, he said. The more assimilated the better.

My own nieces and nephews faced similar challenges, I told Oscar.

It's great to be Italian American, German American, Mexican American, Oscar explained, but I taught my daughter to be American, period.

Assimilation is too powerful of a force, I argued, and there's little resistance, especially among the young. In my own family, I told Oscar, the younger generation in my family is losing the mother tongue and at times I rebel by blasting "Despacito," hoping a Luis Fonsi song with Justin Bieber will at least make my nephews curious about their grandparents' native language. No such luck. Cristian's headphones don't come off as he plays video games. Toñito sways to the catchy tune, as his mother, Irene, a business administrator, cracks up.

All—Rosalinda, Gena and Trinity—preferred not being spoken to in Spanish, as if the language cheapens them, I often say, trying to guilt trip them. We all speak English, the universal language. Some, like my niece Camille, retain both. My brother Frank, a former border patrol detention guard, and his wife, Mari, our former waitress at Freddy's Café, married and raised their children—Jasmine, Luzely Wendy, Erica, Carlos—to be bilingual, bicultural. They speak Spanish so fluently I often forget they speak English even better.

Dave interrupted our conversation about language, music, saying, I have zero interest in Justin Bieber no matter the language. Besides, Dave had bigger problems. He confessed at times he didn't understand his customers' inner conflicts, hypocrisy and fear.

They come in and eat your food and admire the music, the artwork, the tequila, the mezcal, and then they vote a crazy man into the White House who hates Mexicans, he said. And I always thought of myself as Italian. But they hate me, the Mexican in me. That just ain't right. You get me?

He had married an Italian American girl, Lauren, from South Philly. They were now parents of Luca, a toddler with a remarkable resemblance to Dave, even the way he toddled around Tequilas as though he owned the place, with flailing arms and a big, drooling laugh.

He also worried his father might give up on the United States and go back to Mexico permanently like that bird his grandmother talked about. He'd return to his nest.

You can't go back anymore, he told his father across the table. You have two nests.

I will never leave my family, David said, looking at Luca.

Dave wasn't convinced.

For binational birds, finding home solely in one place was complicated, I told Dave. We were pulled in both directions. We learned this over three decades through our shared journey.

I want my kid to have a grandfather, he added. We need Dad to be a part of our lives, but I think Dad likes it there in Guadalajara. He looks different, like he belongs. Cheerful. He even has a New Age look, wearing untucked striped linen shirts. Look at his beard. What's up with that?

Primo interrupted David, who was about to set his son straight.

Mexico can't take away your father, Primo told Dave. Not Mexico. Not Marité. No one. David is an immigrant and, like those before him, he has built, with much determination, hardship and creativity, his own Mexico, here in Philadelphia. He doesn't need to be back in Mexico. He lives in the Mexico he has built for himself and for us. A Mexico more real than the one we left behind.

Mexican food had grown into an empire worth $38 billion nationwide. Tequilas was no longer some exotic place with *enchiladas poblanas*. The dish was as common as pasta, pizza, hamburgers and sushi. Tequilas had become a quintessential American success story. David was now one of the most respected restaurateurs not just in Philadelphia but in the country. His regular customers included Philadelphia Eagles owner Jeffrey Lurie and his wife, Tina Lai.

Goddamn it, that's America, Primo said. Mexicans almost single-handedly rebuilt Center City Philadelphia with their sweat and sleepless nights. They played a key role in reviving the Italian Market, keeping schools open, generating income for new businesses. Keeping the nation's immigrant spirit alive.

They paid property taxes, either through paying for homes or renting from landlords. They paid income taxes and social security taxes, without any benefits after retirement. For example, in 2010, the Social Security Administration estimated $13 billion went into the social security trust fund from undocumented workers. And only $1 billion was paid out to them.

A burden to U.S. taxpayers? Primo asked. Bullshit.

As usual, Primo helped put things in perspective. He apologized for his absence over the years. And yet he still commanded our attention. He had pulled me out of my lonely isolation in Philadelphia so many years ago and now he was pulling us out of something just as bad, a stranger in America. He did it here, where the Quakers sought to create a utopia of tolerance and acceptance. Americans might end up walling themselves off from everybody, but they were no different from Germans, Italians or the Irish. The "Americans" would eventually look around and realize the enemies they had created in their own heads had grown into something else: Americans like them.

Primo turned to his longtime obsession, Huntington, the Harvard scholar who had long predicted a clash of civilizations.

Huntington was right, Primo said. No migration in the past had influenced the United States as much as the Mexican migration. The problem with Huntington's theory is that he ended with the wrong conclusion. Mexicans were not a threat but represented one of the greatest contributions to America: social, economic political and cultural greatness.

Where were you more Mexican? Primo asked us again.

I looked at David and knew Primo was right. No other country could have made us more Mexican than right here inside Tequilas.

David folded his arms and shook his head in agreement. He had lived more than half of his life in Philadelphia.

I cannot leave Philadelphia behind, just as I cannot leave Guadalajara for good, he said. How many people can say they are truly binational? Not many, I think. What was once an emotional baggage is now a privilege, David said.

I told David I'd been away from Mexico for more than two years and I hadn't gone nuts yet, but that was probably because I knew I could always go back.

America gave you the possibility to develop your Mexican-ness, I said. Isn't that what you're trying to say, Primo? That in itself was worth the sacrifice.

Your Mexican identity grew, Primo echoed. You sacrificed and became more Mexican and something else.

You didn't have that possibility in Mexico, I said. The United States, its spirit, its meaning, has transformed us. Somehow, we had crossed over, organically, without much of a fuss. Until now.

Americans fell in love with you, David, and the restaurant you built, Primo said. They are so fascinated, they're copying your food, tequila, mezcal, even your music. That's what the United States does when it wants to adopt you. They copy you. It's called flattery. Mainstream acceptance.

Ken was quiet, as usual. Until he, too, confessed—ironically: I never felt as Mexican in New Mexico as I did here with you guys.

Ken wasn't just a lawyer; notwithstanding the debacle with David, Ken has always been a serial entrepreneur. Over the years, he's launched radio, television and tech businesses and now was closing in on that license to sell pot, as he built a venture capital fund in California's tech world.

I'm in business to subsidize my public interest work, he said.

Ken confessed he fixated on the one job he's always wanted. Mayor of Philadelphia.

I'm biding my time, he said, conceding he thought about running again, someday.

We need every vote, white, African American, Asian, Muslim, Hispanic to turn Pennsylvania blue again. He was reenergized and wanted to give elections another chance, he said. Voting was the only way to help revive America. He too wanted to make a difference, prove that as the latest guests on the grand stage of America we had something to prove. We belong. We now had to step up our game and strengthen what felt like a fragile democracy. Help save our country.

I don't give Trump credit for anything, Ken said. But the one thing this election has revealed is the gap between rich and poor, educated and uneducated and the tribal society we're in danger of becoming. Going into the future you need leaders who have feet in both camps, with enough empathy to lead in a racially majority-minority world. Leadership that's going to keep us from becoming a tribal society in the future.

We raised our glasses to Ken and began to enjoy the tequila even more, waiting for Primo to continue, and he did.

That's America. This is the only place where the Quakers could be Quakers in the New World, he said. You three are more gringo than the gringos because many have forgotten the dream. You live that dream daily. That's America.

DAVID AND I RETREATED to the Cueva for a nightcap, or two. Each time, we tried to outdo the last by coming up with new music selections to surprise each other. One night we listened to Miguel Bosé's "Amo" fifty consecutive times, memorizing every lyric; lately, Juana Molina, Calle 13, Zoe and Soda Stereo's "La Ciudad de La Furia" with singer Gustavo Cerati leading us into delicious agony.

This time no music. Just confessions.

After the election, I cried for Luca, David said, and for the country that awaits him.

Lately, David had become obsessed with Philadelphia's history, which was really the country's story. He visited Independence Hall, read the Declaration of Independence and walked across Washington Park to the gravesite of Benjamin Franklin. He kept a copy of the U.S. Constitution at his desk.

I departed Philadelphia and, in between flights on my way to a fellow-ship at the University of California at San Diego, David texted me from the balcony of his apartment, which overlooked Center City Philadelphia and its newest landmarks.

I'm here raising my glass for my homeland which opened its arms to me and allowed me to be myself, it read. To America, which in its origins gave humanity a reason to believe in humanity.

For three days the fog swept across the Pacific Ocean, cutting off most of the view from my window in La Jolla.

It was hard to look out the window and tell where I was.

California had learned from its past cruel treatment of its immigrants and was now so progressive and above the fray that it almost felt like it had seceded from the rest of the nation. The Golden State reminded me of our values as Americans. I liked waking up three hours behind the East Coast. Time was slower. It felt as if we didn't care about the mess growing in Washington. A handwritten sign outside a window of a UCSD dorm summed up the sentiment: Fuck Trump.

Outside my window, five boys and a girl played basketball. I heard the sharp sound of the basketball being dribbled on cement. Each bounce brought memories of the San Joaquin Valley and playing ball with my brothers.

After three sunny days, it rained again in Southern California, rained as hard as it had the day of my uncle's funeral. It poured torrents. I thought of those heavy clouds that teased us mercilessly. The clouds that scorched the land with drought and death. But here, there was a sudden release.

A weight lifted, and so did the fog. The sky was so blue I could almost pat it gently.

30.

My Homelands

My brother Edmundo, Mundito to us, rests from grilling and is enjoying a beer. He is glued to his smartphone. "What is Life" followed by "My Sweet Lord" by George Harrison are playing, rediscovered by a new generation after a summer blockbuster movie.

Inside our house, my mother is also cooking and I have little choice but to wait in anticipation. There is something artistic about the way she moves about the kitchen cooking, the little things she says, the snippets of songs she sings. It all goes into her rice, tacos, enchiladas, *menudo* and *caldo de res*.

She's poetic, lyrical in her creations. I take out my cell phone and record her, hoping to keep the moment ingrained forever.

My new office is now nestled in the mountains of El Paso. From my desk I can see green vegetation, ocotillos standing tall and strong, purple sagebrush blowing during the summer monsoon rains. My brothers, sisters, nephews and nieces are with me to celebrate the Fourth of July and help me clear old furniture and files. Gena, my niece, leads the effort. She helps me pack old reporter's notebooks from three decades and stack them in boxes in the garage, including some my mother saved from my days as a reporter in Philadelphia. I brushed my finger over notebooks that read "Campbells, Chicago, Kennett Square, Freddy's Café . . ." I unloaded a trunk full of books, research hidden away inside my VW Bora, with its Mexico City plates to remind me of another life and place, a time tucked back in La Condesa neighborhood surrounded by Parque Mexico and trees that touched the sky. My heart still aches.

In my office, there is a fresh coat of soft blue paint on the walls that replaced a bright orange palette. A large wooden desk faces the mountains named after pioneer Benjamin Franklin Koons. The space is minimal now with only a work station and a printer.

The space is clear, and so is my mind.

Angela is back in El Paso, too. She left the Cronkite School of Journalism at ASU and, like me, was eager to be a full-time journalist again. She took a job covering the border for the *Albuquerque Journal*.

Can we live without one another, you and I, like Mexico and the United States? Can we even imagine that? What better place than here, what better time than now to be home and tell new and old stories?

She just smiled.

I'm back in the city that taught me about reporting stories made of delicate threads that reporters are tasked with unraveling. Stories that bind us. This city feels neither fully American nor Mexican but something in between. It's an eclectic, dynamic city where a musician turned city councilman and U.S. Representative with roots in Ireland named Beto O'Rourke aspires to be a U.S. senator from Texas, a state toying with shades of purple. And it's O'Rourke, the underdog, not his Cuban American opponent, Ted Cruz, running unofficially as the Spanish-speaking Hispanic candidate. This region is surrounded by desert and a long history of isolation, generating the kind of fierce independence needed to survive the elements of the earth and the fickle will of opportunistic politicians who pretend to know and understand the *frontera*. Few do. Here on the border, this remoteness shapes our character—our songs, our poetry and literature, our own state of mind.

El Paso, one of America's great cities, with its sundried splendor, is under construction. New roads, bridges, overpasses, expanding highways—all rise up to better connect us to the rest of the world, providing a route for the burgeoning city and booming trade between Mexico and the United States. El Paso itself is constantly trying to be something else, always pulled by the needs and mercurial moods of Mexico City, Washington and New York, where purse strings and political winds blow. We share a state border with New Mexico and an international border with Mexico. We're a model of tolerance, learning to get along in order to push forward. These days we're erasing our history, literally knocking down historic buildings, razing entire neighborhoods—including *Duranguito*—and searching for an identity not fully defined. We seem to be looking far and wide for someone else to label us when, deep down, we know who we are. We are citizens of a region known as Paso del Norte, a historic crossroads for Native

American tribes, for Spaniards in the New World, for American pioneers pushing west, African Americans stationed at Fort Bliss who later chose to retire here, including the mother of Khalid, Grammy-nominated singer.

It's the Ellis Island of the Southwest. This region has long welcomed newcomers of different cultural and religious backgrounds, including Mennonites, Mormons, Asians, Middle Easterners and Africans. In recent years, mothers and fathers with children have made it over this stretch of border from their violence-wracked homelands of Venezuela, Honduras, Guatemala and El Salvador. Most face an uphill battle to stay. My sister Linda, an immigration attorney, focused many of her efforts on helping some of the most vulnerable people who come to the U.S., including Central American families, most of whom are detained asylum seekers.

Across generations, El Paso was often the first to welcome the biggest wave of Mexicans. We became a majority–minority community in the 1920s, following the Mexican Revolution, and since then, a rite of passage for people who traveled through here filled with hope on their way north and left behind pieces of themselves, from mementos to bones in the desert. Some succeeded and reconnected with relatives and friends and jobs. Some died in their effort, having drowned in the Rio Grande, succumbed to the sweltering desert, suffocated in eighteen-wheeler trucks or railroad boxcars.

These deaths haunt us.

These memories are a heaviness we carry.

The older I become, the more I realize that maybe nothing really changes. Now talk of walling off the U.S. from Mexico, and inevitably a piece of who we are, seems to only test our resolve and history. When Tijuana was plunged into drug violence and Americans stayed away, the city was forced to look inward, take a critical look and rebuild. San Diego came to realize it was better off economically and culturally connected to Tijuana rather than living in isolation. *Calibaja* is a term coined for a region that pays homage to the blending of Southern California and Baja California, miles of beaches, stunning sunsets, fine wine and food, including the best *chilaquiles* I've tasted, made by men and women with no plans to cross the border. Similarly, the Americanization of Mexico is racing. Mexican schoolchildren are now required to learn English.

I see glimpses of El Paso also reclaiming its past, rebuilding an old trolley line that may eventually reconnect two sister cities, two countries again. Paseo de Las Luces will soon extend across the border from South El Paso Street—where Freddy's once welcomed bridge crossers— to Juárez Avenue, shining light on our commonalities, not our differences. As if to underscore our resilience, one of the overpasses under construction in El Paso curves and seems to be headed directly for Juárez, looming over the rusted steel fence that our neighbors refer to as a wall. Here on the border we make wings and fly above it. It is in between these two worlds that I have returned to live.

My new assignment as a Mexico Border correspondent for the *Dallas Morning News* is to explain this misunderstood region of ten million people to a nation divided and torn, hateful and suspicious, as if their country was stolen from under them.

I looked around and smiled to myself. My family is here. When I left for Philadelphia I was afraid that the humble foundation that kept us together as a family would collapse around us. But our bond held. Although many of my siblings left, they, like me, have returned to the border. Tested. Stronger.

Linda and Monica went away and came back home to jump-start their own business, LINK, a college advising business meant to empower high school students and encourage them to look beyond the familiar to the unknown, even if it means leaving their comfort zones. Their philosophy is rooted in the idea that education is the key to so many of our society's problems and strife, which means if we can get it right, the possibilities are endless. They also work with DACA recipients, the Dreamers. Their entire business model is built on encouraging people to dream through education.

Mundito was promoted to regional manager of a prosthetics clinic. Juan is an accountant. Panchito, or Frank, is a security guard. Mario and David work in the delivery business, from cookies to bread to auto parts. Both are worried about automation killing their jobs. Mario's company has been downsizing. David drives a truck from the border to Trump's Midwest, part of the supply chain, just-in-time delivery system that contributes to more than half a trillion dollars in U.S.-Mexico trade.

How long before robots drive my truck? David asks. Ten, twenty years? I don't know, but I'd start looking at plan B, I respond.

As night falls, my parents join me in the living room before heading to bed. The voice of Univision anchorman Jorge Ramos blares.

No nos vamos a sentar. No nos vamos a callar y no nos vamos a ir. My mother looks to my father and mimics the latest public announcement by

Univision, one of the two Spanish-language TV networks—Telemundo the second—sparring nightly for top ratings with ABC, CBS, FOX and NBC. The networks reached some 50 million *hispanohablantes* in the U.S., a greater number of Spanish speakers than in Spain.

Did you hear that? my mother says, referring to the ad on the TV. We're not going to sit down. We're not going to be quiet. We're not leaving.

Jorge is right, she concludes.

Just get everyone to vote next time, I remind her.

Yes, my father adds. Vote. *No se hagan gueyes, pendejos.* Don't fool around.

They retreat to bed. I watch the sky darken before it lights up again in dramatic fashion.

I make a mad dash into my parents' bedroom to urge them to come outside.

I love it when the sky is this black: it's the perfect backdrop for fireworks, I tell them, trying to nudge them up to watch the fireworks with me. My father is wearing his sleep mask to help him with apnea.

What's there to celebrate? he says. I'm staying in bed.

I'll go without him, my mother says. I like the *pólvora*.

That's the gunpowder used to make fireworks in Mexico. That's how we called the fireworks show back in San Luis de Cordero, on the twenty-fifth of August, when the town breaks into a huge party to celebrate its founding, she says.

This is the first time he doesn't watch the fireworks with us, I say.

He's just tired, she says. Emotionally drained. We all are.

We step outside. There are just enough clouds floating to keep the stars away and make the fireworks burn that much brighter.

Magical, I tell Mama.

I put my arm around Mama and point to fireworks in another direction. It seems we can hear noises coming from the edge of the river, people celebrating beyond the shadows, near a fence that symbolizes America's latest gasp of resistance to its own immigrant story. Where some imagine bad hombres, danger, we see beauty in the borderlands.

In redefining who we are as Americans, we had to reach this turning point of division, nativism, fear in order to take that next step to become part of the fabric of this country, to belong, even if we already do. We've done this for centuries, beginning with the Founding Fathers gathering over a document in Philadelphia. And in my own lifetime, on that wintry night when Ken, David, Primo and I met and forged ahead.

I look at my mother and think only of all she has been through, what she has gone through to give us the life we have in this country. She could be angry or bitter. Instead she is grateful and forgiving. She stands beside me, petite under my arm, hopeful for the future of both her countries.

San Luis de Cordero is where my umbilical cord is buried. Love for Mexico City runs red in my veins. The *tierra* of the San Joaquin Valley is burned into my memory and fingertips. I hold Philadelphia in my mind. El Paso in my soul and heart. The Rio Grande and its gentle Rio Bravo Waters flow through me.

This is home, the epicenter of my homelands.

ACKNOWLEDGMENTS

Looking back, it feels like I began this book before I was born.

I wish to thank my parents, Juan Pablo Corchado and Herlinda Jimenez de Corchado, for teaching me about empathy and bringing me along to witness the greatest migration of Mexicans through their lives and experiences. They gave me the earliest understanding of a complex issue that's haunted us for decades. They often provided much-needed inspiration when I hit writer's block.

All my love to Angela Kocherga for supporting me through the story I needed to write, oftentimes sharing the reporting and experiences between two countries. You're still my light on the darkest roads.

At the Wylie Agency, thank you to Jessica Freidman for your friendship and professional guidance over the years. To Jin Auh for seeing the value in this project and then going into battle to make sure the story was told. To Cristóbal Pera, who as editorial director of Random House Mondadori and later my agent at Wylie, helped me reshape my original idea over tequilas in Mexico City. Now as publishing director at Vintage Español, he remains as invested in the story.

At Bloomsbury, I'm indebted to Anton Mueller for taking a simple idea and pushing me to think bigger, broader. To Jenna Dutton, Grace McNamee, Tara Kennedy for their patience in making the work a reality. *Salud*.

Thank you to Lauren Courcy Villagran, for again nudging me out of my comfort zone as a reporter and steadfastly helping me fine-tune my voice as a writer.

I'm especially thankful to my gifted sister Linda, an immigration attorney and a talented writer with her own book to pursue. She helped me through endless rewrites, constantly reminding me that it's not about writing, but rewriting.

I'm grateful to Lauren Eades for providing research and editing support throughout this process: from the time when this book was merely an idea floating around in Milo's on Calle Amsterdam in Colonia La Condesa to the final stages of editing.

I'm also grateful to researchers Courtney Columbus and Sara Jones. Photojournalists Billy Calzada, Erich Schlegel and Courtney Pedroza for providing pictures that ingrained moments forever. Thank you, too, John Carlano, Hidemi Yakota, Julie Amparano and Hilary Dick, for digging into your photo treasure troves and finding some gems.

During the research and writing of this book I was fortunate to have been able to rely on the support of Arizona State University and its top Walter Cronkite Journalism Program. I was inspired by many of my future colleagues, including the infamous Ms: Mauricio Casillas, Miguel Otárola and Molly Bilker.

I also relied on the support of the Woodrow Wilson Center's Mexico Institute in Washington, D.C. Thank you, Duncan Wood, Christopher Wilson, Eric Olson, Andrea Tanco, Andrea Conde Ghigliazza, Ximena Rodriguez and Carlos Castillo Perez.

For the long conversations that helped provide a richer understanding, thank you to Bernardo Ruiz, Andrew Selee, Shannon O'Neil, Jim Dickmeyer, James Hollifield, Luisa del Rosal, Tony Garza, Carlos Bravo Regidor, Sergio Silva Castaneda, David Shirk and Rafael Fernández de Castro. Thank you, authors and *cabrónes* Philip Connors and Benjamin Alire Sáenz. At Pew Research Center, thank you, Jeffery S. Passel and Mark Hugo Lopez.

I'm thankful to the Lannan Foundation, whose support included a residency in Marfa, complete with the nightly roar of a Union Pacific Train and a wild turkey in the backyard; and the Institute of Politics at the University of Chicago: David Axelrod, Alicia Sams, Steve Edwards and Ashley Jorn. Many thanks for the coffee, tequila, and talks, Miguel Toro, Claudia Barrera, Manuel Toral, Gerardo Serna, Dominic Bracco, David Ansari, Najla Ayoubi, Tony Blinken, Bob Dold, Jennifer Granholm, Steven Greenhouse and Shailagh Murray.

Much gratitude to the best student ambassadors who made my time at the University of Chicago hopeful: Michelle Shim, Olivia Shaw, Nicole Somerstein and Ella Deeken.

Thank you, too, Enrique Davila and Jonathan Acevedo.

Special thanks to Emilio Kourí, Brodwyn Fischer, Mauricio Tenorio.

My deepest gratitude to the USMEX Program at the University of California, San Diego, for luring me back to California and providing research, writing time and a beloved dorm with a view to the Pacific Ocean. Thank you, Melissa Floca and Greg Mallinger and USMEX fellows, particularly Alina R. Méndez, Tania Islas Weinstein, Thomas Passananti, Emilio de Antuñano Villarreal and Jaime Arredondo Sanchez Lira.

Enormous gratitude to Gordon Hanson at UCSD School of Global Policy and Strategy.

I enriched my insight from a number of terrific books, including *Ringside Seat to a Revolution* by David Dorado Romo; *Mexicans in the Remaking of America* by Neil Foley; *The Other Americans* by Joel Millman; *Latino Americans* by Ray Suarez; *Walls and Mirrors: Mexican Americans, Mexican Immigrants, and the Politics of Ethnicity* by David Gutiérrez; *Two Nations Indivisible* by Shannon O'Neil; *Dreamland* by Sam Quinones; *Border Games* by Peter Andreas; *Becoming Mexican American* by George J. Sánchez; *Latinos* by Earl Shorris; *Mexicanos* by Manuel G. Gonzales; *Anglos and Mexicans in the Making of Texas* by David Montejano; *Wetback Nation* by Peter Laufer; *The Making of the Mexican Border* by Juan Mora-Torres, *The Labyrinth of Solitude* by Octavio Paz; *The Fight in the Fields: Cesar Chavez and the Farmworkers Movement* by Susan J. Ferriss and Ricardo Sandoval; *Detroit's Mexicantown* by Maria Elena Rodriguez; *El Pueblo Mexicano en Detroit y Michigan: A Social History* by Dennis Nodin Valdés; *Los Mexicanos en Estados Unidos* by Roger Díaz de Cossío, Graciela Orozco and Esther González; *Philadelphia: A 300-Year History*; and *Larry Kane's Philadelphia*.

My gratitude to the *camineros* for much needed encouragement: Ricardo Sandoval, Cecilia Ballí, Ernesto Torres, Dudley Althaus, Gilbert Bailon, Alfredo Carbajal, Jason Buch and Vianna R. Davila, all great storytellers.

My colleagues Maria Sacchetti, Cindy Carcamo, Dianne Solis, Susan J. Ferriss and Julia Preston, the best immigration reporters I know.

Throughout this journey, I relied on my experiences over thirty years as a journalist. I took my first steps as a pup reporter at the *El Paso Herald-Post* and the *Ogden Standard-Examiner* in Utah. In my time in Mexico I told many stories that ended up in my previous book, *Midnight in Mexico: A Reporter's Journey Through a Country's Descent into Darkness* and the pages of the *Dallas Morning News*.

Thank you for your support and patience, Mike Wilson, Robyn Tomlin, Keith Campbell, Tom Huang, Tim Connolly and Alfredo Carbajal.

To my family, the Corchados and Jimenezes on both sides, *los quiero*. *Gracias*.

Foremost, I spent three decades interviewing the main characters in this book, fact-checking their accounts with those who know them, as well as my own notes, recordings and interviews. Thank you, David, Ken and Primo for unselfishly sharing your story, which is really the story of millions of Americans and Mexicans in their search for a better life.

A NOTE ON THE AUTHOR

Alfredo Corchado is the Mexico Border correspondent for the *Dallas Morning News* and author of *Midnight in Mexico: A Reporter's Journey Through a Country's Descent into Darkness*. Born in Durango, Mexico, he was raised in California and Texas. Corchado began his career in journalism in El Paso, Texas, before working for the *Wall Street Journal*. He is a Nieman, Woodrow Wilson, Rockefeller, Lannan, USMEX and IOP fellow, and the winner of the Maria Moors Cabot Prize and Elijah Parish Lovejoy Award for Courage in Journalism. He is also a former director of the Borderlands Program at the Walter Cronkite School of Journalism at Arizona State University. He has reported on the reach of Mexican drug cartels into the United States, the plight of Mexican and Central American immigrants in the U.S. and government corruption on both sides of the border. He was inducted into the Texas Institute of Letters in 2018. Corchado lives between El Paso and Mexico City but calls the border home.